UrText Supplement

for 'A Course In Miracles'

Providing the original (Ur) text that has been further edited and published as various versions of the 'A Course In Miracles'. *This supplement contains only the first eight chapters of the UrText,* as these are the most changed in all the versions of the Course. There is a substantial amount of communication from the Source in these first eight chapters, that has been left out of all published versions of the full Course.

The full UrText is available online and in hard copy also from other sources. This supplement is intended as a teaching supplement; not as a technical reference to the original Course notes and UrText. It is intended to 'feel more reader friendly' for meditative study times of the Course material.

This supplement retains the original wording as provided in online pdf versions of the UrText, but formatting of paragraph breaks, indents, highlighting, and occasional emphasis with added italics has been added for studying purposes. This supplement is focused on clearly conveying the Message the Course intends. It also contains numerous footnotes to all the bible references in the Course.

Original Author: The Source, through the persona of Jesus of Nazareth.

Received by: Helen Schucman

Edited to the original UrText by: William T. Thetford and Helen Schucman

Formatting in this supplement: Tim Bickel

Provided by:

Awake Living Center

Provided by the *Awake Living Center*

12130 W. Ridge Rd
E. Springfield, PA 16411
(814) 922-7058
www.awakelivingcenter.com

The Awake Living Center is a group of people dedicated to attaining and teaching the full Awakening the 'A Course In Miracles' teaches. Our single function, both mindfully and physically, is to provide a constant reference to the most simple Truth that 'The Truth is true, and nothing else is true.'

In the natural desire of awaken mind to share, we extend this desire to facilitate others in their own growing awareness. This is done through weekly groups and much personal 'plugging in' to keep only the Truth as our only goal, and to return to it sooner than later when we find we have slipped from awareness of it.

Physically, we are a small community of shared living; we also provide meditative retreats, and an always open space for resting in or sharing the joy of bright awake awareness.

Not all our 'members' are physically close to us, and we are glad to extend our circle of support and single-focus to join and stay connected with anyone else dedicated to their awakening. We all need each other, as a constant reminder of the Truth of our Being, and … to share the joy of bright awareness with.

This UrText Supplement is available on the Awake Living Center website as a web page, a searcher, and as a pdf file you can download.

The 'Urtext' and 'A Course In Miracles', as well as this Supplement format, are public domain documents and may be freely used, shared, and enjoyed by anyone with no permission needed.

UrText Supplement
ISBN-10: 1512288160   ISBN-13: 978-1512288162

Table of Contents

Forward..i
   What Is This Supplement?..i
   The Nature Of Channeling..iv
Chapter 1 – Introduction To Miracles...1
   A. Introduction...1
   B. Principles Of Miracles..1
      a. The Relationship of Miracles and Revelation.....................................10
      b. The Concept Of Lack..37
   C. Distortions of Miracle Impulses..40
Chapter 2 - The Illusion Of Separation..45
   A. Introduction...45
   B. The Re-interpretation of Defenses..51
      a. Reinterpretation Of Some "Dynamic" Concepts................................54
      b. The Atonement As Defense..56
   C. Healing as Release from Fear...62
   D. Fear as Lack of Love...68
   E. The Correction for Lack of Love...70
   F. The Meaning of the Last Judgment...81
Chapter 3 - Retraining The Mind..83
   A. Introduction...83
   B. Special Principles for Miracle Workers..89
   C. Atonement without Sacrifice...90
   D. Miracles as Accurate Perception...97
   E. Perception versus Knowledge...98
   F. Conflict and the Ego..101
   G. The Loss of Certainty..105
   H. Judgment and the Authority Problem...113
   I. Creating versus the Self-Image..117
Chapter 4 – The Root Of All Evil..120
   A. Introduction...120
   B. Right Teaching and Right Learning...122
   C. The Ego and False Autonomy...128
   D. Love without Conflict...133
   E. The Escape from Fear...137
      a. This Need Not Be..137
   F. The Ego-Body Illusion..140
   G. The Constant State..143

    H. Creation and Communication..148
    I. True Rehabilitation...150
Chapter 5 – Healing And Wholeness...152
    A. Introduction...152
    B. Healing as Joining..153
    C. The Mind of the Atonement..154
    D. The Voice for God..156
    E. The Guide to Salvation..159
    F. Therapy and Teaching..162
    G. The Two Decisions...166
    H. Time and Eternity..169
    I. The Eternal Fixation...173
Chapter 6 – Attack And Fear..177
    A. Introduction...177
    B. The Message of the Crucifixion..178
    C. The Uses of Projection...183
    D. The Relinquishment of Attack..187
    E. The Only Answer..188
    F. "To Have, Give All to All"..192
    G. "To Have Peace, Teach Peace to Learn It"...195
    H. "Be Vigilant Only for God and His Kingdom"...198
Chapter 7 - The Consistency Of The Kingdom..202
    A. Introduction...202
    B. Bargaining versus Healing..202
    C. The Laws of Mind..204
    D. The Unified Curriculum..206
    E. The Recognition of Truth..208
    F. Healing and the Changelessness of Mind...212
    G. From Vigilance to Peace..216
    H. The Total Commitment..220
    I. The Defense of Conflict..224
    J. The Extension of the Kingdom..226
    K. The Confusion of Strength and Weakness..228
    L. The State of Grace..230
Chapter 8 – The Journey Back...233
    A. Introduction...233
    B. The Direction of the Curriculum..233
    C. The Rationale for Choice...234
    D. The Holy Encounter...236
    E. The Light of the World..239

F. The Power of Joint Decision...244
G. Communication and the Ego-Body Equation...247
H. The Body as Means or End..251
I. Healing as Corrected Perception..254
J. The Acceptance of Reality..257
K. The Answer to Prayer...260

Forward

What Is This Supplement?

This version of the 'A Course In Miracles' Ur text supplement arises from my personal experiences of awakening. I started using the Course in 1990. By the end of the first year I had started facilitating a weekly Course group and have pretty much had at least one weekly meeting ever since.

In the years since, I have observed my own awakening, and the awakening of many, many others. It is clear that those who choose to accept the totality of what the Truth in the Course offers, experience rapid and deep transformations in their lives – becoming peaceful, stable, loving and helpful people – some in a matter of weeks and months. Whereas those who seek to use the Course to just bring 'god-power' to their continuing separated existence as a human being – still have the same drama-trama and issues raging in their lives ten and twenty years later.

The Course is very simple and very specific. Yet it is so easy for a human mind to completely miss 'getting it,' over and over and over. I find that including more of the dialog between Bill and Helen and Jesus that went on as the Course was originally transmitted helps open our individual minds to better reception, and transformation, from that same Source.

When we come to an inspired source of Truth intending to learn from it, a funny thing happens that makes no sense to our intellectual mind. What happens is, because of our intention to realize Truth, we join with the Source itself. We are no longer reading the words and trying to understand ideas and concepts. We move directly to 'absorbing mode,' And while in that mode, It is actively changing HOW our mind works. That is why we can reread our favorite spiritual teaching over and over and feel like we get new and deeper insight from it every time.

By including more of the dialog, I find a mind is moved TO the same receptive state that was going on during the transmission from Jesus to Helen and Bill (and the world.) In this dialog, we can see and feel the extremely personal connection we have to God's channel. He, or It, depending on how we care to label it, can be seen to be intimately and knowledgeably involved with EVERY aspect of our life, from what is best to have for breakfast, to how to accept complete awakening – all the time. The Source is always present and acting WITH us. This is a very, very helpful experience to get and accept. It will replace years and decades of 'studying what the Course says' – with ever growing and deepening experiences of direct insightful 'knowing,' appropriate to every moment at hand.

Forward

We will find that our initial extremely chaotic separated mind will bounce all over the place – in awareness – with great rapidity. And we will find, the Source follows with us guiding us right through it all, until the chaos and desire for separated thinking is undone and we are just at peace through and through.

To that end, I have taken what has been called the UrText, an early typed version of the notes that Helen recieved from Jesus. I have kept the majority of the reported aside dialogs that went on between the Giver and Receivers in the process. As will be seen, Helen's mind was quite fragmented and scattered initially as far as her ability to receive consistently and clearly.

The published versions of the Course have all come from various people taking this jumble and deciding to order it into a presentable printed form. This supplement retains the original order and content of the material received, but adds formatting. One, I highlight the personal dialog between Helen and Bill and the Voice – Jesus. These highlights are merely to serve as indicators that the stream is going to shift gears. I find this is less jolting to my mind when I am warned a shift is coming, so I can stay more in a meditative state while reading this. And two, I add additional paragraph breaks, indents, and italics emphasis where they seem natural.

One key format I retain from the original transmissions is the Source's use of all caps to indicate emphasis. When we 'hear' the inner Voice for ourselves, the emphasis on INDIVIDUAL words, and even parts of words is VERY clear. So, I retain that mode of emphasis in the text.

Another element I remain aware of is - the process of channeling itself. I had just begun doing some channeling before I discovered the Course existed. Because of my little experience with the phenomena of channeling, when I did pick up the Course it had a very, very strong impact. I recognized instantly that this was a powerful and very pure channel of connection to our Source. Personally, I felt a huge relief in discovering that this existed. I cried for three days in an ongoing emotional release, before I could continue actually reading what the Course had to say.

The point being – every one channels, and at much more frequent intervals than we suspect. It comes through as insights and intuition. It is why we can occasionally help a friend feel better for no discernible reason or ability of our own. So, I find reading the dialog of the Communication also reawakens or stimulates my own channeling ability. And I would like to see it do likewise for you.

'Channeling' is just a particular subset of our ability to use our own higher awake, or Christ, mind. If fact, channeling is any use of the mind where we let our 'input' be received from something beyond our own personal intellect and opinions. Channeling is not necessarily plugged into higher Christ awareness; we can also plug into the collective subconscious' continuing desire for separation and spew all kinds of stuff trying to glorify and justify continuing human separated existence. Like tuning to a particular TV channel – what we receive when channeling depends on what we want.

But if some part of our mind, as had Helen's and Bill's, has already decided to reconnect with the One Whole Mind's Truth, then that channel can be extremely clear and powerful for real Truth. In the personal dialogs we can see where It overrode what they wanted or intended to think or make of something, and It could give very clear guidance to reorient their minds to Truth. Here then, we can see that this focused ability called channeling, is really no more than our growing awareness and its ability to 'listen' only to our own higher Mind, the Holy Spirit, to guide our decisions and to unfold our life.

A second area where I have observed procrastination for decades (even in myself) is in becoming willing 'to hear.' The Course repeats very, very frequently that awakening is about learning to listen to OUR OWN ONENESS with the Higher Mind-Spirit that gives us the Life that we are. There is a great reluctance to actually open up and 'hear' for ourselves – and particularly – to trust it. Yet developing that orientation to our Being in Truth IS what awakening is. So, again, reading the personal dialogs, is a happy re-reminder that I can, and should, for the sake of my own growing peace and awareness, be listening more myself and looking out less to any external form of Truth transmission, including the Course. 'Hearing' more and more blends into relaxed Being where we just KNOW. Channeling is a beginning, perhaps a contrived opening of our mind. But it lets the Light (Awareness) in, and we gradually get more comfortable with ever increasing levels of it. Until we finally accept we ARE that Light, not who we thought we were in separation, and then we can permanently relax into that Being and trust it for input regarding all the seeming little and important details and decisions in every aspect of living while we are still on planet earth.

I have developed a version of this on the Awake Living Center website. But many have asked if there is a printed equivalent, as they prefer reading non-electronically. That is why this version is made available in print too.

I have made an effort to retain every meaningful statement between Source and Helen and Bill. Yet I have taken the liberty, listening to my own inner Source to rearrange it moderately so exchanges are flow and connect more smoothly; like moving a dialog for correction adjacent to the area of the passage that is being corrected. I also have added more emphasis through indents and breaking out single important lines to stand alone; but keeping the original words and flow in the order as it was given.

Above all, the thing to constantly remember is: The Course is not special. It is not the Truth. It is words, symbols and ideas to teach us where to find the Truth in our own mind. It directs us where to look in our mind for it, and gives us many clues, like Love and Forgiveness, so we can recognize it when we come across it. The Course is a pointer – that I

Forward

love. So I continue to use it. So far, it is the most direct and uncompromised transmission about Truth that I have found.

But it is not special. Any child that can read and write or type, could channel its equivalent and do so not even using any religious term or symbol that we would recognize; and yet it still would be as true as the Course. To gain what It is teaching we have to constantly both Love and appreciate it without doubt or reservation, while simultaneously letting all its words and ideas continually fall away to make room for our own still place of Knowing, that it intends to produce in us.

The purpose of the Course is to restore our own awareness of our own right mind. I just find this arrangement of words and ideas helpful to me, and some others, toward that end. And so I share it.

The Nature Of Channeling

Connecting to our Source is always intense, exciting, and fun if we will let it be. The Source knows EVERY thought, feeling and experience, past and present, in our mind. This in itself can produce uncomfortable feelings initially, until we learn the Source is truly 100 percent non-judgmental.

It is playful and will produce humorus perspectives on anything – if we will let it. It can easily produce puns or show us double and even triple levels of meaning in a word or phrase. This often appears to be extremely irreverent to our old (and erroneous) established beliefs about God and life itself.

During a dissertation of any particular topic, the Source may flicker many brief awarenesses TO us, of many seemingly scattered thoughts and experiences we have had. It can take off on any one of those. Part of learning to channel better is to learn to ask It if this is the appropriate time for our thinking to go in a particular direction.

It will NEVER fight our choice. But if we are trying to produce a certain outcome, like receiving guidance on getting a particular stuck issue in our mind undone, or in streaming a message such as the Course, if we ask where to direct our mind, the Source will direct it most efficiently and beneficially for us. We can see in the early dialogs that Helen struggles with this – a plethora of ideas, puns, and insights are available to her. Sometimes she decides to pursue them then and there, and there is a lengthy divergence from the core message the Course intends. Other times, she is more open to guidance and lets her mind be brought back to and re-focused on the intended use of the moment.

This can also be seen in comments the Source makes for corrections. Seemingly out of nowhere, It addresses a particular point that can be better clarified – because a lingering question about it still exists in their minds.

The Nature Of Channeling

As we work with learning to listen better, channeling becomes integrated into a moment to moment habitual activity of frequently opening our mind to see if It has something better to say than what I am inclined to think alone. In time, this opening becomes 'wordless.' We just learn how to briefly, but very frequently, pause in our thinking-feeling-reacting human activity with the intention of receiving THOUGHT. We can do this between thoughts while speaking, or listening to another. And eventually, we can do it with every breath we take. Initially, developing the habit of asking about – everything – can seem like an annoying and cluttered mind process. It becomes our smooth and natural primary mind process as time goes by.

As I mentioned above, connecting with our Higher Source – IS extremely personal feeling. Our initial inclination in 'asking' is for us to pose a question and then to expect a literal answer, like getting a text on our cell phone. Sometimes it does work that way, but the more natural and real channel is different.

When we pause, which is stilling our mind, we can learn to temporarily have an instant of 'no thought.' We formulate our question. That question doesn't have to be 'right' for the Source already knows all about it, being part of us. But we ask our question, then let It answer. Often the initial answer is a better form of our own question. We are given better awareness of what we are actually trying to do – behind our original question. And sometimes the answer comes while we are still struggling to select the best vocabulary to formulate the question.

For example, maybe we can't pay a bill, or have some situation we see is insolvable. We will tend to formulate our own answer then ask for that. That is vary non-optimal. Instead we learn to step back with the 'problem' and open our mind with an ATTITUDE like: 'See this topic I've got going on here? See my flummoxed feelings and anxiety about this? Bring me to peace with this.' Then we do that pausing thing with no thought. And we wait for the answer to come – through our own thoughts - now that we are not insisting on thinking them for our self, but rather, are willing to let them be given to us.

The answer may appear immediately; it will if 'necessary' as in 'Hey! Step back! That bus is not going to stop.' But more likely, it will arise in a moment of peace when we are not thinking about the topic at all. That is why showers are so great for insightful moments. Or when we are mentally preoccupied with some basically mindless task like cutting the grass, washing the dishes or cooking supper. Then all at once, we get a new perspective and new idea.

The answer may also come through unfolding. That is, the only thought I get right now is 'Hey! I haven't talked to Fred for a while. I should give him a call.' And that leads to some information or idea. Then the next step is given and so on, and one day we realize that everything has been taken care of and we no longer are concerned with that issue, topic

Forward

or problem, And we learn the Answer always does come and we will always be directed to receive it – so I don't even have to worry about my own remaining noisy mind or apparent stupidity any more; my Source if always bigger than my reluctance – to have everything solved. Once I learn that, peace reigns in new levels in my life.

All these aspects are reflected in the dialogs of the Course UrText. Reading through them prompts a familiarity in our own mind as to what we COULD be doing – in communication with our Source. And as that reminder, they are extremely helpful.

A last note: our separated mind thinks it is special and has its own important private thoughts. Like, what applies to Bill and Helen, I couldn't possibly know, and besides, it wouldn't be relevant to me anyway. Well, the truth is: ALL Mind is exactly the same. Here in the real feeling illusion of separation it is always both projecting itself as separated, and at least occasionally, working to return to awareness of its Real Nature in One Mind. Once we see that all topics and issues and problems are irrelevant because they are all the same, without my personal glorification of their specialness stamped on them, we then see we can learn from any situation as 'they' are all just 'me' anyway. It is a big step in accepting Oneness, Wholeness, or our Reality, when we can happily just BE that other person. That doesn't make sense to our ego-brain mind, I know. But it is easy to do. Then we are learning through a billion incarnations of 'me' and not continually plodding alone through every newly conceived permutation of problemness we can invent.

If we read the dialogs between Bill and Helen and Jesus with a truly open mind, we get actual real flashes of experiencing the mind-awareness they are in at the moment of the communication. And we gain; we see the equivalent of that mind error as we have hidden it in our story of our self, and we receive the solution for it specifically.

It is hard to keep in mind initially; we are not reading printed words when we read the Course; we are approaching our own personal connection to Source, for that is what the Course represents. And the Connection to Source becomes alive and real in the present for the plugging in we did through the willingness to pick up the book and read it.

May you have fun developing your own listening.

Tim

Chapter 1 – Introduction To Miracles

A. Introduction

1   It is crucial to say first that this is a required course. Only the time you take it is voluntary. Free will does not mean that you establish the curriculum. It means only that you can elect what to take when. It is just because you are not ready to do what you should elect to do that time exists at all.

    You will see miracles through your hands through me.

    You should begin each day with the prayer

        "Help me to perform whatever miracles you want of me today"

B. Principles Of Miracles

1. The first thing to remember about miracles is that there is no order of difficulty among them. One is not harder or bigger than another. They are all the same.

2. Miracles do not matter. They are quite unimportant.

3. They occur naturally as an expression of love. The real miracle is the love that inspires them. In this sense, everything that comes from love is a miracle.

    This explains the first point related to the lack of order. ALL expressions of love are maximal.

    This is why the "thing in itself", i.e. the miracle, does not matter. The only thing that matters is the Source, and this is far beyond human evaluation.

2   Q and A re: first 3 points.) [H = Helen Schucman, B=Bill, S: Source (Jesus)]

    Q. H: Would you regard this communication as a kind of miracle?

    A. S: There is nothing special or surprising about this at all. The ONE thing that happened was the Universal Miracle which was the experience of intense love that you have felt. Don't get embarrassed by the idea of love. Embarrassment is only a form of fear, and actually a particularly dangerous form because it reflects egocentricity.

    Do not feel guilty about the fact that you are doubting this. Just re-read them and their truth will come to you. I love you, and I am not afraid or embarrassed or doubtful. MY strength will support you, so don't worry and leave the rest to me. But when you see B., be SURE you tell him how much he helped you through by giving you the right

Chapter 1 – Introduction To Miracles

message, and don't bother with worrying about how you received it. That doesn't matter either. You were just afraid.

H: fearful in taxi about a communication which related Dave's healing and Jonathan's hernia. She thought it would be safer to dissociate the two.

S: Instructions were: refer to Principle **1.** and re-read NOW.

4. ALL miracles mean Life, and God is the giver of Life. He will direct you VERY specifically.

Plan ahead is good advice in this world, where you should and must control and direct where you have accepted responsibility.

But the Universal Plan is in more appropriate hands. You will know all you need to know. Make NO attempts to plan ahead in this respect.

5. Miracles are habits, and should be involuntary. They should not be under conscious control. Consciously selected miracles are usually misguided, and this will make the talent useless.

6. Miracles are natural. When they do NOT occur something has gone wrong.

7. Miracles are everyone's right, but purification is necessary first.

8. Miracles are a form of healing. They supply a lack, and are performed by those who have more for those who have less.

9. Miracles are a kind of exchange. Like all expressions of love, which are ALWAYS miraculous in the true sense, the exchange reverses the physical laws.

10. A miracle is a reversal of the physical order because it brings more love to the giver AND the receiver.

11. A miracle is misunderstood when it is regarded as a spectacle. The use of miracles as a spectacle to INDUCE belief is wrong. They are really used for and by believers.

H. has some fear about **11.** and doubt about **9.** and **10.**. Probably doubt induced by fear of **11.**.

B. Principles Of Miracles

3   S: When you say "If you want me to I will" please add "and if you DON'T want me to I won't." This is the RIGHT use of inhibition. There has to be SOME control over learning for channelizing purposes. Remember retroactive inhibition which should be easy enough for you.

Sometimes the new learning is the more important, and HAS to inhibit the old. It's a form of correction.

12. Prayer is the medium of miracles. Prayer is the natural communication of the Created with the Creator. Through prayer, love is received, and through miracles love is expressed.

13. Miracles are thought-creations. Thought can create lower-order or higher-order realities. This is the basic distinction between intellectualization and thinking. One creates the physical, and the other the spiritual, and we believe in what we create.

14. A miracle is a beginning and an end(ing). It thus abolishes time. It is always an affirmation of re-birth, which seems to go back, but really goes forward. It undoes the past in the present, and thus releases the future.

15. Miracles attest to truth. They are convincing because they arise from conviction. Without conviction, they deteriorate into magic, which is mindless, and therefore destructive, or rather, the uncreative use of Mind.

16. Each day should be devoted to miracles. God created time so that man could use it creatively, and convince himself of his own ability to create. Time is a teaching device, and a means to an end. It will cease when it is no longer useful for facilitating learning.

2   SPECIAL INSTRUCTIONS: Notes on this course have to be taken only under good learning conditions. The same goes for review periods. I will tell you when, but REMEMBER TO ASK.

17. Miracles are teaching devices for demonstrating that it is more blessed to give than to receive. They simultaneously increase the reserve strength of the giver, and supply the lack of strength in the receiver. BE VERY CAREFUL in interpreting this.

2   INSTRUCTIONS: The purpose of this course is integration. I told you that you will not be able to use it right until you have taken it. As long as your identification vacillates, (and B's is weak) you cannot accept the gift that belongs to you. You are still vacillating

Chapter 1 – Introduction To Miracles

between recognizing the gift and throwing it away. B regards himself as too weak to accept it. You do not yet know its healing power. After you have passed the course, you will accept it and keep it and use it. That is the final exam, which you will have no trouble in passing. Midterm marks are not entered on the permanent record.

18. Miracles are the absence of the body. They are sudden shifts into invisibility, away from lower order reality. That is why they heal.

19. A miracle is a service. It is the maximal service that one soul can render another. It is a way of loving your neighbor [1] as yourself. The doer recognizes his own and his neighbor's inestimable value simultaneously.

2   S: This is why no areas of hatred can be retained. If you retain them, your own value is no longer inestimable because, you are evaluating it as X or infinity minus that amount. This is meaningless mathematically, which uses the term "inestimable" only in the very literal sense. Pun intended especially for B, who originally did not get it. Intended as a special sign of love.

20. Miracles rest on the law and order of eternity, not of time.

2   Miracles are an industrial necessity. Industry depends on cooperation, and cooperation depends on miracles. [2]

21. Miracles are cobwebs of iron. They unite human frailty to the strength of God.

2   A miracle reawakens the awareness that the spirit, and not the body, is the altar of Truth. This is the recognition that leads to the healing power of the miracle.

3   H. considered changing "iron" to "steel."

S: No. Steel would NOT be a better word. Steel is very useful but it would have to be tempered by fire. Iron is the raw material. The point of miracles is that they replace fire, thus making it unnecessary.

22. Miracles are natural expressions of total forgiveness. Through miracles, man accepts God's forgiveness by extending it to others. The second step is inherent in the first, because light cannot tolerate darkness. Light dispels darkness automatically, by definition.

---

1   Leviticus 19:18, Mark 12:31, Mat 19:19. 22:39, Luke 10:27, Romans 13:9 all refer to loving neighbours as thyself.
2   See also, this section: Principle **21**, p3 and Principle **23**, p3

B. Principles Of Miracles

23. Miracles are associated with fear only because of the fallacy that darkness can hide. Man believes that what he cannot see does not exist, and his physical eyes cannot see in the dark. This is a very primitive solution, and has led to a denial of the spiritual eye, which always depends on light. Remember the Biblical injunction: "May I never forget that THINE eye is ever upon me, beholding the evil and the good."[3]

2   There are two stages, one lower and one higher, which are involved in the escape from darkness:

> 1. the recognition that darkness CANNOT hide. This usually does entail fear.
> 2. The recognition that there is nothing you WANT to hide, even if you could. This brings escape from fear.

3   S: Re Principle **21** - cobwebs of iron. "This is upside down as stated. The part about 'uniting human frailty with the strength of God' is all right, but the explanation stops too soon. If iron is the 'raw material', cobwebs can't become the iron. That is only the way it seems, because cobwebs are associated with the frailty and iron with strength. If you look carefully at the phrasing, you will see it is reversed (Principle **9.** already tells you that miracles reverse the physical or lower order laws.)

4   The raw material, or iron, is heavy but crude, and stands for the body, which is a crude creation. The cobweb concept is closer to how the body SHOULD be regarded, i.e., as an airy and temporary home, which can just be blown away with a slight breeze.

5   The point, Principle **21.**, should read "A miracle reawakens the awareness that the spirit, and not the body, is the altar of Truth. This is the recognition that leads to the healing power of the miracle."

24. A miracle rearranges the order of perception, and places the levels in their true perspective. This heals at all levels, because all sickness comes from confusing the levels.

2   Tell B. about the idea (which is still dim to H.) that the reason is not that you (plural) distantiate, doubt, or cannot believe. It is more of a reaction formation against a pull which you both recognize is so intense that you are afraid that you will be uprooted. But remember that a cobweb is really stronger than the iron, if you see it properly. This fear is also why you couldn't get the point straight.

3   By the way, it is not true that you are both 'JUST SCRIBES'. You might remember that the Scribes were very wise and holy man and are even sometimes spelled with a capital S. If you want to go further, you might change the meaning of 'just' from 'merely'

---

[3] Proverbs 15:3 The eyes of the LORD are in every place, keeping watch upon the evil and the good.

Chapter 1 – Introduction To Miracles

to 'honest', a term used in the Bible in association with 'might' or 'strength.' Tell B. you couldn't make that pun if the original phrasing had been singular.

4   H. aside: about liking the first about assumption failure more.

S: It was cuter, but this one MEANS more. The REAL reason you don't like it is because it refers to you in a VERY lofty position. This makes you nervous.

5   S: Correction (Principle **20**): And don't lose sight of the emphasis on cooperation, or the NOT SINGULAR. That point about "industrial necessity" should read "corporate," referring to the body of Christ which is a way of referring to the Church. But the Church of God is only the sum of the souls he created, which IS the corporate body of Christ. Correct to read: "A Miracle makes souls one in God," and leave in the next part about cooperation.

6   S: Further correction: "God" should read "Christ." The Father and the Son are not identical, but you CAN say "Like Father, LIKE Son."

7   S: Remind B. to get another notebook. I don't give up as easily as HE does. If I could get YOU to listen, which was a miracle in itself, I can get him to register. He should appreciate this more than anyone else, having had some trouble with this problem himself.

8   "LORD HEAL ME" IS THE ONLY LEGITIMATE PRAYER. This also means "Lord atone for me," because the only thing man should pray for is forgiveness. He HAS everything else.

9   Now take this personally, and listen to Divine logic: If, when you have been forgiven, you have everything else, and If you have been forgiven Then you HAVE everything else.

10   This happens to be the simplest of all propositions:

         If P then Q. P. Therefore, Q.

11   The real question is, is P true? If you will review the evidence, I think you will find this inescapable. I went on very personal record to this effect, and I am the only completely True Witness for God. You have every right to examine MY credentials—in fact, I urge you to do so. You haven't read the Bible in years.

12   S: Special Explanatory Note: As soon as you (H and B) have entered the second phase, you will be not only willing to enter into communion, but will also understand peace and joy. Your commitment is not yet total. That is why you still have more to learn than to teach. When your equilibrium stabilizes, you can teach AS MUCH as you learn. This will give you the proper sense of balance. Meanwhile, remember that NO EFFORT IS WASTED. Unless you remember this, you cannot avail yourself of MY efforts, which are limitless.

B. Principles Of Miracles

13   (Have a good day.) Since only eternity is real, why not use the illusion of time constructively? You might remember that "underneath are the Everlasting Arms."[4]

14   BIBLICAL QUOTATION: "If you are ashamed of me before men, I will be ashamed of you before God,[5]" (H. questions as misquoted.) is interpreted as a threat ONLY as long you remain in the first step. [6]

15   What it REALLY means is that if you are ashamed of me (or embarrassed by love), you will project and therefore make it impossible for me to reach you. Make every effort you can NOT to do this. I will help you as much as you will let me.

25. Miracles make time and tide wait for all men. They can heal the sick and raise the dead because man himself made both death and taxes, and can abolish both.

Note: Tax also means "strain." One definition for miracles is: "That which, or one who, is of surpassing excellence or merit." From Dictionary, third definition

From Notes: S: "As long as you take accurate notes, every word is meaningful. But I can't always get through. Whenever possible, I will correct retroactively. Be sure to note all later corrections. They mean that you are more receptive than you were when I tried before.

2   That's right - YOU are a miracle. God creates only "that which, or one who, is of surpassing excellence or merit." Man is capable of this kind of creation, too, being in the image and likeness [7] of his own Creator. Anything else is only his own nightmare, and does not exist. Only the Creations of Light are real.

26. Miracles are a part of an interlocking chain of forgiveness which, when completed, is the Atonement. This process works all the time and in all dimensions of time.

2   S: (e.g. given of H. report rewrite for Esther!) Esther had hurt something you loved, by writing a report you regarded as very bad. You atoned for her by writing one in her name that was very good. Actually, it was not your responsibility professionally to do this, but because you DO love the Shield you recognized that in this case, you ARE your

---

4 Deuteronomy 33:27 The eternal God is thy dwelling place, And underneath are the everlasting arms: And he thrust out the enemy from before thee, And said, Destroy.

5 Mark 8:38 "For whosoever shall be ashamed of me and of my words in this adulterous and sinful generation, the Son of man

6 Chapter 2 E. The Correction For Lack Of Love, p1-3

7 Genesis 1:26-27 Then God said, "Let Us make man in Our image, according to Our likeness; let them have dominion over the fish of the sea, over the birds of the air, and over the cattle, over all the earth and over every creeping thing that creeps on the earth." So God created man in His own image; in the image of God He created him; male and female He created them.

Chapter 1 – Introduction To Miracles

brother's keeper. While you did not cancel Esther's sin (later defined as "lack of love") you DID cancel out its EFFECTS.

3   Someday I want to tell Esther that not only is she forgiven but that the effects of all her sins are canceled. This is what I have already told you. When I can tell her, she will be afraid for a long time, because she will remember many things, consciously or unconsciously, including the Shield report, a lack of love which you canceled out in advance by a miracle of devotion.

4   I am in charge of the process of Atonement, which I undertook to begin. My Atonement was for the canceling out of all sins (i.e., lack of love) which human beings could not otherwise correct. That is what the Biblical statement "underneath are the Everlasting Arms" means.

5   H. explanation: This means that He will backstop whenever human miracles will not suffice for atonement purposes. However, it is perfectly clear that when a person can atone by miracles, both giver and receiver are atoning. It is better to atone this way because of the mutual benefits involved.

"Inasmuch as you do it unto the least of these, my children" really ends with "you do it unto yourself and ME. [8] " The reason why YOU come before me is because I do not need miracles for my own Atonement, but I stand at the end in case YOU fail temporarily.

6   S: SPECIAL EXPLANATION: (In response to H. request re possible corrections.) Change the word "sin" to "absence of love." Sin is a man-made word with threat connotations which he made up himself. No REAL threat is involved anywhere. Just because "nature abhors a vacuum," which is true enough, it does NOT follow that "a vacuum is filled with hellfire." Nothing is gained by frightening yourself, and it is very destructive. Miracles need freedom from fear. Part of their Atonement value involves just that. Note that the word "atone" really means "undo."

7   The purpose of the Atonement is to restore everything TO you. That is, to restore the awareness. (Later clarification.) You had everything when you were created, just as everyone did.

8   Having been restored to your original state, you naturally become part of the Atonement yourself. You now share MY inability to tolerate the lack of love in yourself and in everyone else, and MUST join the GREAT CRUSADE to correct it. The slogan for this Crusade is "Listen, Learn, and DO."

---

[8] Matthew 25:40 (ASV) And the King shall answer and say unto them, Verily I say unto you, Inasmuch as ye did it unto one of these my brethren, even these least, ye did it unto me.

B. Principles Of Miracles

9   This means:

> Listen to My Voice,
> Learn to undo the error,
> and DO something to correct it.

The first two are not enough. The real members of MY party are ACTIVE workers.

27. The power to work Miracles BELONGS to you. I will create the right opportunities for you to do them. But you must be ready and willing to do them, since you are already able to. Doing them will bring conviction in the ability. I repeat that you will see Miracles through your hands through MINE. Conviction really comes through accomplishment. Remember that ability is the potential, Achievement is its expression, and Atonement is the Purpose.

28. A miracle is a Universal Blessing from God through Me to all My Brothers.

2   S: Explanation: You once said that souls cannot rest until everyone has found salvation. This happens to be true.

3   It is the privilege of the forgiven to forgive. The Disciples were officially and specifically told to heal others, as Physicians of the Lord.[9] They were also told to heal themselves, and were promised that I would never leave them or forsake them[10]. Atonement is the natural profession of the Children of God,[11] because they have professed Me.

---

9   Luke 9:1 Then he called his twelve disciples together, and gave them power and authority over all devils, and to cure diseases. 2 And he sent them to preach the kingdom of God, and to heal the sick.
Luke 10:9 And heal the sick that are therein, and say unto them, The kingdom of God is come nigh unto you.

10 Hebrews 13:5 Let your conversation be without covetousness; and be content with such things as ye have: for he hath said, I will never leave thee, nor forsake thee.

11 Matthew 5:9 Blessed are the peacemakers: for they shall be called the children of God.
Romans 8:16 The Spirit itself beareth witness with our spirit, that we are the children of God: 17 And if children, then heirs; heirs of God, and joint-heirs with Christ; if so be that we suffer with him, that we may be also glorified together. 18 For I reckon that the sufferings of this present time are not worthy to be compared with the glory which shall be revealed in us. 19 For the earnest expectation of the creature waiteth for the manifestation of the sons of God.
Also: Luke 20:36, John 11:51

Chapter 1 – Introduction To Miracles

4   S: (ASIDE.) Tell B that that is what Professor really means. As an Assoc. Prof., he must become associated with My strength. As an Asst. Prof., you must assist both him and Me. The Children need both strength and help. You cannot help until you are strong. The Everlasting Arms are your strength,[12] and the Wisdom of God[13] is your help.

5   "Heaven and Earth shall pass away [14] " means that they will not always exist as separate states. My Word, which is the Resurrection and the Life, [15] shall not pass away, because Life is Eternal. YOU are the work of God, and His Work is wholly loveable and wholly loving. This is how a man MUST think of himself in his heart, because this is what he IS.

6   S: ADD: "As a man thinketh in his heart, so is he." [16]

a. The Relationship of Miracles and Revelation

1   Remember the point about Miracles as a means of organizing different levels of consciousness. Miracles come from the below conscious or subconscious level. Revelations come from the above conscious level. The conscious level is in between and reacts to either sub or super-conscious impulses in varying ratios. Freud was right about the classification, but not the names. He was also right that the content of consciousness is fleeting. Consciousness is the level which engages in the world, and is capable of responding to both external and internal impulses. Having no impulses from itself, and being primarily a mechanism for inducing response, it can be very wrong.

2   Revelations induce complete but temporary suspension of doubt and fear. They represent the original form of communication between God and His Souls, before the intrusion of fire and ice made this impossible. It should be noted that they involve an extremely personal sense of closeness to Creation, which man tries to find in sexual relationships. This confusion is responsible for the depression and fear which are often associated with sex.

---

12 Deuteronomy 33:27 The eternal God is thy refuge, and underneath are the everlasting arms: and he shall thrust out the enemy from before thee; and shall say, Destroy them.

13 Ezra 7:25 And thou, Ezra, after the wisdom of thy God, that is in thine hand, set magistrates and judges, which may judge all the people that are beyond the river, all such as know the laws of thy God; and teach ye them that know them not.

14 Mark 13:31 "Heaven and earth shall pass away: but my words shall not pass away."
Also Matthew 24:25 and Luke 21:33

15 John 11:25: Jesus said to her, "I am the resurrection and the life. He who believes in Me, though he may die, he shall live.

16 Proverbs 23:7 "For as he thinks in his heart, so is he.

B. Principles Of Miracles

3   Sex is often associated with lack of love, but Revelation is PURELY a love experience. Physical closeness CANNOT achieve this.

As was said before, the subconscious impulses properly induce Miracles, which ARE interpersonal, and result in closeness to others.

This can be misunderstood by a personally willful consciousness as an impulse toward sexual gratification.

4   For example, if the identification is with the body, consciousness may distort superconscious impulses by denying their Source, and seeking their impact in the orgasm. This is the result of the "mistaken identity" confusion.

5   If you will look back at the description of the EFFECTS of Revelation (p2 above) you will see that there ARE some similarities in the experiential results but hardly in the content.

6   The Revelation unites Souls directly with God

7   The Miracle unites Souls directly with each other.

8   Neither emanates from consciousness, but both are EXPERIENCED there. This is essential, because consciousness is the state which PRODUCES action, though it DOES NOT Inspire it.

9   Man is free to believe what he chooses. What he DOES attests to what he believes.

10   The deeper levels of his subconscious always contain the impulse to Miracles, but he is free to fill its superficial levels, which are closer to consciousness, with the impulses of this world and to identify himself with them. This results in denying himself access to the miracle level underneath. In conscious actions, then, his interpersonal relationships also become superficial, and miracle-inspired relating becomes impossible.

29. Miracles are a way of EARNING release from fear.

2   Revelation induces a state in which fear has ALREADY BEEN abolished. Miracles are thus a means, and Revelations are an end. In this sense, they work together.

3   S: Tell B. that miracles DO NOT depend on Revelation. They INDUCE it. He is quite capable of miracles already, but he is still too fearful for Revelations.

4   S: to H. Note that YOUR Revelation occurred specifically after you had engaged at the visionary level in a process of DENYING fear.

5   Revelation is intensely personal, and is actually not translatable into conscious content at all. That is why any attempt to describe it in words is usually incomprehensible, even to the writer himself at another time. This is why the Book of

Chapter 1 – Introduction To Miracles

Revelations is essentially incomprehensible. Revelation induces ONLY experience. Miracles, on the other hand, induce interpersonal ACTION. In the end, these are more useful, because of their IMPERSONAL nature.

6   In this phase of learning, working miracles is more valuable because freedom from fear cannot be thrust upon you. The experience cannot last.

7   S: Tell B. that your propensity for Revelations, which is very great, is the result of a high level of past communion. Its transitory nature comes from the descent into fear, which has not yet been overcome. His own "suspended" state mitigates both extremes. This has been very apparent in the course of both of your recent developmental patterns.

8   S: Miracles are the essential course of ACTION for both of you. They will strengthen him and stabilize you.

9   S: NOTE that the much more personal than usual notes you are taking today reflect the Revelatory experience. This does NOT produce the more generalizeable quality which this course is aimed at. They may, nevertheless, be of great help to B. personally, since you asked for something that WOULD help him personally. It depends on how he listens, and how well he understands the COOPERATIVE nature of your joint experience. You can help only by reading this note FIRST. Ask him later if this should be included in the written part of the course at all or whether you should keep these notes separately. He is in charge of these decisions.

10 S: Tell B. he should try to understand the VERY important difference between Christ-control and Christ-guidance. This is what made him fearful yesterday.

30. Miracles praise God through men. They praise God by honoring his Creations, affirming their perfection. They heal because they deny body-identification and affirm Soul-identification. By perceiving the Spirit, they adjust the levels and see them in proper alignment. This places the Spirit at the center, where Souls can communicate directly.

31. Miracles should inspire gratitude, not awe. Man should thank God for what he really is. The Children of God are very holy. The miracle honors their holiness.

2   God's Creations cannot lose their holiness, although it can be hidden. The miracle uncovers it, and brings it into the light where it belongs.

3   Holiness can never be really hidden in darkness, but man can deceive himself on this point. This illusion makes him fearful, because in his heart he KNOWS it is an illusion. Like all illusions, he exerts enormous efforts to establish their validity. The miracle sets validity where it belongs. Eternal validity belongs only to the Soul. The miracle

B. Principles Of Miracles

acknowledges only the Truth. It thus dispels man's illusions about himself, and puts him into communion with himself and with God.

32. Christ inspires all miracles, which are essentially intercessions. They intercede for man's holiness, and make him holy. They place man beyond the physical laws, and raise him into the sphere of celestial order. In this order, man IS perfect.

2   The Soul never loses its communion with God. Only the mind and body need Atonement. The miracle joins in the Atonement of Christ by placing the mind in the service of the Spirit. This establishes the proper function of mind, and abolishes its errors.

33. Miracles honor man, BECAUSE he is lovable. They dispel illusions about himself, and perceive the light in him. They thus atone for his errors by freeing him from his own nightmares. They release him from a prison in which he has imprisoned himself. By freeing his mind from illusions, they restore his sanity, and place him at the feet of Jesus.[17]

    S: Tell B:

2   A man's mind can be possessed by illusions, but his Spirit is eternally free. If a mind creates without love, it can create an empty shell. This CAN be possessed by evil. But the Atonement restores the Soul to its proper place. Unless there is emptiness there is no danger, and emptiness is a false creation. The mind that serves the Spirit is invulnerable.

    H. Note: Biblical quotation re healing of devil possessed man, in which the sufferer was subsequently found healed in his right mind, and sitting at feet of Jesus.

34. The miracle restores the Soul to its fullness. By atoning for lack, it establishes perfect protection. The strength of the Soul leaves no room for intrusions. The forgiven are filled with the Soul, and their Soul forgives in return. It is the duty of the released to release their brothers.

2   The forgiven ARE the means of Atonement. Those released by Christ must join in releasing their brothers, for this is the plan of Atonement. Miracles are the way in which minds that serve the spirit unite with Christ for the salvation,or release, of all God's Creations.

---

[17] The account of "Legion" - Mark 5: 1-15: And they came to Jesus and saw him who had been demon-possessed, and had the legion, sitting and clothed and right-minded, the one who had the legion. And they were afraid.

Chapter 1 – Introduction To Miracles

3   MockedH: commented on awakening with the phrase "God is not Mocked,"[18] with anticipation of punishment.

4   S: INTERPRETATION: "God is not mocked" was intended as reassurance. You are afraid that what you wrote last night was contradictory, conflicting with some earlier points, especially because you were writing while you were all doped up. Remember, "God is not mocked" under any circumstances.

5   S: Tell B. that there are certain advantages in being a Psychologist. A major one is the understanding of projection, and the extent of its results. Possession is very closely related to projection. "Lucifer "[19] could be literally translated "Light Bearer. " He literally PROJECTED himself from Heaven. Projection still has this "hurling" connotation, because it involves hurling something you DO NOT want, and regard as dangerous and frightening, to someone else. This is the opposite of the Golden Rule, and having placed this rule upside down, the reverse of miracles, or projection, follows automatically.

35. One of the major problems with miracle workers is that they are so sure that what they are doing is right, because they KNOW it stems from love, that they do not pause to let ME establish MY limits.

2   S: The correction lies in accepting what is true in YOURSELF, by bringing ALL that you are into light. (H. fearful of writing next part.) Cayce[20] was wrong about Possession, and he was also wrong about hurting himself.

3   While what he,Cayce, did came from Me, he could NOT be induced to ask me each time whether I wanted him to perform this PARTICULAR miracle. If he had, he would not have performed any miracles that could not get through constructively, and would thus have saved himself unnecessary strain. He burned himself out with indiscriminate miracles, and to this extent did not fulfill his own full purpose, and was also subject to the Scribal error I mentioned at the start. The Disciples were also prone to this.

4   The answer is NEVER perform a miracle without asking me IF you should. This spares you from exhaustion, and because you act under direct communication the trance[21]

---

18 Gal 6:7 "Be not deceived; God is not mocked: for whatsoever a man soweth, that shall he also reap."
Also Job 13:9 Will it be well when He searches you out? Or can you mock Him as one mocks a man?
19 Isa 4:12 KJV: How are you fallen from heaven, O Lucifer, son of the morning! how are you cut down to the ground, who did weaken the nations!
20 Edgar Cayce – 'The Sleeping Prophet' Founder of A.R.E. - Association for Research And Enlightenment. The first distributed copy of the typed Course text was sent to the A.R.E., which Helen was familiar with. That version of the Course has been labeled the HLC version, for Hugh Lyn Cayce, Edgar's son, then running the association.

B. Principles Of Miracles

becomes unnecessary. Because miracles are expressions of love, it does NOT follow that they will always be effective. I am the only one who can perform miracles indiscriminately, because I AM the Atonement. You have a ROLE in Atonement, which I will dictate TO you.

5   Remember, you already have a point about the involuntary nature of miracles [22]. We also have established the fact that everything involuntary belongs under Christ-control, NOT under yours. Under Christ-control, Miracles REPLENISH the doer as well as the receiver.

6   Possession really means "Not under Christ-Control," thus making him vulnerable to projection. The references (Edgar Cayce) to the earth-bound entering bodies really refer to the "taking over" by their own earth-bound "thoughts." This IS Demon Possession. After all, Lucifer fell, but he was still an angel. He is thus the symbol for man. Atonement is the knowledge that the belief that angels can fall is false. It is true that mind can create projections as well as miracles, but it's NOT true that projections are REAL. Any psychologist should understand this. This is what is meant by "The Truth shall set you free."[23]

7   Christ-controlled miracles are part of the Atonement, but Christ-guidance is personal, and leads to PERSONAL salvation. The impersonal nature of miracles is an essential ingredient, because this enables Me to control their distribution as I see fit.

8   Christ-guidance, on the other hand, leads to the highly PERSONAL experience of Revelation. This is why it involves PERSONAL choice. A guide does NOT control, by definition, but he does DIRECT, leaving the following up to you. "Lead us not into temptation"[24] means "guide us out of our own errors." Note that the word is "lead," NOT order.

9   "Take up thy cross and follow me "[25] should be interpreted to read "Recognize your errors and choose to abandon them by following My guidance."

10 Tell B. when he is afraid of Possession, he need only remember that error cannot really threaten Truth, which ALWAYS can withstand its assaults. ONLY the error is really vulnerable. The "Princes of this World"[26] are princes only because they are really angels. But they are free to establish their kingdom where they see fit.

---

22 This section: Principle 5.
23 John 8:32 and ye shall know the truth, and the truth shall make you free.
24 Matthew 6:13 And lead us not into temptation, but deliver us from evil:
25 Mark 10:21 "And Jesus looking upon him loved him, and said unto him, One thing thou lackest: go, sell whatsoever thou hast, and give to the poor, and thou shalt have treasure in heaven: and come, take up the cross, and follow me."
26 I Corinthians 2:6 Howbeit we speak wisdom among them that are perfect: yet not the wisdom of this world, nor of the princes of this world, that come to nought:

Chapter 1 – Introduction To Miracles

> If you will remember that ALL princes INHERIT their power from the Father, the right choice becomes inevitable.
>
>> The soul is in a state of grace forever.
>> Man's reality is ONLY his soul.
>> Therefore, man is in a state of Grace forever.

11 Atonement undoes all errors in this respect, and thus uproots the REAL source of fear. If you will check back at the reference to uprooting [27], you will understand it better in this context.

12 S: Tell B. that:

13 WHENEVER God's reassurances are experienced as threat, it is ALWAYS because man is defending his misplaced and misdirected love and loyalty. That is what projection always involves.

14 "Casting spells" merely means "affirming error," and error is lack of love. When man projects this onto others, he DOES imprison them, but only to the extent that he reinforces errors they have already made. This distortion makes them vulnerable to the curse of others, since they have already cursed themselves. The miracle worker can only bless, and this undoes the curse and frees the soul from prison.

15 S: Tell B. that his slip about (rivet [28]) should be noted:

16 Some slips reach consciousness from the un-Christ-controlled subconscious, and betray a lack of love.

17 But other slips come from the superconscious, which IS in communion with God, and which can also break into consciousness.

18 S: B's slip (rivet) was an expression of a Soul gaining enough strength to request freedom from prison. It will ultimately DEMAND it.

19 S: Special Revelation for H.

> You are wholly lovely. A perfect shaft of pure light. Before your loveliness the stars stand transfixed, and bow to the power of your will.
>
> What do children know of their creation, except what their Creator tells them?
>
> You were created ABOVE the angels because your role involves creation as

---

[27] This section Principle 24, p2
[28] Refers to some Bill comment never revealed.
   Further forward references to it at:
   This Chapter Principle 42, p14 [as river]
   Chapter 5 I. The Eternal Fixation, p14.

B. Principles Of Miracles

> well as protection.
>
> > You who are in the image of the Father need bow only to HIM, before whom I kneel with you.
>
> S: NOTE: This revelation was permitted because you did NOT project onto B. the blame for your omission to ASK ME if you should transcribe the notes. The fact that HE should have done so does not exempt you from your own omission.
>
> > Thanks for blessing him with a miracle rather than cursing him with projection.
>
> S: NOTE FURTHER: HE needn't feel concerned about it either; so he forgot? It happens all the time, until the habit of asking becomes involuntary.

20 S: re H. meeting with Dr. Wise and Dr. Damrosch. Dr. D permitted an opportunity for questioning in his capacity as chairman of the flu board for asking re B's flu shot. This was an example of how miracles should work. You did not jump into the question yourself, and even though you DID rush for the phone on Red's advice, you exerted no pressure on B's reluctance.

This gave ME a chance to let you leave it to the real expert, whom I sent to answer the question.

36. Miracles are examples of right thinking. Reality contact at all levels becomes strong and accurate, thus permitting correct delineation of intra-and interpersonal boundaries. As a result, the doer sees the truth as God created it. [This is what is meant by the point on "perspective adjustment." Principle **24**]

37. A miracle is a correction factor introduced into false thinking by ME.

It acts as a catalyst, shaking up erroneous perception and snapping it into place. This correction factor places man under the Atonement principle, where his perception is healed. Until this has occurred, perception of the Divine Order is impossible. True depth perception becomes possible only at the highest order of perceptual integration.

38. The Spiritual eye is the mechanism of miracles, because what the Spiritual eye perceives IS truth. The Spiritual eye perceives both the Creations of God AND the creations of man. Among the creations of man, it can also separate the true from the false by its ability to perceive totally rather than selectively. It thus becomes the proper instrument for reality testing, which always involves the necessary distinction between the true and the false.

Chapter 1 – Introduction To Miracles

39. The miracle dissolves error because the Spiritual eye identifies error as false or unreal. This is the same as saying that by seeing light, darkness automatically disappears.

2   Darkness is lack of light. It does not have unique properties of its own. It is an example of the scarcity fallacy, from which only error can proceed. Truth is always abundant. Those who perceive and acknowledge that they have everything have no need for driven behavior of any kind.

3   Miracles are a blessing from parents to children. This is just another way of phrasing the previous point about "from those who have more to those who have less." Children do NOT belong to parents, but they DO need to share their greater abundance. If they are deprived, their perception becomes distorted. When this occurs, the whole family of God, or the Sonship, is impaired in its relationships.

4   Ultimately, every member of the family of God must return. The miracle calls to him to return, because it blesses and honors him even though he may be absent in spirit.

40. The miracle acknowledges all men as your brothers and Mine. It is a way of perceiving the Universal Mark of God in them.

2   S: Tell B. that this is the true "strawberry mark" of Brotherhood. This is just a sign of special concern for him, because he keeps worrying about this.

You might add that his false idea about his own exclusion from Universal Love is fallacious in your terms, and arrogant in his. HIS real specialness does NOT stem from exclusion, but from inclusion. ALL My Brothers are special. He should stop interpreting this as "all except B." This is ridiculous!

Tell him that the implied lack of love that his version contains is WAY off the Mark, and misses the level of right thinking entirely. He MUST heal his perception in this respect. He MUST work a miracle on behalf of himself here before he can effect miracles as creative energizers, which they are. (See the point, Principle **24**, about miracles as a perception corrector)

3   S: Tell B. that 50,000,000 Frenchmen CAN be wrong, because the notion is too fragmented. What CAN'T be wrong is the Universal Sonship of which he is a part.)

4   God WOULD be mocked if ANY of his creations lacked holiness. The Creation IS whole. The mark of Wholeness is Holiness, not holes. THE SONSHIP HAS NO HOLES ANYWHERE.

41. Wholeness is the perceptual content of the miracle. It thus corrects, or atones for, the faulty perception of lack.

B. Principles Of Miracles

2   We now turn to the fundamental distinction between miracles and projection. The stimulus MUST precede the response, and must also determine or influence the kind of response that is evoked. The relationships of S and R (stimulus and response) are EXTREMELY intimate. (The behavioristic terminology is because this part deals with behavior.)

3   Behavior IS response, so that the question "response to what?" becomes crucial.

4   Stimuli of all kinds are identified through perception. You perceive the stimulus and behave accordingly. It follows, then, that:

> As ye perceive
> So will ye behave

5   H: Raises point that Biblical language is hardly behavioristic terminology.

6   S: Answer: No, but they needn't be OUT of accord with each other, either.)

7   Consider the Golden Rule again. [29] You are asked to behave towards others as you would have them behave toward you. This means that the perception of both must be accurate, since the Golden Rule is the Order for appropriate behavior. You can't behave appropriately unless you perceive accurately, because appropriate behavior DEPENDS on lack of level confusion. The presence of level confusion ALWAYS results in variable reality testing, and hence variability in behavioral appropriateness.

8   All forms of self-image debasement are FUNDAMENTAL perceptual distortions. They inevitably produce either self-contempt or projection, and usually both.

9   Since you and your neighbor are equal members of the same family, as you perceive both, so will you behave toward both.

> The way to perceive for Golden Rule behavior is to look out from the perception of your own holiness and perceive the holiness of others.

10   S: B. and you need considerable clarification of the channel role. Look carefully at Mrs. Albert. She is working miracles every day, because she knows who she is. I emphasize again that your tendency to forget names is not hostility, but a fear of involvement or RECOGNITION. You had misinterpreted human encounters as opportunities for magic rather than for miracles and so you tried to PROTECT THE NAME. This is a very ancient and primitive way of trying to protect a person.

11   S: NOTE The very old Jewish practice of changing the name of a person who is very ill, so that when the list is given to the Angel of Death, the person with that name will not be found.

---

[29] This section: Principle 34, p2

Chapter 1 – Introduction To Miracles

12   This is a good example of the curiously literal regression which can occur in very bright people when they become afraid. You and B. both do it. Actually, it is a device closely related to the phobia, in the sense that they both narrow fear to a simple aspect of a much larger problem in order to enable them to avoid it.

13   A similar mechanism works when you get furious about a comparatively minor expression by someone to whom you are ambivalent. A good example of this is your response to Jonathan, who DOES leave things around in very strange ways. Actually, he does this because he thinks that by minor areas of disorganization he can protect his stability. I remind you that you have done this yourself for years, and should understand it very well. This should be met with great charity, rather than with great fury.

14   The fury comes from your awareness that you do not love Jonathan as you should, and you narrow your lack of love by centering your hate on trivial behavior in an attempt to protect him from it. You also call him Jonathan for the same reason. [30]

15   Note that a name is a human symbol that "stands for" a person. Superstitions about names are very common for just that reason. That is also why people sometimes respond with anger when their names are spelled or pronounced incorrectly.

16   Actually, the Jewish superstition about changing the names was a distortion of a revelation about how to alter or avert death. What the revelation's proper content was that those "who change their mind" (not name) about destruction (or hate) do not need to die. Death is a human affirmation of a belief in hate. That is why the Bible says "There is no death,"[31] and that is why I demonstrated that death does not exist. Remember that I came to FULFILL the law[32] by RE-INTERPRETING it. The law itself, if properly understood, offers only protection to man. Those who have not yet "changed their minds" have entered the "hellfire" concept into it.

17   Remember, I said before that because "nature abhors a vacuum," [33] it does NOT follow that the vacuum is filled with hell fire. The emptiness engendered by fear should be replaced by love, because love and its absence are in the same dimension, and correction cannot be undertaken except WITHIN a dimension. Otherwise, there has been a confusion of levels.

---

30 This section: Principle 3 p2
31 2 Timothy 1:10 But has now been revealed by the appearing of our Savior Jesus Christ, who has abolished death and brought life and immortality to light through the gospel, ;
Revelation 21:4 And God will wipe away every tear from their eyes; there shall be no more death, nor sorrow, nor crying. There shall be no more pain, for the former things have passed away."
32 Matthew 5:17 Do not think that I came to destroy the Law or the Prophets. I did not come to destroy but to fulfill.
33 This section: Principle 26, p6

B. Principles Of Miracles

18   Returning to Mrs. Albert, she corrected your error about her name without embarrassment and without hostility, because she has NOT made your own mistake about names.

19   S: She is not afraid, because she knows she is protected. She made the correction ONLY because you were inaccurate, and the whole question of embarrassment did not occur to her.

20   She was also quite unembarrassed when she told you that everything has to be done to preserve life, because you never can tell when God may come and say "Get up, Dave," and then he will.

21   She did not ask what YOU believed first, and afterwards merely added "and it's true, too." The RIGHT answer to the SCT item is: WHEN THEY TOLD ME WHAT TO DO, I "referred the question to the only REAL authority."

22   H: note: If you ask somebody what he believes before you tell him what you believe, then you are implying that you will say what he approves. This is not "the real authority."

23   You took a lot of notes on "Those who are ashamed of Me before men, them will I be ashamed of before God."[34] This was rather carefully clarified, even though the quotation is not quite right, but it doesn't matter.

24   The important thing is that elsewhere in the Bible it also says "Those who represent, or plead for, Me to men will be represented, or pleaded for, BY Me before God."[35]

Note: This quotation is also not the correct Biblical phrasing, but it IS what it means. Note that one who represents also "witnesses for." The quotation thus means that you represent or "witness for" the authority in whom you believe.

25   Your witnessing DEMONSTRATES your belief, and thus strengthens it.

26   I assure you that I will "witness for" anyone who lets me, and to whatever extent he himself permits it.

27   Those who witness for me are expressing, through their miracles, that they have abandoned deprivation in favor of the abundance they have learned BELONGS to them.

> [Isaiah 43:10 :
> "You are My witnesses," says the LORD,
> "And My servant whom I have chosen,
> That you may know and believe Me,
> And understand that I am He.

---

34   Matthew 10:33 But whosoever shall deny me before men, him will I also deny before my Father which is in heaven. Also Mark 8:38 and Luke 9:2

35   Matthew 10:32 Every one therefore who shall confess me before men, him will I also confess before my Father which is in heaven.

Chapter 1 – Introduction To Miracles

> Before Me there was no God formed,
> Nor shall there be after Me.
> I have declared and saved,
> I have proclaimed,
> And there was no foreign god among you;
> Therefore you are My witnesses,"
> Says the LORD, "that I am God."
>
> ...added for reference]

42. A MAJOR contribution of miracles is their strength in releasing man from his misplaced sense of isolation, deprivation, and lack. They are affirmations of Sonship, which is a state of completion and abundance.

2   B's very proper emphasis on "changing your mind" needs clarification.

3   Whatever is true and real is eternal, and CANNOT change or be changed. The Soul is therefore unalterable because it is ALREADY perfect, but the mind can elect the level it chooses to serve. The only limit which is put on its choice is that it CANNOT serve two masters.[36]

4   While the ballot itself is a secret one, and the right to vote is fully protected, voting ALWAYS entails both election AND rejection. If two candidates are voted for, for the same position, the machine cancels the ballot automatically.

5   This is necessary, because a split vote does not represent ANY REAL allegiance.

> Free will is the attribute of the mind, NOT the Soul. The Soul always remains changeless, because it never leaves the sight of God.

6   The Creation of the Soul is already fully accomplished. The mind, if it votes to do so, becomes a medium by which the Soul can create along the line of its own creation. If it does not freely elect to do so, it retains this creative ability, but places itself under tyrannous rather than authoritative control. As a result, what it creates is imprisonment, because such are the dictates of tyrants.

7   To "change your mind" means to place it at the disposal of True authority. The miracle is thus a sign that the mind has elected to be guided by Christ in HIS service. The abundance of Christ is the natural result of choosing to follow him.[37]

---

36 Luke 16:13 No servant can serve two masters: for either he will hate the one, and love the other; or else he will hold to one, and despise the other. Ye cannot serve God and mammon.
37 Matthew 4:19 Then He said to them, "Follow Me, and I will make you fishers of men."

B. Principles Of Miracles

8   S: P.S. The reason you have been late recently (for work) because you were taking dictation is merely because you didn't remember to ask me when to stop. This is an example of the "indiscriminate or uncontrolled" miracle-working we already spoke of. It is well-meant but ill-advised.

9   I prompted that call from Jack (taxi man – couldn't pick H. up, etc.) to show you that this is not necessary. Also, the other man needed the money more today.

10   NOTE that you managed to fill your scribal role with no interruptions, and were also on time.

11   NOTE also that you closed the book and put it aside WITHOUT consulting me.

         ASK "Is that all?"

         ANSWER: No: Add the following: These notes are serving, among other things, to replace the "handwriting on the wall" which you once saw next to your own altar, which read "You have been weighed in the balance and found wanting."

12   Scribes MUST learn Christ-control, to replace their former habits, which DID produce scarcity rather than abundance. From errors of this kind, the sense of deprivation IS inevitable, but very easily corrected.

13   Both of you are involved with unconscious distortions (above the miracle level), which are producing a dense cover over miracle-impulses which makes it hard for them to reach consciousness.

14   S: The following is in relation to question about sex. Tell B. "the one more river [38]" is related to sex. You might even explain it to him as a "tidal wave," a term which he will understand. YOU won't.

         Sex and miracles are both WAYS OF RELATING.

         The nature of any interpersonal relationship is limited or defined by what you want it to DO which is WHY you want it in the first place.

         Relating is a way of achieving an outcome.

15   Indiscriminate sexual impulses resemble indiscriminate miracle impulses in that both result in body image misperceptions.

16   The first is an expression of an indiscriminate attempt to reach communion through the body. This involves not only the improper self identification, but also disrespect for the individuality of others.

---

[38] Regarding slip (rivet vs river) discussed in Chapters 1 and 5:
This section: Principle 35, p14, p16
Chapter 5 I. The Eternal Fixation, p14

Chapter 1 – Introduction To Miracles

17   Self-control is NOT the whole answer to this problem, though I am by no means discouraging its use.

18   It must be understood, however, that the underlying mechanism must be uprooted, a word you both should understand well enough by now not to regard it as frightening.

19   ALL shallow roots[39] have to be uprooted, because they are not deep enough to sustain you. The illusion that shallow roots can be deepened and thus made to hold is one of the corollaries on which the reversal of the Golden Rule,[40] referred to twice before, is balanced.[41]

As these false underpinnings are uprooted, or given up, equilibrium is experienced as unstable. But the fact is that NOTHING is less stable than an orientation which is upside down. Anything that holds it this way is hardly conducive to greater stability.

20   The whole danger of defenses lies in their propensity to hold misperceptions rigidly in place. This is why rigidity is regarded AS stability by those who are off the mark.

21   S: NOTE The only final solution - (no, Helen, this has nothing to do with the Nazi use of the term. You just got frightened again.) One of the more horrible examples of inverted or upside down thinking (and history is full of horrible examples of this) is the fact that the Nazis spelled their appalling error with capital letters. I shed many tears over this, but it is by no means the only time I said "Father, forgive them for they know not what they do."[42]

22   All actions which stem from reverse thinking are literally the behavioral expressions of those who know not what they do. Actually, Jean Dixon was right in her emphasis on "Feet on the ground and fingertips in the Heaven," though she was a bit too literal for your kind of understanding. Many people knew exactly what she meant, so her statement was the right miracle for them.

23   For you and Bill, it would be better to consider the concept in terms of reliability and validity. A rigid orientation can be extremely reliable, even if it IS upside down. In fact, the more consistently upside down it is, the more reliable it is, because consistency always held up better mathematically than test-re-test comparisons, which were ALWAYS on shaky ground. You can check this against Jack's notes if you wish, but I assure you its true. Split-half reliability is statistically a MUCH stronger approach. The reason for this is that correlation which is the technique applied to test-re-test

---

39   Luke 8:13 But the ones on the rock are those who, when they hear, receive the word with joy; and these have no root, who believe for a while and in time of temptation fall away.

40   Matthew 7:12 Therefore, whatever you want men to do to you, do also to them, for this is the Law and the Prophets.

41   This section: Principle 34, p2; Principle 41, p7,p9

42   Luke 23:34 Then said Jesus, Father, forgive them; for they know not what they do.

B. Principles Of Miracles

comparisons, measures only the EXTENT OF association, and does not consider the Direction at all.

24 But two halves of the same thing MUST go in the same direction, if there is to be accuracy of measurement. This simple statement is really the principle on which split half reliability, a means of estimating INTERNAL consistency, rests.

25 Note, however, that both approaches leave out a very important dimension. Internal consistency criteria disregard time, because the focus is on one-time measurements. Test-retest comparisons are BASED on time intervals, but they disregard direction.

26 It is possible, of course, to use both, by establishing internal consistency AND stability over time. You will remember that Jack once told his class that the more sophisticated statisticians are concentrating more and more on reliability, rather than validity. The rationale for this, as he said, was that a reliable instrument DOES measure something. He also said, however, that validity is still the ultimate goal, which reliability can only serve.

27 I submit (I'm using Jack's language in this section, because it always had a special meaning for you. So did Jack.) Your confusion of sex and statistics is an interesting example of this whole issue. Note that night you spent in the scent of roses doing a complex factorial analysis of covariance. It's a funny story to others, because they see a different kind of level confusion than the one you yourself were making. You might recall that YOU wanted that design, and Jack opposed it. One of the real reasons why that evening was so exhilarating was because it represented a "battle of intellects," (both good ones, by the way), each communicating exceptionally clearly but on opposite sides. The sexual aspects were naturally touched off in both of you, because of the sex and aggression confusion.

28 It is especially interesting that after the battle ended on a note of compromise with your agreeing with Jack, he wrote in the margin of your notes "virtue is triumphant." (H. note re submission-dominance, feminine-masculine roles, entered into this.) While this remark was funny to both of you at the time, you might consider its truer side. The virtue lay in the complete respect each of you offered to the other's intellect. Your mutual sexual attraction was also shared.

29 The error lay in the word "triumphant." This had the "battle" connotation, because neither of you was respecting ALL of the other. There is a great deal more to a person than intellect and genitals. The omission was the Soul.

30 I submit that if a mind (Soul) is in valid relationship with God, it CAN'T be upside down. Jack and the other very eminent methodologists have abandoned validity in favor of reliability because they have lost sight of the end and are concentrating on the means.

Chapter 1 – Introduction To Miracles

31   Remember the story about the artist who kept devoting himself to inventing better and better ways of sharpening pencils. He never created anything, but he had the sharpest pencil in town. (The language here is intentional.)

32   Sex is often utilized on behalf of very similar errors. Hostility, triumph, vengeance, self-debasement, and all sort of expressions of the lack of love are often VERY clearly seen in the accompanying fantasies.

But it is a PROFOUND error to imagine that, because these fantasies are so frequent, or occur so reliably, *that this implies validity.* Remember that while validity implies reliability the relationship is NOT reversible. You can be wholly reliable, and ENTIRELY wrong.

33   While a reliable test DOES measure something, what USE is the test unless you discover what the "something" is? And if validity is more important than reliability, and is also necessarily implied BY it, why not concentrate on VALIDITY and let reliability fall naturally into place?

34   Intellect may be a "displacement upward," but sex can be a "displacement outward." How can man "come close" to others through the parts of him which are really invisible? The word "invisible" means "cannot be seen or perceived." What cannot be perceived is hardly the right means for improving perception.

35   The confusion of miracle impulse with sexual impulse is a major source of perceptual distortion, because it INDUCES rather than straightening out the basic level-confusion which underlies all those who seek happiness with the instruments of the world. A desert is a desert is a desert. You can do anything you want in it, but you CANNOT change it from what it IS. It still lacks water, which is why it IS a desert

S: to H. Bring up that dream about the Bluebird. While H. was looking for this dream, she came across another. The message was to bring both, as an excellent example of how extremely good H. had become over the intervening 25 years at sharpening pencils. [43] Note that the essential content hasn't changed; it's just better written.

The thing to do with a desert is to LEAVE.

43. Miracles arise from a miraculous state of mind. By being One, this state of mind goes out to ANYONE, even without the awareness of the miracle worker himself. The impersonal nature of miracles is because Atonement itself is one, uniting all creations with their Creator.

---

[43] This section: Principle 41, p31

B. Principles Of Miracles

44. The miracle is an expression of an inner awareness of Christ and acceptance of his Atonement. The mind is then in a state of Grace, and naturally becomes gracious, both to the Host within and the stranger without. By bringing in the stranger, he becomes your brother. [44]

2   The miracles you are told NOT to perform have not lost their value. They are still expressions of your own state of Grace, but the ACTION aspect of the miracle should be Christ-controlled, because of His complete Awareness of the Whole Plan.

The impersonal nature of miracle-mindedness ensures YOUR own Grace, but only Christ is in a position to know where Grace can be BESTOWED.

45. A miracle is never lost. It touches many people you may not even know, and sometimes produces undreamed of changes in forces of which you are not even aware. This is not your concern. It will also always bless YOU. This is not your concern, either. But it IS the concern of the Record. The Record is completely unconcerned with reliability, being perfectly valid because of the way it was set up. It ALWAYS measures what it was supposed to measure.[45]

2   **S: I want to finish the instructions about sex, because this is an area the miracle worker MUST understand.**

3   Inappropriate sex drives, or misdirected miracle-impulses, result in guilt if expressed, and depression if denied.

We said before that ALL real pleasure comes from doing God's will. Whenever it is NOT done an experience of lack results. This is because NOT doing the will of God IS a lack of self.

4   Sex was intended as an instrument for physical creation to enable Souls to embark on new chapters in their experience, and thus improve their Record. The pencil was NOT an end in itself. It was an aid to the artist in his own creative endeavors. [46]

---

44   Matthew 25:35 For I was hungry and you gave Me food; I was thirsty and you gave Me drink; I was a stranger and you took Me in;

45   [Tim note:] Akashic Records is a term used by Edgar Cayce. It refers to THE collective thought, or story of separation in the One Mind of God's Son. This is the collective 'story' that makes the world at large (seem to be there and to be real), and it is also the script that generates its flow (how it changes with time) This generation is largely unconscious, giving rise to the appearance that 'things just happen to us.' Growing awareness and use of the miracle-oriented state of mind can override this unconscious flow of world events. Experiences in the world always produce a healing experience – if we let them. That, is what is 'measured.'

46   This section: Principle 41, p31

Chapter 1 – Introduction To Miracles

As he made new homes for Souls and guided them through the period of their own developmental readiness, he learned the role of the father himself. The whole process was set up as a learning experience in gaining Grace.

5   The pleasure which is derived from sex AS SUCH is reliable only because it stems from an error which men shared. AWARENESS of the error produces the guilt. DENIAL of the error results in projection. CORRECTION of the error brings release.

6   The only VALID use of sex is procreation. It is NOT truly pleasurable in itself.

> "Lead us not into Temptation" means:
> "Do not let us deceive ourselves into believing that we can relate in peace to God or our brothers with ANYTHING external."

7   The "sin of onan"[47] was called a "sin" because it involved a related type of self-delusion; namely, that pleasure WITHOUT relating can exist.

8   To repeat an earlier instruction, the concept of either the self or another as a "sex-OBJECT" epitomizes this strange reversal. [As B. put it, and very correctly, too,] It IS objectionable, but only because it is invalid. Upside down logic produces this kind of thinking.

9   Child of God, you were created to create the good, the beautiful, and the holy. Do not lose sight of this.

> [You were right in telling B. to] Invite Me to enter anywhere temptation arises. I will change the situation from one of inappropriate sexual attraction to one of impersonal miracle-working.

The concept of changing the channel for libidinal expression is Freud's greatest contribution, except that he did not understand what "channel" really means.

10   The love of God, for a little while, must still be expressed through one body to another. That is because the real vision is still so dim. Everyone can use his body best by enlarging man's perception, so he can see the real VISION. THIS VISION is invisible to the physical eye.

> The ultimate purpose of the body is to render itself unnecessary.
> Learning to do this is the only real reason for its creation.

---

47   Genesis 38:8 And Judah said unto Onan, Go in unto thy brother's wife, and marry her, and raise up seed to thy brother. 9 And Onan knew that the seed should not be his; and it came to pass, when he went in unto his brother's wife, that he spilled it on the ground, lest that he should give seed to his brother. 10 And the thing which he did displeased the Lord: wherefore he slew him also.

B. Principles Of Miracles

11   S: NOTE Scribes have a particular role in the Plan of Atonement, because they have the ability to EXPERIENCE revelations themselves, and also to put into words enough of the experience to serve as a basis for miracles.

       (This refers to experiences at the visionary level, after which H. wrote "If you will tell me what to do, I will to do it." She had not known that the word "to" was inserted, and had merely intended to write "I will do it." This recognition had a terrific impact on H.)

12   This is why you EXPERIENCED that revelation about "I will to do" VERY personally, but also WROTE IT: What you wrote CAN be useful to miracle workers other than yourself. We said before that prayer is the medium of miracles. The miracle prayer IS what you wrote, i.e. "If you will tell me what to do, I will to do it."

13   S: Correction next day: This is not a complete statement, because it does not exclude the negative. We have already told you to add "and NOT to do what you would not have me do." in connection with miracles. [48] The distinction has also been made here between "miracle-mindedness" as a STATE, and "miracle-doing" as its expression.

46. Your miracle-mindedness needs YOUR careful protection, because it is a state of miracle-READINESS. This is what the Bible means in the many references to "Hold yourself ready" [49] and other similar injunctions.

2   Readiness here means keep your perception right side up, (or valid), so you will ALWAYS be ready, willing, and able. These are the essentials for "listen, learn, and do." You must be

>READY to listen
>WILLING to learn
>and ABLE to do

3   Only the last is involuntary, because it is the APPLICATION of miracles which must be Christ-controlled.

---

48   This section: Principle 10, p3
49   Ecclesiastes 5:1 Keep thy foot when thou goest to the house of God, and be more ready to hear, than to give the sacrifice of fools: for they consider not that they do evil.
Titus 3:1 Put them in mind to be subject to principalities and powers, to obey magistrates, to be ready to every good work,
1 Peter 3:15 But sanctify the Lord God in your hearts: and be ready always to give an answer to every man that asketh you a reason of the hope that is in you with meekness and fear:
1 Peter 5:2 Feed the flock of God which is among you, taking the oversight thereof, not by constraint, but willingly; not for filthy lucre, but of a ready mind;

Chapter 1 – Introduction To Miracles

But the other two, which are the voluntary aspects of miracle-mindedness, ARE up to you.

> The miracle prayer is therefore:
> "If you will tell me what to do, I will to do it."
> "and NOT to do what you would not have me do."

This prayer is the door that leads out of the desert forever.

4   To channelize DOES have a "narrowing down" connotation, though NOT in the sense of lack. The underlying state of mind, or Grace is a total commitment. Only the DOING aspect involves the channel at all. This is because doing is always specific.

5   As Jack said, "A reliable instrument must measure something," but a channel is also valid.

6   A channel must learn to do ONLY what it is supposed to do. Change the prayer to read:

> If you will tell me what to do,
> ONLY THAT I will to do.

7   NOTE H. objects to doggerel sound of this, and regards it as very inferior poetry.
       S: ANSWER: It's hard to forget, though.

47. The Revelation is literally unspeakable, because it is an experience of unspeakable love. The word "Awe" should be reserved only for revelations, to which it is perfectly and correctly applicable. It is NOT appropriately applied to miracles, because a state of true awe is worshipful. It implies that one of a lesser order stands before the Greater One. This is the case only when a Soul stands before his Creator. Souls are perfect creations, and should be struck with awe in the presence of the Creator of Perfection.

2   The miracle, on the other hand, is a sign of love among equals. Equals cannot be in awe of each other, because awe ALWAYS implies inequality. Awe is not properly experienced even to me.

       S: to H. That is why in that short introductory vision, I knelt beside you, FACING the light.

3   An Elder Brother is entitled to respect for his greater experience, and a reasonable amount of obedience for his greater wisdom. He is also entitled to love, because he is a brother, and also to devotion, if he is devoted. It is only my own devotion that entitles me

B. Principles Of Miracles

to yours. But you will notice that I have knelt at your altar as readily as I would ever have you kneel at mine.

4
>There is nothing about me that you cannot attain. I have nothing that does not come from God. The main difference between us as yet is that I have NOTHING ELSE. This leaves me in a state of true holiness, which is only a POTENTIAL in you.

5 "No man cometh to the Father but by me[50]" is among the most misunderstood statements in the Bible. It DOES NOT mean that I am in anyway separate (or different) from you, EXCEPT IN TIME. Now, we know that time does not exist.

Actually, the statement is much more meaningful if it is considered on a vertical rather than a horizontal axis. Regarded along the vertical, man stands below me, and I stand below God. In the process of "rising up," I AM higher. This is because without me the distance between God and man is too great for man to encompass. I bridge the distance as an Elder Brother[51] to man, on the one hand, and a Son of God on the other. My devotion to my brothers has placed me in charge of the Sonship, which I can render complete only to the extent I can SHARE it.

6 This appears to contradict another statement: "I and my Father are one.[52]" It doesn't. There are still separate parts in the statement, in recognition of the fact that the Father is GREATER. Actually, the original statement was "are of one KIND."

7 The Holy Spirit is the Bringer of Revelations, not miracles. Revelations are INDIRECTLY inspired by me, because I am close to the Holy Spirit, and alert to revelation-readiness in my brothers.

I can thus BRING DOWN to them more than they can DRAW down to themselves. Jean Dixon's description is perhaps a better statement of my position. Because my feet are on the ground and my hands are in heaven, I can bring down the glories of Heaven to my brothers on earth.

48. The Holy Spirit is the Highest Communication Medium. Miracles do not involve this type of communication, because they are TEMPORARY communicative devices. When man can return to his original form of communication with God by direct REVELATION, the need for miracles is over. The Holy Spirit mediates higher to lower

---

50 John 14:6 "Jesus saith unto him, I am the way, and the truth, and the life: no one cometh unto the Father, but by me."
51 Romans 8:29 For whom He foreknew, He also predestined to be conformed to the image of His Son, that He might be the firstborn among many brethren.
52 John 10:30 I and my Father are one.

Chapter 1 – Introduction To Miracles

order communication, keeping the direct channel from God to man open for revelation. Revelation is NOT reciprocal. It is always FROM God TO man. This is because God and man are NOT equal. The miracle is reciprocal because it ALWAYS involves equality.

2   In the longitudinal, or horizontal, plane, the true equality of all men in the Sonship appears to involve almost endless time. But we know that time is only an artifact introduced as a learning aid.

49.   The miracle is a learning device which lessens the need for time. The sudden shift from horizontal to vertical perception which the miracle entails introduces an interval from which the doer and the receiver both emerge much farther along in time than they would otherwise have been.

50.   A miracle has thus the unique property of abolishing time by rendering the space of time it occupies unnecessary. There is NO relation between the time a miracle TAKES and the time it COVERS. It substitutes FOR learning that might have taken thousands of years. It does this by the underlying recognition of perfect equality and holiness between doer and receiver on which the miracle rests.

It is unstable, but perfectly consistent, i.e., it does not occur predictably across time, and it rarely occurs in comparable forms. But within ITSELF it is perfectly consistent. Since it contains NOTHING BUT an acknowledgment of equality and worth, all parts ARE equal. This establishes the prerequisite for validity.

2   We said before that the miracle abolishes time. It does this by a process of COLLAPSING it. It thus abolishes certain INTERVALS within it. It does this, however, WITHIN the larger temporal sequence.

3   The validity of the miracle, then, is PREDICTIVE, not logical, within the temporal schema. It establishes an out-of-pattern time interval, which is NOT under the usual laws of time. Only in this sense is it timeless. By collapsing time, it literally saves time, much the way "daylight saving time" does. It rearranges the distribution of light.

4   The miracle is the only device which man has at his immediate disposal for controlling time. Only the Revelation TRANSCENDS it, having nothing to do with time at all. The miracle is much like the body, in that both are learning aids which aim at facilitating a state in which they are unnecessary. When the Soul is finally in the original state of direct communication, neither the body nor the miracle serves any purpose.

5   While he is IN the body, however, man can choose between loveless and miraculous channels of creativity. He can create an empty shell,[53] but he DOES NOT create nothing at all. He can wait, delay, paralyze himself, reduce his creativity almost to nothing, and

---

53 See previous: Principle 33, p2; forward ref: Ch. 2 A. p3

B. Principles Of Miracles

even introduce a real developmental arrest or regression. But he CANNOT abolish his creativity. He CAN destroy his medium of communication, but NOT his potential.

6   He was NOT created by his own free will. Only what HE creates is his to decide. The basic decision of the miracle-minded is NOT to wait on time any longer than is necessary. Time can waste, as well as be wasted. The miracle-worker, therefore, accepts the time-control factor of the miracle gladly, because he knows that every collapse of time brings all men closer to the ultimate RELEASE from time, in which the Son and the Father ARE one.

7   The real meaning of "are of one kind" is "of one mind or will." When the will of the Sonship and the Father are one, their perfect accord IS Heaven.

8   S: ASIDE: Tell B. he is right in providing you with the consistent strength you need to get, and he needs to offer. Your instability and his weakness have resulted from bad karmic choices, and your relationship NOW is crucial for the future. You must both exert every effort to restore it to what it once was. Both of you are correcting where you have failed before. This has already enabled you to fulfill a very unexpected role in your own joint salvation, and the salvation of many other children I will entrust increasingly to you. These are by no means chosen at random. B. should know that his preparation is not only in terms of sharing in the results of your better application of some rather unusual talents. His own role, which he will understand after his preparation is complete, will be equally surprising. He will need your help then, as you need his strength now.

9   Note that you DO NOT need his help as a scribe, because you developed this ability by your own efforts, and finally placed them at MY disposal. By lending you his strength, he strengthens himself. When he gains this through his own efforts, he will need your help in a very unexpected way. But this is just another example of the reciprocal nature of miracles.

10   Equality does not imply homogeneity NOW. When EVERYONE has EVERYTHING, individual contributions to the Sonship will no longer be necessary. When the Atonement has been completed, ALL talents will be shared by ALL of the Sons of God. God is NOT partial. All of his children have His total love, and all of his gifts are given freely to everyone alike.

11   "Except you become as little children"[54] means unless you fully recognize your complete dependence on God, you cannot know the real power of the Son in his true relationship with the Father.

12   S: You and B:

---

[54] Matthew 18:3: And said, "Assuredly, I say to you, unless you are converted and become as little children, you will by no means enter the kingdom of heaven.

Chapter 1 – Introduction To Miracles

13   You DO have special talents which are needed for the Celestial speedup at this time. But note that the term speed-up is not one which relates to the TRANSCENDING of time.

14   When time is abolished, and all of the Sons of God have come home, no special agents will be necessary. But do not underestimate the power of special agents now, or the great need there is for them. I do not claim to be more than that myself. No one in his Right Mind, (a term which should be specially noted) ever wants either more or less than that. Those who are called on to witness for me NOW are witnessing for all men, as I am.

15   The role of the Priestess was once to experience Revelations and to work miracles. The purpose was to bring those not yet available for direct Revelations into proper focus for them. Heightened perception was always the essential Priestess attribute.

16   This is the first time that H. ever said that she would be honored if there were any notes.

17   H: Neither B. nor I is really clear about how sexual-impulses can be directly translated into miracle-impulses.

18   S: The fantasies that I mentioned yesterday (refers to a discussion H. and B. had) provide an excellent example of how you switch. Now switch the pronoun references, or it will be too confusing.

19   Fantasies are distorted forms of thinking, because they always involve twisting perception into unreality. Fantasy is a debased form of vision. Visions and Revelations are closely related. Fantasies and projection are more closely associated, because both attempt to control external reality according to false internal needs. "Live and let live" happens to be a very meaningful injunction. Twist reality in any way, and you are perceiving destructively. Reality was lost through usurpation, which in turn produced tyranny. I told you, you were now restored to your former role in the Plan of Atonement. But you must still choose freely to devote your heritage to the greater Restoration. As long as a single slave remains to walk the earth, your release is not complete. Complete restoration of the Sonship is the only true goal of the miracle-minded.

20   Sexual fantasies are distortions of perception by definition. They are a means of making false associations, and obtaining pleasure from them. Man can do this only because he IS creative. But although he can perceive false associations, he can never make them real except to himself. As was said before, man believes in what he creates. If he creates a miracle, he will be equally strong in his belief in that.

>   The strength of his conviction will then sustain the belief of the miracle receiver.

B. Principles Of Miracles

21 NO fantasies, sexual or otherwise, are true. Fantasies become totally unnecessary as the Wholly satisfying nature of reality becomes apparent. The sex impulse IS a miracle impulse when it is in proper focus. One individual sees in another the right partner for "procreating the stock,"[55] and also for their joint establishment of a creative home. This does not involve fantasy at all. If I am asked to participate in the decision, the decision will be a Right one, too.

22 In a situation where you or another person, or both, experience inappropriate sex impulses, KNOW FIRST that this is an expression of fear. Your love toward each other is NOT perfect, and this is why the fear arose. Turn immediately to me by denying the power of the fear, and ask me to help you to replace it with love. This shifts the sexual impulse immediately to the miracle-impulse, and places it at MY disposal.

23 Then acknowledge the true creative worth of both yourself AND the other one. This places strength where it belongs. Note that sexual fantasies are ALWAYS destructive, or depleting, in that they perceive another in an inappropriate creative role. Both people are perceived essentially as "objects" fulfilling THEIR OWN pleasure drives. This dehumanized view is the source of the DEPLETING use of sex. Freud's description is purely NEGATIVE, i.e., as a release from the UNPLEASANT. He also observed that the tension from id impulses never completely abates.

24 What he should have said is that the shift from miracle-impulses to sexual impulses was debilitating in the first place, because of the level-confusion involved. This set up a state in which real release was impossible. Note also that Freud's notion of sex was as a device for inducing RELAXATION, which he confused with PEACE.

25 Inappropriate sex relaxes only in the sense that it may induce physical sleep. The miracle, on the other hand, is an ENERGIZER. It always strengthens, and never depletes. It DOES induce peace, and by establishing tranquility, not relaxation, it enables both giver and receiver to enter into a state of Grace. Here his miracle-mindedness - not release from tension - is restored.

26 Tension is the result of a building-up of unexpressed miracle-impulses. This can be truly abated only by releasing the miracle-drive, which has been blocked.

> Converting it to sexual libido merely produces further blocking. Never foster this illusion in yourself, or encourage it in others.
> An "object" is incapable of release, because it is a concept which is deprived of creative power. The recognition of the real creative power in yourself AND others brings release because it brings peace.

---

[55] 'S: Wolff was not too far off here" - possibly refering to: (Google this:) "ATLANTA JOURNAL-RECORD OF MEDICINE B. WOLFF - January 1, 1902"

Chapter 1 – Introduction To Miracles

27   The peace of God which passeth understanding CAN keep your hearts now and forever.[56]

28   S: There are only two short additions needed here:

29   Your earlier acute problem in writing things down came from a MUCH earlier misuse of very great scribal abilities. These were turned to secret rather than shared advantage, depriving it of its miraculous potential, and diverting it into possession. This is much like the confusion of sex impulses with possession-impulses. Some of the original material is still in the Temple. This is why you became so afraid about Atlantis. B. has his own reasons.

30   Retain your miracle-minded attitude toward Rosie VERY carefully. She once hurt both of you, which is why she is now your servant. But she is blessed in that she sees service as a source of joy. Help her straighten out her past errors by contributing to your welfare now.

31   Special Revelation re H. - OMISSION 1 (The following was in notes but omitted from typed text:).

"Priestess, a brother has knelt at your shrine. Heal Him through Me."

H: I have an idea that the shrine merely represented the "altar within," which the Priestess served. I imagine that the communication form was direct, and the "brother" always nameless. I – the Priestess responded automatically by praying directly to God, standing with upraised arms to draw down a blessing on her brother, who knelt outside. Her response was completely automatic and impersonal. She never even thought of checking the outcome, because there WAS no doubt.

32   H: question re past memories.

33   S: ANSWER: As long as you remember ALWAYS that you never suffered anything because of anything that anyone ELSE did, this is not dangerous.

34   Remember that you who want peace can find it only by complete forgiveness. You never really WANTED peace before, so there was no point in knowing how to get it. This is an example of the "need to know" principle, which was established by the Plan of Atonement long before CIA.

35   No kind of knowledge is acquired by anyone unless he wants it, or believes in some way he NEEDS it. A psychologist does NOT need a lesson on the hierarchy of needs as such, but like everyone else, he DOES need to understand his own.

---

[56] Philippians 4:7 And the peace of God, which passeth all understanding, shall guard your hearts and your thoughts in Christ Jesus.

B. Principles Of Miracles

b. The Concept Of Lack

1   This particular set of notes will be the only one which deals with the concept of "lack," because while the concept does not exist in the Creation of God, it is VERY apparent in the creations of man. It is, in fact, the essential difference.

2   A need implies lack, by definition. It involves the recognition, conscious or unconscious, and at times, fortunately, superconscious, that you would be better off in a state which is somehow different from the one you are in.

3   Until the Separation, which is a better term than the Fall, nothing was lacking. This meant that man had no needs at all. If he had not deprived himself, he would never have experienced them.

4   After the Separation, needs became the most powerful source of motivation for human action. All behavior is essentially motivated by needs, but behavior itself is not a Divine attribute. The body is the mechanism for behavior. (Ask any behaviorist, and he's RIGHT, too.)

5   You tell your own classes that nobody would bother even to get up and go from one place to another if he did not think he would somehow be better off. This is very true.

6   Believing that he COULD be "better off" is the reason why man has the mechanism for behavior at his disposal. This is why the Bible says "By their DEEDS ye shall know them."[57]

7   A man acts according to the particular hierarchy of needs he establishes for himself. His hierarchy, in turn, depends on his perception of what he IS, i.e., what he LACKS. This establishes his own rules for what he needs to know.

8   Separation from God is the only lack he really needs to correct. But his Separation would never have occurred if he had not distorted his perception of truth, and thus perceived himself as lacking.

9   The concept of ANY sort of need HIERARCHY arose because, having made this fundamental error, he had already fragmented himself into levels with DIFFERENT needs. As he integrates, HE becomes one, and his ONE need becomes one accordingly. Only the fragmented can be confused about this.

10   Internal integration within the self will not correct the lack fallacy, but it WILL correct the NEED fallacy. (S: Thank you for writing this as given.) Unified need produces unified action, because it produces lack of ambivalence.

---

[57] Matthew 7:16-20 "By their fruits ye shall know them. Do men gather grapes of thorns, or figs of thistles? Even so every good tree bringeth forth good fruit; but the corrupt tree bringeth forth evil fruit. A good tree cannot bring forth evil fruit, neither can a corrupt tree bring forth good fruit. Every tree that bringeth not forth good fruit is hewn down, and cast into the fire. Therefore by their fruits ye shall know them."

Chapter 1 – Introduction To Miracles

11 The concept of need hierarchy, a corollary to the original error, requires correction at its OWN level, before the error of levels itself can be corrected. Man cannot operate, or behave, effectively while he operates at split levels. But as long as he does so, he must introduce correction from the bottom UP.

12 This is because he now operates in space, where "up" and "down" are meaningful terms. Ultimately, of course, space is as meaningless as time. The concept is really one of space-time BELIEF. The physical world exists only because man can use it to correct his UNBELIEF, which placed him in it originally. As long as man KNEW he did not need anything, the whole device was unnecessary.

13 The need to know is not safely under man's control at this time. It is MUCH better off under mine. Let's just leave it at that.

14 Specific question raised by B re sex under existing conditions. H. raised previous question about the past, which has just been answered.[58]

15 S: The other question, however, I am more than willing to answer, because it is appropriate for NOW. You and B. both chose your present sex partners shamefully, and would have to atone for the lack of love which was involved in any case.

16 You selected them precisely BECAUSE they were NOT suited to gratify your fantasies. This was not because you wanted to abandon or give up the fantasies, but because you were AFRAID of them. You saw in your partners a means of protecting against the fear, but both of you continued to "look around" for chances to indulge the fantasies.

17 The dream of the "perfect partner" is an attempt to find EXTERNAL integration, while retaining conflicting needs in the self.

18 B. was somewhat less guilty of this than you, but largely because he was more afraid. He had abandoned the hope of finding a perfect partner in a neurotic sense of despair of finding it. You, on the other hand, insisted that the hope was justified. Neither of you, therefore, was in your Right Mind.

19 As was said before, homosexuality is INHERENTLY more risky (or error prone) than heterosexuality, but both can be undertaken on an equally false basis. The falseness of the basis is clear in the accompanying fantasies. Homosexuality ALWAYS involves misperception of the self OR the partner, and generally both.

---

58 [Tim note:] There seems to have been a lot of dialog between Bill, Helen, and Jesus that was never shared. It also seems that they chose to include some portions of dialog that they deemed generally useful. Hence there are these rather cryptic and partial comments and questions, that Jesus proceeds to answer. This section is just one example of this. However, these partial dialogs are still very useful for self-awareness.

B. Principles Of Miracles

20   Penetration DOES NOT involve magic, nor DOES ANY form of sexual behavior. It IS a magic belief to engage in ANY form of body image activity at all. You neither created yourselves, nor controlled your creation. By introducing levels into your own perception, you opened the way for body-image distortions.

    The lack of love, or faulty need-orientation, which led to your particular person (not OBJECT) choices CAN BE corrected within the existent framework, and would HAVE to be in the larger interest of overall progress. The situation is questionable largely because of its inherent vulnerability to fantasy-gratification. Doing the best you can WITHIN this limitation is probably the best corrective measure at present. Any relationship you have undertaken for whatever reasons becomes a responsibility.

21   If you shift your own needs, some amount of corresponding shift in the need-orientation of the other person MUST result, This will be beneficial, even if the partner was originally attracted to you BECAUSE of your disrespect. Teaching devices which are totally alien to a learner's perceptual system are usually merely disruptive. Transfer depends on SOME common elements in the new situation which are understandable in terms of the old.

22   Man can never control the effects of fear himself, because he has CREATED fear and believes in what he creates. In attitude, then, though not in content, he resembles his own Creator, who has perfect faith in His Creations because he Created them. All creation rests on belief, and the belief in the creation produces its existence. This is why it is possible for a man to believe what is not true for anyone else. It is true for him because it is made BY him.

23   Every aspect of fear proceeds from upside down perception. The TRULY creative devote their efforts to correcting this. The neurotic devotes his to compromise. The psychotic tries to escape by establishing the truth of his own errors. It is most difficult to free him by ordinary means, only because he is more stable in his denial of truth.

24   The miracle makes no distinction among degrees of misperception. It is a device for perception-correction which is effective quite apart from either the degree or the direction of the error. This is its TRUE indiscriminateness.

25   Christ-controlled miracles are selective only in that they are directed toward those who can use them for THEMSELVES. Since this makes it inevitable that they will extend them to others, a very strong chain of Atonement is welded. But Christ-control takes no account at all of the MAGNITUDE of the miracle itself, because the concept of size exists only in a plane that is itself unreal. Since the miracle aims at RESTORING reality, it would hardly be useful if it were bound by the laws of the same error it aims to

Chapter 1 – Introduction To Miracles

correct. Only man makes that kind of error. It is an example of the "foolish consistency" his own false beliefs have engendered.

26   Both the power and the strength of man's creative will must be understood, before the real meaning of denial can be appreciated and abolished. Denial is NOT mere negation. It is a positive miscreation. While the miscreation is NECESSARILY believed in by its own creator, it does not exist at all at the level of true Creation.

27   The miracle compares the creations of man with the higher level of creation, accepting what is in ACCORD as true, and rejecting the DISCORDANT as false. This is why it is so closely associated with validity. Real validity is both true AND useful, or better, it is useful BECAUSE it is true.

28   All aspects of fear are untrue, because they DO NOT exist at the higher creative levels, and therefore do not exist at all. To whatever extent a man is willing to submit his beliefs to the real test of validity, to that extent are his perceptions healed, or corrected.

29   In sorting out the false from the true, the miracle proceeds much along the lines suggested very correctly by B., i.e.:

> If perfect love casts out fear,[59]
>   And if fear exists,
>   Then there is NOT perfect love.
> But
>   Only perfect love really exists.

30   Therefore, if there is fear, it creates a state which does not exist. Believe THIS and you WILL be free. Only God can establish this solution, for THIS faith IS His gift.[60]

C. Distortions of Miracle Impulses

1   Man must contribute to his readiness here as elsewhere. The readiness for faith, as for everything else that is true, entails the two steps necessary for the release from fear.

2   Denial of fear, in human terms, is a strong defense because it entails two levels of error:

> 1) That truth CAN be denied and
> 2) That absence of truth can be effective.

---

59 1 John 4:18 There is no fear in love; but perfect love casts out fear, because fear involves torment. But he who fears has not been made perfect in love.

60 Ephesians 2:8 For by grace you have been saved through faith, and that not of yourselves; it is the gift of God,

C. Distortions of Miracle Impulses

3   EXPERIENCING fear, which is more characteristic of B., involves only the second error. However, these differences do not affect the power of the miracle at all, since only truth and error are its concern.

4   S: YOU are both more miracle-minded, and less able to recognize fear because of your stronger, but split, identification. B., also characteristically, is less miracle-minded, but better able to recognize fear, because his identification is more consistently right but weaker.

5   Together, the conditions needed for consistent miracle-mindedness, the state in which fear has been abolished, can be particularly well worked out. In fact, it WAS already well worked out before.

6   S: to H. Your idea about the real meaning of "possession" should be clarified. Your own denial of fear (this refers to a visionary experience of H.) introduced some error variance, but not really a significant amount. However, there is always a chance that as the size of the sample increases, what was non-significant before may ATTAIN significance, so we had better get this out of the way now while you are still within the safety margin.

7   Fear of possession is a perverted expression of the fear of the irresistible attraction.

    S: Aside. Yes, this DOES apply to homosexuality, among other errors, where the whole concept of possessing, or "entering" is a key fear. It is a symbolic statement of an inverted decision NOT to enter into, or possess, the Kingdom. In physical terms, which it emphasizes because of the inherent error of Soul avoidance, REAL physical creation is avoided, and fantasy gratification is substituted.

8   The truth is still that the attraction of God is irresistible at ALL levels, and the acceptance of this totally unavoidable truth is only a matter of time. But you should consider whether you WANT to wait, because you CAN return now, if you choose.

    S: Note to H: You are writing this with improper motivation, but we will try anyway. If you are to stop, do so immediately.

9   Possession is a concept which has been subject to numerous distortions, some of which we will list below:

10

1. Possession can be associated with the body only. If this occurs, sex is particularly likely to be contaminated. Possession versus being possessed is apt to be seen as the male and female role. Since neither will be conceived of as satisfying alone, and both will be associated with fear, this interpretation is particularly vulnerable to psychosexual confusion.

Chapter 1 – Introduction To Miracles

11   2. From a rather similar misperceptual reference point, possession can also be associated with things. This is essentially a shift from 1), and is usually due to an underlying fear of associating possession with people. In this sense, it is an attempt to PROTECT people, like the superstition about "protecting the name," we mentioned before.

12   Both 1) and 2) are likely to become compulsive for several reasons, including:

      a. They represent an attempt to escape from the real possession-drive, which cannot be satisfied this way.

      b. They set up substitute goals, which are usually reasonably easy to attain.

      c. They APPEAR to be relatively harmless, and thus SEEM to allay fear. The fact that they usually interfere with good interpersonal relationships can be interpreted, in this culture, as a lack of sophistication on the part of the OTHER (not the self), and this induces a false feeling of confidence in the solution, based on reliability NOT validity. It is also fairly easy to find a partner who SHARES the illusion. Thus, we have any number of relationships which are actually ESTABLISHED on the basis of 1), and others which HOLD TOGETHER primarily because of the joint interests in 2).

      d. The manifestly EXTERNAL emphasis which both entail seems to be a safety device, and thus permits a false escape from much more basic inhibitions. As a compromise solution, the ILLUSION of interpersonal relating is preserved, along with the retention of the lack of love component. This kind of psychic juggling leaves the juggler with a feeling of emptiness, which in fact is perfectly justified, because he IS acting from scarcity. He then becomes more and more driven in his behavior, to fill the emptiness.

13   When these solutions have been invested with extreme belief, 1) leads to sex crimes, and 2) to stealing. The kleptomaniac is a good example of the latter.

14   Generally, two types of emotional disturbances result:

      a. The tendency to maintain the illusion that only the physical is real. This produces depression.

      b. The tendency to invest the physical with non-physical properties. This is essentially magic, and tends more toward anxiety-proneness.

      There is also a tendency to vacillate from one to the other, which produces a corresponding vacillation between depression AND anxiety.

Both result in self imposed starvation.

C. Distortions of Miracle Impulses

15
    3. Another type of distortion is seen in the fear of or desire for "spirit" possession. The term "spirit" is profoundly debased in this context, but it DOES entail a recognition that the body is not enough, and investing it with magic will not work. This recognition ACCEPTS the fact that neither 1) nor 2) is sufficient, but, precisely BECAUSE it does not limit fear so narrowly, it is more likely to produce greater fear in its own right.

16
    Endowing the Spirit with human possessiveness is a more INCLUSIVE error than 1) or 2), and a step somewhat further away from the "Right Mind." Projection is also more likely to occur, with vacillations between grandiosity and fear. "Religion" in a distorted sense, is also more likely to occur in this kind of error, because the idea of a "spirit" is introduced, though fallaciously, while it is excluded from 1) and 2).

17
    Witchcraft is thus particularly apt to be associated with 3), because of the much greater investment in magic.

18
    t should be noted that 1) involves only the body, and 2) involves an attempt to associate things with human attributes. Three, on the other hand, is a more serious level confusion, because it endows the Spirit with EVIL attributes. This accounts both for the religious zeal of its proponents, and the aversion, or fear, of its opponents. Both attitudes stem from the same false belief.

19
    This is NOT what the Bible means by "possessed of the Holy Spirit."[61] It is interesting to note that even those who DID understand that could nevertheless EXPRESS their understanding inappropriately.

    The concept of "speaking in many tongues" was originally an injunction to communicate to everyone in his own language, or his own level. It hardly meant to speak in a way that NOBODY can understand.

    This strange error occurs when people DO understand the need for Universal communication, but have contaminated it with possession fallacies. The fear engendered by this misperception leads to a conflicted state in which communication IS attempted, but the fear is allayed by making the communication incomprehensible.

20
    It could also be said that the fear induced selfishness, or regression, because incomprehensible communication is hardly a worthy offering from one Son of God to another.

21
    4. Knowledge can also be misinterpreted as a means of possession. Here, the content is not physical, and the underlying fallacy is more likely to be the confusion of mind and

---

61 Acts 2:4 And they were all filled with the Holy Ghost, and began to speak with other tongues, as the Spirit gave them utterance.

Chapter 1 – Introduction To Miracles

brain. The attempt to unite nonphysical content with physical attributes is illustrated by statements like "the thirst for knowledge."

22 S: No Helen, this is NOT what the "thirst" in the Bible means. The term was used only because of man's limited comprehension, and is probably better dropped.

23 The fallacious use of knowledge can result in several errors, including:
   a. The idea that knowledge will make the individual more attractive to others. This is a possession-fallacy.
   b. The idea that knowledge will make the individual invulnerable. This is the reaction formation against the underlying fear of vulnerability.
   c. The idea that knowledge will make the individual worthy. This is largely pathetic.

24 S: Both you and B. should consider type 4) VERY carefully. Like all these fallacies, it contains a denial mechanism, which swings into operation as the fear increases, thus canceling out the error temporarily, but seriously impairing efficiency.

25 Thus, you claim you can't read, and B. claims that he can't speak. Note that depression is a real risk here, for a Child of God should never REDUCE his efficiency in ANY way. The depression comes from a peculiar pseudo-solution which reads:

   A Child of God is efficient.

   I am not efficient.

   Therefore, I am not a Child of God.

26 This leads to neurotic resignation, and this is a state which merely INCREASES the depression.

27 The corresponding denial mechanism for 1) is the sense of PHYSICAL inability, or IMPOTENCE. The denial mechanism for 2) is often bankruptcy. Collectors of things often drive themselves well beyond their financial means, in an attempt to force discontinuance. If this idea of cessation cannot be tolerated, a strange compromise involving BOTH insatiable possessiveness and insatiable throwing-away (bankruptcy) may result. An example is the inveterate or compulsive gambler, particularly the horse-racing addict. Here, the conflicted drive is displaced both from people AND things, and is invested in animals. The implied DEROGATION of people is the cause of the underlying EXTREME superstition of the horse racing addict.

Chapter 2 - The Illusion Of Separation

A. Introduction

1   This section is inserted here because it deals with a more fundamental misuse of knowledge, referred to in the Bible as the cause of the Fall (or Separation). There are several introductory remarks which are intended to make these explanations less fear-provoking. The first is a couplet which I drew to your attention during the fragments of Midsummer Night's Dream, which you heard last night:

> "Be as thou wast wont to be
> See as thou wast wont to see."

    It is noteworthy that these words were said by Oberon in releasing Titania from her own errors, both of being and perceiving. These were the words which re-established her true identity as well as her true abilities and judgment. The similarity here is obvious.

2   There are also some definitions, which I asked you to take from the dictionary, which will also be helpful. Their somewhat unusual nature is due to the fact that they are not first definitions in their chronological appearance. Nevertheless, the fact that each of them does appear in the dictionary should be reassuring.

> Project (verb): to extend forward or out.
> Project (noun): a plan in the mind
> World: a natural grand division.

    (Note that you originally wrote "word" instead of "world.")

3   We will refer later to projection as related to both mental illness and mental health. It will also be commented on that Lucifer literally projected himself from heaven. We also have observed that man can create an empty shell, but cannot create nothing at all.[62]

    This emptiness provides the screen for the misuse of projection.

4   The Garden of Eden, which is described as a literal garden in the Bible, was not originally an actual garden at all. It was merely a mental state of complete need-lack. Even in the literal account, it is noteworthy that the pre-Separation state was essentially one in which man needed nothing. The Tree of Knowledge, again an overly-literal concept, (as is clearly shown by the subsequent reference to "eating of the fruit of the tree") is a symbolic reference to some of the misuses of knowledge referred to in the section immediately preceding this one. There is, however, considerable clarification of this concept, which must be understood before the real meaning of the "detour into fear" can be fully comprehended.

---

62 Chapter 1 B. Principles Of Miracles Principle 33, p2; Principle 50, p5

Chapter 2 - The Illusion Of Separation

Projection, as defined above, (this refers to the verb) is a fundamental attribute of God, which he also gave to his Son. In the Creation, God projected his Creative Ability out of Himself toward the Souls which He created, and also imbued them with the same loving wish (or will) to create. We have commented before on the FUNDAMENTAL error [63] involved in confusing what has been created with what is being created. We have also emphasized that man, insofar as the term relates to Soul, has not only been fully Created, but also been created perfect. [64] There is no emptiness in him. The next point, too, has already been made, but bears repetition here. The Soul, because of its own likeness to its Creator, is creative. [65] No Child of God is capable of losing this ability, because it is inherent in what he IS.

5   Whenever projection in its inappropriate sense is utilized, it ALWAYS implies that some emptiness (or lack of everything) must exist, and that it is within man's ability to put his own ideas there INSTEAD of the truth. If you will consider carefully what this entails, the following will become quite apparent:

> First, the assumption is implicit that what God has Created can be changed by the mind of Man.

> Second, the concept that what is perfect can be rendered imperfect, or wanting, is intruded.

> Third, the belief that man can distort the Creations of God, including himself, has arisen, and is tolerated.

> Fourth, that since man can create himself, the direction of his own creation is up to him.

6   These related distortions represent a picture of what actually occurred in the Separation. None of this existed before, nor does it actually exist now. The world, as defined above, WAS made as a natural grand division, or projecting outward of God. That is why everything which He Created is like Him.

---

63 Chapter 1 B. Principles Of Miracles, b. The Concept Of Lack, p9
64 Chapter 1 B. Principles Of Miracles Principle 32; Principle 42, p3; Principle 47
65 Chapter 1 B. Principles Of Miracles Principle 16; Principle 25, p2; Principle 38, Principle 42, p6; Principle 45, p9
    Also, Genesis 1:26-27 Then God said, "Let Us make man in Our image, according to Our likeness; let them have dominion over the fish of the sea, over the birds of the air, and over the cattle, over all the earth and over every creeping thing that creeps on the earth." So God created man in His own image; in the image of God He created him; male and female He created them.

A. Introduction

7   It should be noted that the opposite of pro is con. Strictly speaking, then, the opposite of projecting is conjecting, a term which referred to a state of uncertainty or guess work. Other errors arise in connection with ancillary defenses, to be considered later.

For example, dejection, which is obviously associated with depression, injection, which can be misinterpreted readily enough, in terms of possession fallacies (particularly penetration), and rejection, which is clearly associated with denial. It should be noted also that rejection can be used as refusing, a term which necessarily involves a perception of what is refused as something unworthy.

8   Projection as undertaken by God was very similar to the kind of inner radiance which the Children of the Father inherit from Him. It is important to note that the term "project outward" necessarily implies that the real source of projection is internal.

This is as true of the Son as of the Father.

9   The world, in its original connotation, included both the proper creation of man by God, AND the proper creation by man in his Right Mind. The latter required the endowment of man by God with free will, because all loving creation is freely given. Nothing in either of these statements implies any sort of level involvement, or, in fact, anything except one continuous line of creation, in which all aspects are of the same order.

10   When the "lies of the serpent"[66] were introduced, they were specifically called lies because they are not true. When man listened, all he heard was untruth. He does not have to continue to believe what is not true, unless he chooses to do so. All of his miscreations can disappear in the well known "twinkling of an eye,"[67] because it is a visual misperception.

11   Man's spiritual eye can sleep, but as will shortly appear in the notes (reference Bob, elevator operator [68]) a sleeping eye can still see. One translation of the Fall, a view emphasized by Mary Baker Eddy, and worthy of note, is that "a deep sleep fell upon Adam."[69] While the Bible continues to associate this sleep as a kind of anesthetic utilized for protection of Adam during the creation of Eve, Mrs. Eddy was correct in emphasizing that nowhere is there any reference made to his waking up. While Christian Science is clearly incomplete, this point is much in its favor.

---

66 Genesis 3:1 Now the serpent was more subtle than any beast of the field which the Lord God had made. And he said unto the woman, Yea, hath God said, Ye shall not eat of every tree of the garden?

67 1 Corinthians 15:52 In a moment, in the twinkling of an eye, at the last trumpet. For the trumpet will sound, and the dead will be raised incorruptible, and we shall be changed.

68 Chapter 2 B. The Re-interpretation of Defenses, p16

69 Genesis 2:21 And the LORD God caused a deep sleep to fall on Adam, and he slept; and He took one of his ribs, and closed up the flesh in its place.

Chapter 2 - The Illusion Of Separation

12   The history of man in the world as he saw it has not been characterized by any genuine or comprehensive re-awakening, or re-birth.

This is impossible as long as man projects in the spirit of miscreation. It still remains within him to project as God projected his own Spirit to him. In reality, this is his ONLY choice, because his free will was made for his own joy in creating the perfect.

13   All fear is ultimately reducible to the basic misperception of man's ability to USURP the power of God. It is again emphasized that he neither CAN nor HAS been able to do this. In this statement lies the real justification for his escape from fear. This is brought about by his acceptance of the Atonement, which places him in a position to realize that his own errors never really occurred.

14   When the deep sleep fell upon Adam, he was then in a condition to experience nightmares, precisely because he was sleeping. If a light is suddenly turned on while someone is dreaming, and the content of his dream is fearful, he is initially likely to interpret the light itself as part of the content of his own dream. However, as soon as he awakens, the light is correctly perceived as the release from the dream, which is no longer accorded reality. I would like to conclude this with the Biblical injunction "Go ye and do likewise."[70] It is quite apparent that this depends on the kind of knowledge which was NOT referred to by the "Tree of Knowledge" which bore lies as fruit. The knowledge that illuminates rather than obscures is the knowledge which not only makes you free, but also shows you clearly that you ARE free.[71]

15   The preceding sections were inserted because of the necessity of distinguishing between real and false knowledge. Having made this distinction, it is well to return to the errors already listed a while back. [72]It might be well to recapitulate them here.

1) The first involved the fallacy that only the physical is real.

2) The second involved things rather than people.

3) The third involves the endowment of the physical with non-physical properties.

4) And the fourth clarified the misuse of knowledge.

All of them were subsumed under possession fallacies. The denial mechanism for three has already been set forth in some detail, and will also continue after the following:

---

70 Luke 10:37 And he said, He that shewed mercy on him. Then said Jesus unto him, Go, and do thou likewise.
71 John 8:32 And you shall know the truth, and the truth shall make you free."
72 Chapter 1 B. Principles Of Miracles, b. Distortions Of Miracle Impulses, p9 - 21

A. Introduction

16   The corresponding denial mechanism for (1) is the sense of PHYSICAL inability, or IMPOTENCE.

The denial mechanism for (2) is often bankruptcy. Collectors of things often drive themselves well beyond their financial means, in an attempt to force discontinuance. If this idea of cessation cannot be tolerated, a strange compromise involving BOTH insatiable possessiveness and insatiable throwing-away (bankruptcy) may result. An example is the inveterate or compulsive gambler, particularly the horse-racing addict. Here, the conflicted drive is displaced both from people AND things, and is invested in animals. The implied DEROGATION of people is the cause of the underlying EXTREME superstition of the horse racing addict.[73]

17   The alcoholic is in a similar position, except that his hostility is more inward than outward directed.

18   Defenses aimed at protecting (or retaining) error are particularly hard to undo, because they introduce second-order misperceptions which obscure the underlying errors still further.

19   The pseudo-corrective mechanism of (3) is apt to be more varied because of the more inclusive nature of the error, which has already been mentioned. Some of the possibilities are listed below:

20   If "being possessed" is brought to ascendance, a state of some sort of possession by external forces results, but NOT with a major emphasis on attacking others. Attack BY others becomes the more obvious component. In the more virulent forms, there is a sense of being possessed by demons, and unless there is vacillation with a)[74], a catatonic solution is more likely than a paranoid one.

21   The FOCUSED paranoid has become more rigid in his solution, and centers on ONE source of projection to escape from vacillation. It should be noted that this type of paranoia is an upside down form of religion, because of its obvious attempt to unify into oneness.

22   (1), (2), and (4) are more likely to produce neurotic rather than psychotic states, though this is by no means guaranteed. However, (3) is inherently more vulnerable to the psychotic correction, again because of the more fundamental level confusion which is involved. It should be noted, however, that the greater fear which is induced by (3) can ITSELF reach psychotic proportions, thus forcing the individual closer and closer to a psychotic solution.

23   *It is emphasized here that these differences have no effect at all on the miracle, which can heal any of them with equal ease.* This is because of the miracle's inherent

---

[73] This is a repeat of an earlier paragraph: Chapter 1 C. Distortions Of Miracle Impulses, p28
[74] ? Chapter 1 C. Distortions Of Miracle Impulses, p14

Chapter 2 - The Illusion Of Separation

avoidance of within-error distinctions. Its SOLE concern is to distinguish between truth, on the one hand, and ALL kinds of error, on the other. This is why some miracles SEEM to be of greater magnitude than others. But remember the first point in this course, i.e., that there is no order of difficulty in miracles. [75]

24   The emphasis on mental illness which is marked in these notes reflects the "UNDOING" aspect of the miracle. The "DOING" aspect is, of course, much more important. But a true miracle cannot occur on a false basis. Sometimes the undoing must precede it.

25   At other times, both can occur simultaneously, but you are not up to this at the moment.

26   Further, insights into mental illness can be misused, and lead to preoccupation with one's own symptoms. This is why this area is less constructive for most people than a course primarily devoted to mental health. However, some professions will find some principles of mental illness constructive, especially those which are concerned with mental illness in others. This obviously includes psychologists.

27   The obvious correction for ALL types of the possession-fallacy is to redefine possession correctly. In the sense of "taking over," the concept does not exist at all in divine reality, which is the only level of reality where real existence is a meaningful term.

28   No one CAN be "taken over" unless he wills to be. However, if he places his mind under tyranny, rather than authority, he intrudes the submission/dominance onto free will himself. This produces the obvious contradiction inherent in any formulation that associates free will with imprisonment. Even in very mild forms, this kind of association is risky, and may spread quite unexpectedly, particularly under external stress. This is because it can be internally controlled ONLY if EXTERNAL conditions are peaceful. This is not safe, because external conditions are produced by the thoughts of many, not all of whom are pure in heart as yet.

29   Why should you be at THEIR mercy? This issue is VERY closely related to the whole possession issue. You insist on thinking that people CAN possess you, if you believe that their thoughts, or the external environment, can affect you, regardless of WHAT they think. You are perfectly unaffected by ALL expressions of lack of love. These can be either from yourself and others, or from yourself to others, or from others to you.

30   (I'm glad you passed that test. It was crucial. This is ref. to H's reluctance to take dictations as given.)

---

[75] Chapter 1 B. Principles Of Miracles Principle 1

A. Introduction

31 Peace is an attribute in YOU. You cannot find it outside.[76] All mental illness is some form of EXTERNAL searching. Mental health is INNER peace. It enables you to remain unshaken by lack of love from without, and capable, through your own miracles of correcting the external conditions, which proceed from lack of love in others.

B. The Re-interpretation of Defenses

1 When you are afraid of ANYTHING, you are acknowledging its power to hurt you. Remember that where your heart is, there is your treasure[77] also. This means that you believe in what you VALUE.

2 If you are AFRAID, you are VALUING WRONG. Human understanding will inevitably value wrong, and by endowing all human thoughts with equal power, will inevitably DESTROY peace. This is why the Bible speaks of "The peace of God which PASSETH (human) understanding."[78]

THIS peace is totally incapable of being shaken by human errors of any kind. It denies the ability of anything which is not of God to effect you in any way.

3 This is the PROPER use of denial. It is not used to HIDE anything, but it IS used to correct error. It brings ALL error into the light, and since error and darkness are the same, it abolishes error automatically.

4 True denial is a very powerful protective device. You can and should deny any belief that error can hurt you. This kind of denial is NOT a concealment device, but a correction device. The "Right Mind" of the mentally healthy DEPENDS on it.

5 You can do ANYTHING I ask. I have asked you to perform miracles,[79] and have made it VERY clear that these are NATURAL, CORRECTIVE, HEALING, and UNIVERSAL. There is nothing good they cannot do. But they cannot be performed in

---

76 Deuteronomy 4:29 But from there you will seek the LORD your God, and you will find Him if you seek Him with all your heart and with all your soul.
77 Matthew 6:21 For where your treasure is, there your heart will be also.
78 Philippians 4:7 And the peace of God, which surpasses all understanding, will guard your hearts and minds through Christ Jesus.
79 Chapter 1 A. Introduction, p1   You should begin each day with the prayer
      "Help me to perform whatever miracles you want of me today"
  Also, Matthew 10:1 And when He had called His twelve disciples to Him, He gave them power over unclean spirits, to cast them out, and to heal all kinds of sickness and all kinds of disease.

Chapter 2 - The Illusion Of Separation

the spirit of doubt.[80] Remember my own question, before you ask yours "Oh ye of little faith, wherefore didst thou DOUBT."[81]

6   You have asked YOURSELVES why you cannot really incorporate my words.

The idea of cannibalism in connection with the Sacrament is a reflection of a distorted view of sharing. I told you before that the word "thirst" in connection with the Spirit was used in the Bible because of the limited understanding of those to whom I spoke. I also told you NOT to use it. The same holds for expressions like "feeding on."

Symbiosis is misunderstood by the mentally ill, who use it that way. But I also told you that you must recognize your total dependence on God, a statement which you did not like.

7   God and the Souls He created ARE symbolically related. They are COMPLETELY dependent on each other. The creation of the Soul itself has already been perfectly accomplished, but the creation BY Souls has not. God created Souls so He could depend on them BECAUSE He created them perfectly. He gave them His peace so they would not be shaken, and would be unable to be deceived. Whenever you are afraid, you ARE deceived. Your mind is NOT serving your Soul. This literally starves the Soul by denying its daily bread.[82]

8   Remember the poem about the Holy Family which crossed your mind last night:

> "Where tricks of words are never said
>
> And mercy is as plain as bread."

The reason why that had such a strong impact on you originally was because you knew what it MEANT.

9   God offers ONLY mercy. Your own words should ALWAYS reflect only mercy, because that is what you have received, and that is what you should GIVE. Justice is a temporary expedient, or an attempt to teach man the meaning of mercy. Its

---

80 Matthew 14:29 And he said, Come. And when Peter was come down out of the ship, he walked on the water, to go to Jesus. 30 But when he saw the wind boisterous, he was afraid; and beginning to sink, he cried, saying, Lord, save me. 31 And immediately Jesus stretched forth his hand, and caught him, and said unto him, O thou of little faith, wherefore didst thou doubt?
Matthew 17:19-20 Then the disciples came to Jesus privately and said, "Why could we not cast it out?" So Jesus said to them, Because of your unbelief; for assuredly, I say to you, if you have faith as a mustard seed, you will say to this mountain, "Move from here to there, and it will move; and nothing will be impossible for you."
81 Matthew 14:31 And immediately Jesus stretched forth his hand, and caught him, and said unto him, O thou of little faith, wherefore didst thou doubt?
82 Matthew 6:11 Give us this day our daily bread.

B. The Re-interpretation of Defenses

JUDGMENTAL side rises only because man is capable of INJUSTICE if that is what his mind creates.

You are afraid of God's will because you have used your own will, which He created in the likeness of His own, to MISCREATE.

10   What you do NOT realize is that the mind can miscreate only when it is NOT free. An imprisoned mind is not free by definition. It is possessed, or held back, by ITSELF. Its will is therefore limited, and not free to assert itself.

11   The three things that crossed your mind, which was comparatively free at the time, are perfectly relevant:

>   1. It is alright to remember the past, PROVIDED you also remember that ANYTHING you suffer is because of YOUR OWN ERRORS.

>   2. In this context, your remark that "after the burning, I swore if I ever saw him again, I would not[83] recognize him." Note, by the way, that you did not put in the "not" until afterwards. That is because your inherent correction-device was working properly at the moment. The result is that you are NOT DENYING ME.

>   3. The story about Hinda. This was an excellent example of misperception which led to a totally unwarranted fear of a PERSON. (H's story refers to a very young child who fell down the stairs when H. had arms open in a welcoming gesture at bottom of stairs. For years afterwards, Hinda screamed upon seeing H.) The mis-step which caused her fall had nothing at all to do with you, just as your own mis-steps have nothing at all to do with me.

12   Denial of error is a very powerful defense of truth. We have slowly been shifting the emphasis from the negative to the positive use of denial. Remember, we have already stated that denial is not a purely negative (powerless) device; it results in positive miscreation. That is the way the mentally ill DO employ it.

13   But remember a very early thought of your own, "Never underestimate the power of denial." In the service of the "Right Mind," the denial of ERROR frees the mind and re-establishes the freedom of the will. When the will is REALLY free, it CANNOT miscreate, because it recognizes ONLY TRUTH.

---

83   ("Not" was written in later)

Chapter 2 - The Illusion Of Separation

14 Projection arises out of FALSE DENIAL. Not out of its proper use. My own role in the Atonement IS one of true projection, i.e., I can project to YOU the affirmation of truth. If you project error to me (or to yourself) you are interfering with the process. My use of projection, which can also be yours, is NOT based on faulty denial. But it DOES involve the very powerful use of the denial of error.

15

> The miracle worker is one who accepts my kind of denial and projection, unites his own inherent abilities to deny and project with mine, and imposes them back on himself and others. This establishes the total lack of threat anywhere. Together we can then work for the real time of peace, which is Eternal.

16 I inspired Bob (ref. to elevator man who took H. down from her apt.) to make that remark to you, and it is a pity that you heard only the last part. But you can still use that. His remark ended with: "Every shut eye is not asleep." [84] Since your own vision is much improved at the moment, we will go on a while.

a. Reinterpretation Of Some "Dynamic" Concepts

1 Freud's identification of mechanisms was quite correct, as was his recognition of their creative ability. They can INDEED create man's perception, both of himself and his surroundings.

But Freud's limitations induced inevitable limits on his own perception. He made two kinds of errors.

> The first is that he saw only how the mechanisms worked in the mentally ill. The second is his own denial of the mechanism of the Atonement.

Let us take up the first, because a clear understanding of the second depends on it.

2 Denial should be directed only to error, and projection should be limited to truth. You should truly give as you have truly received. The Golden Rule[85] can work effectively only on this basis.

3 Intellectualization is a poor word, which stems from the brain-mind confusion. "Right-Mindedness" is better. This device defends the RIGHT MIND, and gives it

---

84 Chapter 2 A. Introduction, p12
85 Matthew 7:12 Therefore, whatever you want men to do to you, do also to them, for this is the Law and the Prophets.

B. The Re-interpretation of Defenses

control over the body. "Intellectualization" implies a split, whereas "Right-Mindedness" involves healing.

4 Withdrawal is properly employed in the service of withdrawing from the desert.
It is NOT a device for escape, but for consolidation.

There IS only One Mind.

5 Dissociation is quite similar. You should split yourself off from error, but only in defense of integration.

6 Detachment is essentially a weaker form of dissociation.
This is one of the major areas of withholding that both you and B. are engaging in.

7 Flight can be undertaken in whatever direction you choose, but note that the concept itself implies flight FROM something. Flight from error is perfectly appropriate.

8 Distantiation is a way of putting distance between yourself and what you SHOULD fly from.

9 Regression is a real effort to return to your own original state. In this sense, it is utilized to RESTORE, not to go back to the less mature.

10 Sublimation should be associated with the SUBLIME.

11 There are many other so-called "dynamic" concepts which are profound errors due essentially to the misuse of defenses. Among them is the concept of different levels of aspiration, which results from real level confusion.

12 However, the main point to be understood from these notes is that you can defend truth as well as error, and in fact, much better.

13 So far we have concentrated on ends rather than means because unless you regard an end as worth achieving, you will not devote yourself to the means by which it can BE achieved. Your own question enabled me to shift the emphasis from end to means.

(Question asked was "how can we incorporate this material?") You and B. HAVE accepted the end as valuable, thus signifying your willingness to use defenses to ensure it.

14 The means are easier to clarify after the true worth of the goal itself is firmly established.

15 Everyone defends his own treasure. You do not have to tell him to do this, because HE will do so automatically. The real question still remains WHAT do you treasure, and HOW MUCH do you treasure it? [86]

---

[86] Matthew 6:19 Lay not up for yourselves treasures upon earth, where moth and rust doth corrupt, and

Chapter 2 - The Illusion Of Separation

16 Once you learn to consider these two points, and bring them into ALL your actions as the true criteria for behavior, I will have little difficulty in clarifying the means.

You have not learned to be consistent about this as yet.

I have therefore concentrated on showing you that the means ARE available whenever you DO ask.

17 You can save a lot of time, however, if you do not need to extend this step unduly. The correct focus will shorten it immeasurably.

18 S: to H: Papers will be very easy to write as this time is shortened.

b. The Atonement As Defense

1 The Atonement is the ONLY defense which cannot be used destructively. That is because, while everyone must eventually join it, it was not a device which was generated by man. The Atonement PRINCIPLE was in effect long before the Atonement itself was begun. The Principle was love, and the Atonement itself, was an ACT of love. Acts were not necessary before the Separation, because the time-space belief did not exist.

2 It was only after the Separation that the defense of Atonement, and the necessary conditions for its fulfillment were planned. It became increasingly apparent that all of the defenses which man can choose to use constructively or destructively were not enough to save him. It was therefore decided that he needed a defense which was so splendid that he could not misuse it, although he COULD refuse it. His will could not turn it into a weapon of attack, which is the inherent characteristic of all other defenses. The Atonement thus becomes the only defense which was NOT a two-edged sword.[87]

3 The Atonement actually began long before the Crucifixion. Many Souls offered their efforts on behalf of the Separated Ones but they could not withstand the strength of the attack, and had to be brought back. Angels came, too, but their protection was not enough, because the Separated ones were not interested in peace. They had already split

---

 where thieves break through and steal: 20 But lay up for yourselves treasures in heaven, where neither moth nor rust doth corrupt, and where thieves do not break through nor steal: 21 For where your treasure is, there will your heart be also.
 Luke 6:45 A good man out of the good treasure of his heart bringeth forth that which is good; and an evil man out of the evil treasure of his heart bringeth forth that which is evil: for of the abundance of the heart his mouth speaketh.

87 Psalm 149:6 Let the high praises of God be in their mouth, And a two-edged sword in their hand,

B. The Re-interpretation of Defenses

themselves, and were bent on dividing rather than reintegrating. The levels they introduced into themselves turned against each other, and they, in turn, turned against each other. They established differences, divisions, cleavages, dispersion, and all the other concepts related to the increasing splits they produced.

4 Not being in their Right Minds, they turned their defenses from protection to assault, and acted literally insanely. It was essential to introduce a split-proof device which could be used ONLY to heal, if it was used at all.

5 The Atonement was built into the space-time belief in order to set a limit on the need for the belief, and ultimately to make learning complete. The Atonement IS the final lesson. Learning itself, like the classrooms in which it occurs, is temporary. Let all those who overestimate human intelligence remember this.

(H. questions last sentence, which she perceives as threatening.)

The ability to learn has no value when change of understanding is no longer necessary. The eternally creative have nothing to learn. Only after the Separation was it necessary to direct the creative force to learning, because changed behavior had become mandatory.

6 Human beings can learn to improve their behavior, and can also learn to become better and better learners. This increase serves to bring them in closer and closer accord with the Sonship. But the Sonship itself is a perfect creation, and perfection is not a matter of degree. Only while there are different degrees is learning meaningful. The evolution of man is merely a process by which he proceeds from one degree to the next. He corrects his previous missteps by stepping forward. This represents a process which is actually incomprehensible in temporal terms, because he RETURNS as he goes forward.

7
> The Atonement is the device by which he can free himself from the past as he goes ahead. It UNDOES his past errors, thus making it unnecessary for him to keep retracing his steps without advancing toward his return.

8 In this sense, the Atonement saves time, but, like the miracle which serves it, does not abolish it. As long as there is need for Atonement, there is need for time. But the Atonement, as a completed plan, does have a unique relationship TO time. Until the Atonement is finished, its various phases will proceed IN time, but the whole Atonement stands at its end. At this point, the bridge of the return has been built.

9 S: Note to H. The reason this is upsetting you is because:

The Atonement is a TOTAL commitment. You still think this is associated with loss. This is the same mistake ALL the Separated ones make, in one way or another. They

Chapter 2 - The Illusion Of Separation

cannot believe that a defense which CANNOT attack also IS the best defense. Except for this misperception, the angels COULD have helped them.

What do you think "the meek shall inherit the earth"[88] MEANS?

They will literally take it over because of their strength. A two-way defense is inherently weak, precisely BECAUSE it has two edges it can turn against the self very unexpectedly. This tendency CANNOT be controlled EXCEPT by miracles.

> The miracle turns the defense of Atonement to the protection of the inner self, which, as it becomes more and more secure; assumes its natural talent of protecting others. The inner self knows itself as both a brother AND a son.

10 The above notes were taken with great difficulty by H., and constitute the only series thus far that were written very slowly. When H. asked about this, she was told, "don't worry about the notes. They are right, but YOU are not sufficiently Right-Minded yet to write about the Atonement with comfort. You will write about it yet with joy.

11 Aside from H: Last night I felt briefly but intensely depressed, temporarily under the impression that I was abandoned. I tried, but couldn't get through at all. After a while, I decided to give up for the time being, and He said, "don't worry. I will never leave you or forsake you." I did feel a little better, and decided I was really not sick, so I could return to my exercises. While I was exercising, I had some part-vision experiences which I found only mildly frightening at times, and quite reassuring at others.

12 I am not too sure of the sequence, but it began with a VERY clear assurance of love, and an equally clear emphasis on my own great value, beauty, and purity. Things got a little confusing after that. First, the idea of "Bride of Christ" occurred to me with vaguely inappropriate "undertones." Then there was a repetition of "the way of Love," and a restatement of an earlier experience, now as if it were FROM Him TO me: "Behold the Handmaid of the Lord; Be it done unto you according to His Word."[89]

This threw me into panic before, but at that time, it was stated in the more accurate Biblical phrasing: "Be it done unto ME according to HIS Word."

13 This time I was a bit uneasy, but remembered I had misperceived it last time, and was probably still not seeing it right. Actually, it is really just a statement of allegiance to the Divine Service, which can hardly be dangerous.

---

88 Psalm 37:11 But the meek shall inherit the earth; and shall delight themselves in the abundance of peace. Matthew 5:5 Blessed are the meek: for they shall inherit the earth.
89 Luke 1:38 "And Mary said, Behold, the handmaid of the Lord; be it unto me according to thy word. And the angel departed from her."

B. The Re-interpretation of Defenses

14   Then there was a strange sequence, in which Christ seemed to be making very obvious advances, which became quite sexual in my perception of them. I ALMOST thought briefly that he turned into a devil. I got just a LITTLE scared, and the possession idea came in for a while, but I thought it SO silly, that there is no point in taking it seriously.

15   (As I am writing this, I remember that thing in the book about the demon lover, which once THROUGH me (note spelling, "threw") into a fit. I am upset, but the spelling slip is reassuring.)

16   This morning we reviewed the whole episode. He said he was "VERY pleased at the COMPARATIVE lack of fear, and also the concomitant awareness that it WAS misperception. This showed much greater strength, and a much increased Right-Mindedness. This is because defenses are now being used much better, on behalf of truth MORE than error, though not completely so.

17   The weaker use of mis-projection is shown by my recognition that it can't REALLY be that way, which became possible as soon as denial was applied against error, NOT truth. This permitted a much greater awareness of alternative interpretations.

18   It was also explained (the shift to the passive form instead of "He also explained" should be noted. This is an expression of fear.) "Remember the section in "Letters from the Scattered Brotherhood" you read last evening about 'Hold fast', and please do so."

19   Note by H. re B's remark concerning next message paragraph (p40):

    H: Yes, but I doubt if it says this is inevitable. It may entail more mis-will than we think. The above may have been too passively interpreted.

    S: Note that B. Did NOT ask MY will re same. If he had, HE would have felt better.

20   You know that when defenses are disrupted there is a period of real disorientation, accompanied by fear, guilt, and usually vacillations between anxiety and depression. This process is different only in that defenses are not being disrupted, but re-interpreted, even though it may be experienced as the same thing.

21   In the re-interpretation of defenses, they are not disrupted but their use for ATTACK is lost. Since this means they can be used only ONE way, they became MUCH stronger, and much more dependable. They no longer oppose the Atonement, but greatly facilitate it. The Atonement can only be accepted within you.

22   S: You have perceived it largely as EXTERNAL thus far, and that is why your EXPERIENCE of it has been minimal. You have been SHOWN the chalice many times, but have not accepted it "for yourself." Your major improper use of defenses is now largely limited to externalization. Do not fail to appreciate your own remarkable progress

Chapter 2 - The Illusion Of Separation

in this respect. You perceived it first as a vessel of some sort whose purpose was uncertain but which might be a piss-pot. You DID notice, however, that the INSIDE was gold, while the OUTSIDE, though shiny, was silver. This was a recognition of the fact that the INNER part is more precious than the OUTER side, even though both are resplendent, though with different value.

23   The re-interpretation of defenses is essential to break open the INNER light. Since the Separation, man's defenses have been used almost entirely to defend themselves AGAINST the Atonement, and thus maintain their separation. They generally see this as a need to protect the body from external intrusion, and this kind of misperception is largely responsible for the homosexual fallacy, as well as your own pregnancy fears. The so-called "anal" behavior is a distorted attempt to "steal" the Atonement, and deny its worth by concealing it, and holding onto it with a bodily receptacle, which is regarded as particularly vicious. "Oral" fantasies are rather similar in purpose, except that they stem more from a sense of deprivation, and insatiable thirst which results. "Anal" fallacies are more of a refusal to give, while oral fantasies emphasize a distorted need to take. The main error in both is the belief that the body can be used as a means for attaining Atonement.

24   Perceiving the body as the Temple is only the first step in correcting this kind of distortion.

25   (H. scalded hand, and looked for butter to put on. It occurred to her that the Atonement was the cure. Burn appeared to be minimal, and caused little discomfort.)

26   Seeing the body as the Temple alters part of the misperception, but not all of it. It DOES recognize, however, that the concept of addition or subtraction in PHYSICAL terms is not appropriate.

But the next step is to realize that a Temple is not a building at all. Its REAL holiness lies in the INNER altar, around which the building is built. The inappropriate emphasis which men have put on beautiful Church BUILDINGS is a sign of their own fear of Atonement, and unwillingness to reach the altar itself.

The REAL beauty of the Temple cannot be seen with the physical eye. The spiritual eye, on the other hand, cannot see the building at all, but it perceives the altar within with perfect clarity. This is because the spiritual eye has perfect vision.

27   For perfect effectiveness, the chalice of the Atonement belongs at the center of the inner altar, where it undoes the Separation, and restores the wholeness of the Spirit. Before the Separation, the mind was invulnerable to fear, because fear did not exist. Both the Separation and the fear were MISCREATIONS of the mind, which have to be undone.

B. The Re-interpretation of Defenses

This is what the Bible means by the "Restoration of the Temple."[90] It DOES NOT mean the restoration of the building, but it DOES mean the opening of the altar to receive the Atonement.

28 This heals the Separation, and places within man the one defense against all Separation-mind errors which can make him perfectly invulnerable.

29 The acceptance of the Atonement by everyone is only a matter of time.

In fact, both TIME and MATTER were created for this purpose.

This appears to contradict free will, because of the inevitability of this decision. If you review the idea carefully, you will realize that this is not true. Everything is limited in some way by the manner of its creation. Free will can temporize, and is capable of enormous procrastination. But it cannot depart entirely from its Creator, who set the limits on its ability to miscreate by virtue of its own real purpose.

30 The misuse of will engenders a situation which, in the extreme, becomes altogether intolerable. Pain thresholds can be high, but they are not limitless. Eventually, everybody begins to recognize, however dimly, that there MUST be a better way. As this recognition is more firmly established, it becomes a perceptual turning-point. This ultimately reawakens the spiritual eye[91], simultaneously weakening the investment in physical sight. The alternating investment in the two types or levels of perception is usually experienced as conflict for a long time, and can become very acute.

31 But the outcome is as certain as God. The spiritual eye literally CANNOT SEE error, and merely looks for Atonement. All the solutions which the physical eyes seek, dissolve in its sight. The spiritual eye, which looks within, recognizes immediately that the altar has been defiled, and needs to be repaired and protected. Perfectly aware of the RIGHT defense, it passes over all others, looking past error to truth. Because of the real strength of ITS vision, it pulls the will into its own service, and forces the mind to concur. This reestablishes the true power of the will, and makes it increasingly unable to tolerate delay.

The mind then realizes, with increasing certitude, that delay is only a way of increasing unnecessary pain, which it need not tolerate at all. The pain threshold drops accordingly, and the mind becomes increasingly sensitive to what it would once have regarded as very minor intrusions of discomfort.

32 The Children of God are entitled to perfect comfort, which comes from a sense of perfect trust. Until they achieve this, they waste themselves and their true creative power on useless attempts to make themselves more comfortable by inappropriate means. But the real means is ALREADY provided, and does not involve any efforts on their part at

---
90 John 2:19 Jesus answered and said unto them, Destroy this temple, and in three days I will raise it up.
91 'Spiritual eye' is later referred to as Vision.

Chapter 2 - The Illusion Of Separation

all. Their egocentricity usually misperceives this as personally insulting, an interpretation which obviously arises from their misperception of themselves. Egocentricity and communion cannot coexist. Even the terms themselves are contradictory.

33 The Atonement is the only gift which is worthy of being offered to the Altar of God. This is because of the inestimable value of the Altar itself. It was created perfect, and is entirely worthy of receiving perfection. God IS lonely without His SOULS, and THEY are lonely without Him. Remember the "spiritual" (a VERY good term) which begins with "And God stepped down from Heaven and said: I'M lonely - I'll make ME a World." The world WAS a way of healing the Separation, and the Atonement is the GUARANTEE that the device will ultimately do so.

34 H: request for special message for B.

S: Tell B that his delaying tactics are holding him back. He does not really understand detachment, distantiation, and withdrawal. He is interpreting them as "holding himself aloof" from the Atonement.)

C. Healing as Release from Fear

1 The new emphasis will now be on healing. The miracle is the means, the Atonement the principle, and the healing is the result. Those who speak of "the miracle OF healing" are combining two orders of reality inappropriately. Healing is NOT a miracle. The Atonement, or the final miracle, is a REMEDY. It is purely a means, while any type of healing is a result.

2 The order of error to which Atonement is applied is irrelevant. Essentially, ALL healing is the release from fear. But to undertake this you cannot be fearful yourself.

3 You do not understand healing because of your own fear. I have been hinting throughout (and once stated very directly, because you were unfearful at the time) that you MUST heal others. [92] The reason is that their healing merely witnesses or attests to yours.

4 A major step in the Atonement plan is to undo error at ALL levels. Illness, which is really "not Right Mindedness," is the result of level confusion in the sense that it always entails the misbelief that what is amiss in one level can adversely affect another.

5 We have constantly referred to miracles as the means of correcting level confusion. In reality, all mistakes must be corrected at the level at which they occur. Only the mind is capable of error. The body can ACT erroneously, but this is only because it has responded to mis-Thought. The body cannot create, and the belief that it CAN, a

---

92 Chapter 1 B. Principles Of Miracles Principle 28, p4
    Chapter 1 B. Principles Of Miracles Principle 27, p1-3
    … among others

C. Healing as Release from Fear

fundamental error responsible for most of the fallacies already referred to, produces all physical symptoms.

6   All physical illness represents a belief in magic. The whole distortion which created magic rested on the belief that there is a creative ability in matter, which can control the mind.

This fallacy can work either way; i.e., it can be misbelieved either that the mind can miscreate IN the body, or that the body can miscreate in the mind.

If it can be made clear that the mind, which is the only level of creation, cannot create beyond itself, then neither confusion need occur.

7   The reason why only the mind can create is more obvious than may be immediately apparent. The Soul has been created. The body is a learning device FOR the mind. Learning devices are not lessons in themselves. Their purpose is merely to facilitate the THINKING of the learner. The most that a faulty use of a learning device can do is to fail to facilitate. It does not have the power in itself to introduce actual learning errors.

8   The body, if properly understood, shares the invulnerability of the Atonement to two-edged application. This is not because the body is a miracle, but because it is not inherently open to misinterpretation. The body is merely a fact. Its ABILITIES can be, and frequently are, over evaluated. However, it is almost impossible to deny its existence. Those who do are engaging in a particularly unworthy form of denial.

The use of the word "unworthy" here implies simply that it is not necessary to protect the mind by denying the un-mindful. There is little doubt that the mind can miscreate.

If one denies this unfortunate aspect of its power, one is also denying the power itself.

9   All material means which man accepts as remedies for bodily ills are simply restatements of magic principles.

It was the first level of the error to believe that the body created its own illness.

Thereafter, it is a second mis-step to attempt to heal it through non-creative agents.

It does not follow, however, that the application of these very weak corrective devices are evil. Sometimes the illness has sufficiently great a hold over an individual's mind to render him inaccessible to Atonement. In this case, one may be wise to utilize a compromise approach to mind and body, in which something from the OUTSIDE is temporarily given healing belief.

This is because the last thing that can help the non-Right-Minded, or the sick, is an increase in fear. They are already in a fear-weakened state. If they are inappropriately

Chapter 2 - The Illusion Of Separation

exposed to a straight and undiluted miracle, they may be precipitated into panic. This is particularly likely to occur when upside down perception has induced the belief that miracles are frightening.

10 The value of the Atonement does not lie in the manner in which it is expressed.

In fact, if it is truly used it will inevitably BE expressed in whatever way is most helpful to the receiver, not the giver.

This means that a miracle, to attain its full efficacy, MUST be expressed in a language which the recipient can understand without fear.

It does not follow by any means that this is the highest level of communication of which he is capable. But it DOES mean that it is the highest level of communication of which he is capable NOW.

11 The whole aim of the miracle is to RAISE the level of communication, not to impose regression, as improperly used, upon it.

Before it is safe to let miracle workers loose in this world, it is essential that they understand fully the fear of release.

Otherwise, they may unwittingly foster the misbelief that release is imprisonment, which is very prevalent.

This misperception arose from the attempted protection device (or misdefense):
> that harm can be limited to the body.

This was because of the much greater fear, which this one counteracts, that the mind can hurt itself.

Neither error is really meaningful, because the miscreations of the mind do not really exist. That recognition is a far better protection device than any form of level confusion, because of the advantages of introducing correction at the level of the error.

12 It is essential that the remembrance of the fact that ONLY mind can create at all remain with you.

Implicit in this is the corollary that correction belongs at the thought level, and NOT at either level to which creation is inapplicable. To repeat an earlier statement, and also to extend it somewhat,
> the Soul is already perfect, and therefore does not require correction.
>
> The body does not really exist, except as a learning device for the mind. This learning device is not subject to errors of its own, because it was created, but is NOT creating.

C. Healing as Release from Fear

It should be obvious, then, that correcting the creator (the mind), or inducing it to give up miscreation, is the only application of creation which is inherently meaningful at all.

13   We said before that magic is essentially mindless, or the destructive (miscreated) use of mind. Physical medicines are a form of "spells." In one way, they are a more benign form, in that they do not entail the possession fallacy which DOES enter when a mind believes that it can possess another. Since this is considerably less dangerous, though still incorrect, it has its advantages. It is particularly helpful to the therapist who really wants to heal, but is still fearful himself. By using physical means to do so, he is not engaging in any form of enslavement, even though he is not applying the Atonement. This means that his mind is dulled by fear, but is not actively engaged in distortion.

14   Those who are afraid of using the mind to heal are right in avoiding it, because the very fact that they are afraid HAS made them vulnerable to miscreation. They are therefore likely to misunderstand any healing they might induce, and, because egocentricity and fear usually occur together, may be unable to accept the real Source of the healing. Under these conditions, it is safer for them to rely TEMPORARILY on physical healing devices, because they cannot misperceive them as their own creations. As long as their own vulnerability persists, it is essential to preserve them from even attempting miracles.

15   We said in a previous section that the miracle is an expression of Miracle-Mindedness.[93] Miracle-Mindedness merely means Right-Mindedness in the sense that we are now using it. Right-Mindedness neither exalts nor depreciates the mind of the miracle worker nor of the miracle receiver. However, as a creative act, the miracle need not await the Right-Mindedness of the receiver. In fact, its purpose is to restore him TO his Right Mind. But it is essential that the miracle worker be in his Right Mind, or he will be unable to reestablish Right-Mindedness in someone else.

16   The healer who relies on his own readiness is endangering his understanding.

He is perfectly safe as long as he is completely unconcerned about HIS readiness, but maintains a consistent trust in MINE.[94]

S: Errors of this kind produce some very erratic behavior, which usually point up an underlying unwillingness to co-operate. Note that by inserting the carbon backwards, B. created a situation in which two copies did not exist. This reflected two levels of confidence lack, one in My readiness to heal, and the other in his own willingness to give.

---

93 Chapter 1 B. Principles Of Miracles Principle 46
94 John 14:10 Believest thou not that I am in the Father, and the Father in me? the words that I speak unto you I speak not of myself: but the Father that dwelleth in me, he doeth the works.

Chapter 2 - The Illusion Of Separation

These errors inevitably introduce inefficiency into the miracle worker's behavior, and temporarily disrupt his miracle-mindedness. We might also make very similar comments about your own hesitation about dictating at all. This is a larger error only because it results in greater inefficiency. If you don't say anything, nobody can use it, including Me.

We have established that for all corrective processes, the first step is: know that this is fear. [95] Unless fear had entered, the corrective procedure would never have become necessary. If your miracle working propensities are not working, it is always because fear has intruded on your Right-Mindedness, and has literally upset it, i.e. turned it upside down.

17   All forms of not-Right-Mindedness are the result of refusal to accept the Atonement FOR YOURSELF. If the miracle worker DOES accept it, he places himself in the position to recognize that those who need to be healed are simply those who have NOT done so.

The reason why you felt the vast radiation range of your own inner illumination is because you were aware that your Right-Mindedness IS healing.

> The sole responsibility of the miracle worker
> is to accept Atonement himself.

This means that he knows that mind is the only creative level, and that its errors ARE healed by the Atonement. Once he accepts this, HIS mind can only heal. By denying his mind any destructive potential, and reinstating its purely constructive powers, he has placed himself in a position where he can undo the level confusion of others.

The message which he then gives to others is the truth that THEIR MINDS are really similarly constructive, and that their own miscreations cannot hurt them. By affirming this, the miracle worker releases the mind from over-evaluating its own learning device, the body, and restores the mind to its true position as the learner.

It should be re-emphasized that the body does not learn, any more than it creates. [96] As a learning device, it merely follows the learner, but if it is falsely endowed with self initiative, it becomes a serious obstruction to the learning it should facilitate.

18   ONLY the mind is capable of illumination. The Soul is already illuminated, and the body in itself is too dense. The mind, however, can BRING its own illumination TO the body by recognizing that density is the opposite of intelligence, and therefore

---

95 Previously referenced many times, but defined at: Chapter 2 E. The Correction for Lack of Love, p2
96 Chapter 2 C. Healing As Release From Fear, p7

C. Healing as Release from Fear

unamenable to independent learning. It is, however, easily brought into alignment with a mind which has learned to look beyond density toward light.

19   Corrective learning always begins with awakening the spiritual eye, and turning away from belief in physical sight.

The reason this entails fear is because man is afraid of what his spiritual eye will see, which was why he closed it in the first place.

We said before that the spiritual eye cannot see error, and is capable only of looking beyond it to the defense of Atonement. There is no doubt that the spiritual eye does produce extreme discomfort by what it sees. The thing that man forgets is that the discomfort is not the final outcome of its perception.

When the spiritual eye is permitted to look upon the defilement of the altar, it also looks immediately toward Atonement. Nothing which the spiritual eye perceives can induce fear. Everything that results from accurate spiritual awareness merely is channelized toward correction.

Discomfort is aroused only to bring the need to correct forcibly into awareness.

20   What the physical eye sees is not corrective, nor can it be corrected by any device which can be physically seen. As long as a man believes in what his physical sight tells him, all his corrective behavior will be misdirected.

The reason why the real vision is obscured is because man cannot endure to see his own defiled altar.

But since the altar has BEEN defiled, this fact becomes doubly dangerous unless it IS perceived. This perception is totally non-threatening because of the Atonement. The fear of healing arises in the end from an unwillingness to accept the unequivocal fact that healing is necessary. The fear arises because of the necessary willingness to look at what man has done to himself.

21   Healing was an ability which was lent to man after the Separation, before which it was completely unnecessary. Like all aspects of the space-time belief, healing ability is temporary. However, as long as time persists, healing remains among the stronger human protections. This is because healing always rests on charity, and charity is a way of perceiving the true perfection of another, even if he cannot perceive it himself. Most of the loftier concepts of which man is capable now are time-dependent.

Charity is really a weaker reflection of a much more powerful love-encompassment, which is far beyond any form of charity that man can conceive of as yet.

Charity is essential to Right-Mindedness, in the limited sense to which Right-Mindedness can now be attained. Charity is a way of looking at another AS IF he had already gone far beyond his actual accomplishment in time. Since his own thinking is faulty, he cannot see the Atonement himself, or he would have no need for charity at all. The charity which is accorded him is both an acknowledgment that he IS weak, and a recognition that he COULD BE stronger. The way in which both of these beliefs are stated clearly implies their dependence on time, making it quite apparent that charity lies within the framework of human limitations, though toward the higher levels.

22 We said before, twice in fact, that only Revelation transcends time. [97] The miracle, as an expression of true human charity, can only shorten it at best. [98] It must be understood, however, that whenever a man offers a miracle to another, he IS shortening the suffering of both. This introduces a correction into the Record, [99] which corrects retroactively as well as progressively.

D. Fear as Lack of Love

1 You and B. both You believe that "being afraid" is involuntary. But I have told you many times that only CONSTRUCTIVE acts should be involuntary. We said that Christ-control can take over everything that DOESN'T matter, and Christ-guidance can direct everything that DOES, if you so will.

2 Fear cannot be Christ-controlled, but it CAN be self-controlled.

Fear is always associated with what does not matter.

It prevents Me from controlling it.

The correction is therefore a matter of YOUR will, because its presence shows that you have raised the UNIMPORTANT to a higher level than it warrants. You have thus brought it under your will, where it DOES NOT belong. This means YOU feel responsible for it. The level confusion here is perfectly obvious.

3 The reason that I cannot CONTROL fear for you is that you are attempting to raise to the mind level the proper content of the lower-order reality. I do NOT foster level confusion, but YOU can will to correct it.

---

[97] Chapter 1 B. Principles Of Miracles Principle 50, p4 (only one reference found)
[98] Chapter 1 B. Principles Of Miracles Principle 13; Principle 49; Principle 50, p1 - 4
[99] Akashic Record. A term Edgar Cayce used, referring to the accumulated collective experience in separated consciousness in the One Mind or Sonship. It is also used by other groups and people, but Helen was familiar with Edgar Cayce.
Forward references:
This chapter: E. The Correction For Lack of Love, p26
Chapter 3 C. Atonement Without Sacrifice, p15

D. Fear as Lack of Love

4   You would not tolerate insane behavior on your part, and would hardly advance the excuse that you could not help it. Why should you tolerate insane thinking? There is a fallacy here you would do well to look at clearly.

5   You believe that you ARE responsible for what you DO, but NOT for what you THINK. The truth is that you ARE responsible for what you THINK, because it is only at this level that you CAN exercise choice. What you DO comes from what you think. You cannot separate the truth by giving autonomy to your behavior. This is controlled by Me automatically, as soon as you place what you think under my guidance.

6   Whenever you are afraid, it is a sure sign that you have allowed your mind to miscreate, i.e., have NOT allowed Me to guide it. It is pointless to believe that controlling the outcome of mis-Thought can result in real healing. When you are fearful, you have willed wrongly. This is why you feel you are responsible for it.

7   You must change your MIND, not your behavior, and this IS a matter of will. You do not need guidance EXCEPT at the mind-level. Correction belongs ONLY at the level where creation is possible. The term does not really mean anything at the symptom-level, where it cannot work.

8   The correction of fear IS your responsibility.

When you ask for release from fear, you are implying that it isn't.

You should ask, instead, for help in the conditions which have brought the fear about.

This condition always entails a separated Mind-willingness. At this level, you CAN help it.

9   You are much too tolerant of Mind-wandering, thus passively condoning its miscreation. The particular result never matters, but this fundamental error DOES. The fundamental correction is always the same. Before you will to do anything, ask Me if your will is in accord with Mine. If you are sure that it IS, there will BE no fear.

10   Fear is always a sign of strain, which arises whenever the WILL to do conflicts with WHAT you do. This situation arises in two major ways:

   1. You can will to do conflicting things, either simultaneously or successively. This produces conflicting behavior, which would be tolerable to the self, though not necessarily to others, except for the fact that the part of the will that wants something ELSE is outraged.

   2. You can BEHAVE as you think you should, but without entirely WILLING to do so. This produces consistent behavior, but entails great strain WITHIN the self.

Chapter 2 - The Illusion Of Separation

11   If you think about it, you will realize that in both cases the will and the behavior are out-of-accord, resulting in a situation in which you are doing what you do NOT will. This arouses a sense of coercion, which usually produces rage. The anger then invades the mind, and projection in the wrong sense becomes likely. Depression or anxiety are virtually certain.

12   Remember that whenever there is fear, it is because YOU have NOT MADE UP YOUR MIND. Your will is split, and your behavior inevitably becomes erratic. Correcting at the behavior level can shift the error from the first type to the second, but will NOT obliterate the fear.

13   It is possible to reach a state in which you bring your will under my guidance without much conscious effort, but this implies the kind of habit pattern which you have not developed dependably as yet.

14   S: Tell B. that although he keeps telling you that God will never ask you to do more than you can, he does not understand it himself.

God CANNOT ask more than you WILL. The strength to DO comes from your own undivided will to do. There is NO strain in doing God's will as soon as it is also your own.

15   The lesson here is quite simple, but particularly apt to be overlooked. I will therefore repeat it, URGING you to listen.

> Only your mind can produce fear. It does so whenever it is conflicted in what it wills, thus producing inevitable strain, because willing and doing become discordant. This CANNOT be corrected by better DOING. But it CAN be corrected by higher WILLING.

E. The Correction for Lack of Love

1   After taking the first corrective step, i.e., "Knowing it IS fear," you might benefit temporarily by adding another next step BEFORE going on with the corrective process.

Try saying to yourself that you MUST have willed not to love somehow or somewhere, or that fear which arises from behavior-will conflict could not have happened. Then follow previous instructions.

E. The Correction for Lack of Love

2   If you consider what the process really means, it is nothing more than a series of pragmatic steps in the larger process of accepting the Atonement as THE remedy. From this viewpoint, the steps can be reworded as follows:

   1. Know first this is fear.
   2. Fear arises from lack of love.
   3. The ONLY remedy for lack of love is perfect love.
   4. Perfect love IS the Atonement.

3   The final procedural step (3) is inherent in the last statement (4). We have emphasized that the miracle, or the EXPRESSION of Atonement, is always a sign of real respect from the worthy TO the worthy. This worth IS re-established by the Atonement.

4   It is obvious, then, that when you are afraid you have placed yourself in a position where you NEED Atonement BECAUSE you have DONE something loveless because you WILLED without love. This is precisely the situation for which the Atonement was offered. The need for the remedy inspired its CREATION.

5   As long as you recognize only the NEED for the remedy, you will remain fearful.

However, as soon as you REMEDY it, you have also abolished the fear.

This is how TRUE healing occurs.

6   Everyone experiences fear, and nobody enjoys it. Yet, it would take very little Right-thinking to know why it occurs.

Neither you nor B. have thought about it very much, either.

H: I object at this point to the use of plural verb with a properly singular subject - and remember that last time in a very similar sentence, He said it correctly and I remembered it with real pleasure. This real grammatical error makes me suspicious of the genuineness of these notes.

S: ANSWER: What it really shows is that YOU are not very receptive. The reason it came out that way, is because you are projecting, in the inappropriate way, your own anger, which has nothing to do with these notes. YOU made the error, because you are not feeling loving, so you want me to sound silly, so you won't have to pay attention. Actually, I am trying to get through against considerable opposition, because you are not very happy, and I wish you were. I thought I'd take a chance, even though you are so resistant, because I MIGHT be able to make you feel better. You may be unable not to attack at all, but do try to listen a little, too.

7   Very few people appreciate the real power of the mind. Nobody remains fully aware of it all the time. This is inevitable in this world, because the human being has many things he must do, and cannot engage in constant thought-watching. However, if he

Chapter 2 - The Illusion Of Separation

hopes to spare himself from fear, there are some things he must realize, and realize them fully, at least some of the time.

8
> The mind is a very powerful creator, and it never loses its creative force. It never sleeps. Every instant it is creating, and ALWAYS as you will. Many of your ordinary expressions reflect this. For example, when you say "don't give it a thought," you are implying that if you do not think about something, it will have no effect on you. This is true enough.

9 On the other hand, many other expressions are clear expressions of the prevailing LACK of awareness of thought-power. For example, you say, "just an idle thought," and mean that the thought has no effect. You also speak of some actions as "thoughtless," implying that if the person HAD thought, he would not have behaved as he did. You also use phrases like "thought provoking," which is bland enough, but the term "a provoking thought" means something quite different.

10 While expressions like "think big" give some recognition to the power of thought, they still come nowhere near the truth. You do not expect to grow when you say it, because you don't really believe it. It is hard to recognize that thought and belief combine into a power-surge that can literally move mountains.[100]

11 It appears at first glance that to believe such power about yourself is merely arrogant, but that is not the real reason why you don't believe it.

12 People prefer to believe that their thoughts cannot exert real control because they are literally AFRAID of them. Therapists try to help people who are afraid of their own death wishes by depreciating the power of the wish. They even attempt to "free" the patient by persuading him that he can think whatever he wants, without ANY real effect at all.

13 There is a real dilemma here, which only the truly right-minded can escape. Death wishes do not kill in the physical sense, but they DO kill spiritually. ALL destructive thinking is dangerous. Given a death wish, a man has no choice except to ACT upon his thought, or behave CONTRARY TO it. He can thus choose ONLY between homicide and fear. (See previous notes on will conflicts.[101])

---

100 Matthew 17:20 And Jesus said unto them, Because of your unbelief: for verily I say unto you, If ye have faith as a grain of mustard seed, ye shall say unto this mountain, Remove hence to yonder place; and it shall remove; and nothing shall be impossible unto you.
Also, Luke 17:6 And the Lord said, If ye had faith as a grain of mustard seed, ye might say unto this sycamine tree, Be thou plucked up by the root, and be thou planted in the sea; and it should obey you.
101 This chapter: D. Fear As Lack Of Love, p10

E. The Correction for Lack of Love

14 (H: NOTE I avoided this term in the last series of notes intentionally, because it seemed too Rankian. Apparently, there was a reason why this word should have been used last time. It is used in this section for a very good reason.)

15 The other possibility is that he depreciates the power of his thought. This is the usual psychoanalytic approach. This DOES allay guilt, but at the cost of rendering thinking impotent. If you believe that what you think is ineffectual, you may cease to be overly afraid of it, but you are hardly likely to respect it, either. The world is full of endless examples of how man has depreciated himself because he is afraid of his own thoughts. In some forms of insanity, thoughts are glorified, but this is only because the underlying depreciation was too effective for tolerance.

16
> The truth is that there ARE no "idle thoughts."
> ALL thinking produces form at some level.

The reason why people are afraid of ESP, and so often react against it, is because they KNOW that thought can hurt them. Their OWN thoughts have made them vulnerable.

17 You and B., who complain all the time about fear, still persist in creating it most of the time.

I told you last time that you cannot ask ME to release you from it, because I KNOW it does not exist. YOU don't.

> If I merely intervene between your thoughts and their results, I would be tampering with a basic law of cause and effect, in fact the most fundamental one there is in this world.

I would hardly help if I depreciated the power of your own thinking. This would be in direct opposition to the purpose of this course.

18 It is certainly much more useful to remind you that you do not guard your thoughts at all carefully, except for a relatively small part of the day, and somewhat inconsistently even then. You may feel at this point that it would take a miracle to enable you to do this, which is perfectly true. Human beings are not used to miraculous thinking, but they CAN be TRAINED to think that way.

19 All miracle-workers HAVE to be trained that way. I have to be able to count on them. This means that I cannot allow them to leave their mind unguarded, or they will not be able to help me. Miracle-working entails a full realization of the power of thought, and real avoidance of miscreation. Otherwise, the miracle will be necessary to set the mind ITSELF straight, a circular process which would hardly foster the time-collapse for

Chapter 2 - The Illusion Of Separation

which the miracle was intended. Nor would it induce the healthy respect that every miracle-worker must have for true cause and effect.

20   Miracles cannot free the miracle-worker from fear. Both miracles AND fear come from his thoughts, and if he were not free to choose one, he would also not be free to choose the other. Remember, we said before that when electing one person, you reject another. [102]

21   It is much the same in electing the miracle. By so doing, you HAVE rejected fear. Fear cannot assail unless it has been created. You have been afraid of God, of me, of yourselves, and of practically everyone you know at one time or another.

22   This can only be because you have miscreated all of us, and believe in what you have created. (We spent a lot of time on this before, but it did not help very much.) You would never have done this if you were not afraid of your own thoughts. The vulnerable are essentially miscreators, because they misperceive Creation.

23   You and B. are willing to accept primarily what does NOT change your minds too much, and leaves you free to leave them quite unguarded most of the time. You persist in believing that when you do not consciously watch your mind, it is unmindful.

24   It is time to consider the whole world of the unconscious, or unwatched mind. This will frighten you, because it is the source of fright. You may look at it as a new theory of basic conflict, if you wish, which will not be entirely an intellectual approach, because I doubt if the truth will escape you entirely.

25   The unwatched mind is responsible for the whole content of the unconscious, which lies above the miracle-level. All psychoanalytic theorists have made some contribution to the truth in this connection, but none of them has seen it in its true entirety.

(The correct grammar here is a sign of your better cooperation. Thank you.)

Jung's best contribution was an awareness of individual vs. collective unconscious levels. He also recognized the major place of the religious spirit in his schema. His archetypes were also meaningful concepts. But his major error lay in regarding the deepest level of the unconscious as shared in terms of CONTENT. The deepest level of the unconscious is shared as an ABILITY. As MIRACLE-MINDEDNESS, the content, (or the particular miracles which an individual happens to perform) does not matter at all. They will, in fact, be entirely different, because, since I direct them, I make a point of avoiding redundancy. Unless a miracle actually heals, it is not a miracle at all.

26   The content of the miracle-level is not recorded in the individual's unconscious, because if it were, it would not be automatic and involuntary, which we have said

---

[102] Chapter 1 B. Principles Of Miracles Principle 42, p4

repeatedly it should be. However, the content IS a matter for the Record, which is NOT within the individual himself.

27   All psychoanalysts made one common error, in that they attempted to uncover unconscious CONTENT. You cannot understand unconscious activity in these terms, because "content" is applicable ONLY to the more superficial unconscious levels to which the individual himself contributes. This is the level at which he can readily introduce fear, and usually does.

28   Freud was right in calling this level pre-conscious, and emphasizing that there is a fairly easy interchange between preconscious and conscious material. He was also right in regarding the censor as an agent for the protection of consciousness from fear. HIS major error lay in his insistence that this level is necessary at all in the psychic structure. If the psyche contains fearful levels from which it cannot escape without splitting, its integration is permanently threatened. It is essential not to control the fearful, but to ELIMINATE it.

29   Here, Rank's concept of the will was particularly good, except that he preferred to ally it only with man's own truly creative ability, but did not extend it to its proper union with God's. His "birth trauma," another valid idea, was also too limited, in that it did not refer to the Separation, which was really a FALSE idea of birth. Physical birth is not a trauma in itself. It can, however, remind the individual of the Separation, which was a very real cause of fear.

30   The idea of "will-THERAPY" was potentially a very powerful one, but Rank did not see its real potential because he himself used his mind partly to create a theory OF the mind, but also partly to attack Freud. His reactions to Freud stemmed from his own unfortunate acceptance of the deprivation-fallacy, which itself arose from the Separation. This led him to believe that his own mind-creation could stand only if the creation of another's fell. In consequence, his theory emphasized rather than minimized the two-edged nature of defenses. This is an outstanding characteristic of his concepts, because it was outstandingly true of him.

31   He also misinterpreted the birth-trauma in a way that made it inevitable for him to attempt a therapy whose goal was to ABOLISH FEAR. This is characteristic of all later theorists, who do not attempt, as Freud did, to split off the fear in his own form of therapy.

32   No one as yet has fully recognized either the therapeutic value of fear, or the only way in which it can be truly ended. When man miscreates, he IS in pain. The cause and effect principle here is temporarily a real expeditor. Actually, Cause is a term properly belonging to God, and Effect, which should also be capitalized, is HIS Sonship. This

Chapter 2 - The Illusion Of Separation

entails a set of cause and effect relationships which are totally different from those which man introduced into the Miscreation.

33   The fundamental opponents in the real basic conflict are Creation and miscreation. All fear is implicit in the second, just as all love is inherent in the first. Because of this difference, the basic conflict IS one between love and fear.

34   So much, then, for the true nature of the major opponents in the basic conflict. Since all such theories lead to a form of therapy in which a re-distribution of psychic energy results, it is necessary to consider OUR concept of libido next. In this respect, Freud was more accurate than his followers, who were essentially more wishful. Energy CAN emanate from both Creation AND miscreation, and the particular ratio which prevails between them at a given point in time DOES determine behavior AT that time. If miscreation did NOT engender energy in its own right, it would be unable to produce destructive behavior, which it very patently DOES.

35   Everything that man creates has energy because, like the Creation of God, they come FROM energy, and are endowed by their creator with the power to create. Miscreation is still a genuine creative act in terms of the underlying IMPULSE, but NOT in terms of the CONTENT of the creation. This, however, does not deprive the creation of its OWN creative power. It DOES, however, GUARANTEE that the power will be misused, or USED FEARFULLY.

36   To deny this is merely the previously mentioned fallacy of depreciation. Although Freud made a number of fallacies of his own, he DID avoid this one in connection with libido. The later theorists denied the split-energy concept, not by attempting to heal it, but by re-interpreting it instead of redistributing it.

37   This placed them in the illogical position of assuming that the split which their therapies were intended to heal had not occurred. The result of this approach is essentially a form of hypnosis. This is quite different from Freud's approach, which merely ended in a deadlock.

38   A similar deadlock occurs when both the power of Creation and of miscreation coexist. This is experienced as conflict only because the individual feels AS IF both were occurring AT THE SAME LEVEL. He BELIEVES in what he has created in his own unconscious and he naturally believes it is real BECAUSE he has created it. He, thus, places himself in a position where the fearful becomes REAL.

39   Nothing but level-confusion can result as long as this belief is held in ANY form. Inappropriate denial and equally inappropriate identification of the REAL factors in the basic conflict will NOT solve the problem itself. The conflict CANNOT disappear until it is fully recognized that miscreation is NOT real, and therefore there IS no conflict.

E. The Correction for Lack of Love

This entails a full realization of the basic fact that, although man has miscreated in a very real sense, he need neither continue to do so, nor to suffer from his past errors in this respect.

40 A REDISTRIBUTION of psychic energy, then, is NOT the solution. Both the idea that both kinds MUST exist, and the belief that ONE kind is amenable for use or misuse, are real distortions. The ONLY way is to STOP MISCREATING NOW, and accept the Atonement for miscreations of the past.

Only this can re-establish true single-mindedness. The structure of the psyche, as you very correctly noted yourself, follows along the lines of the particular libido concept the theorist employs.

41 H: I still think it was the other way around .

S: Answer: This confusion arises out of the fact that you DID change the order - several times in fact. Actually, it didn't matter, because the two concepts DO flow from each other. It was a TERRIFIC waste of time, and one in which I hardly care to become engaged myself. PLEASE!

42 Freud's psyche was essentially a good and evil picture, with very heavy weight given to the evil. This is because every time I mentioned the Atonement to him, which was quite often, he responded by defending his theory more and more against it. This resulted in his increasingly strong attempts to make the illogical sound more and more logical.

43 I was very sorry about this, because his was a singularly good mind, and it was a shame to waste it. However, the major purpose of his incarnation was not neglected. He DID succeed in forcing recognition of the unconscious into man's calculations about himself, a step in the right direction which should not be minimized. Freud was one of the most religious men I have known recently. Unfortunately, he was so afraid of religion that the only way he could deal with it was to regard IT (not himself) as sick. This naturally prevented healing.

44 Freud's superego is a particularly interesting example of the real power of miscreation. It is noteworthy throughout the whole development of his theories that the superego never allied itself with freedom. The most it could do in this direction was to work out a painful truce in which both opponents LOST. This perception could not fail to force him to emphasize discontent in his view of civilization.

45 The Freudian id is really only the more superficial level of the unconscious, and not the deepest level at all. This, too, was inevitable, because Freud could not divorce miracles from magic. It was therefore his constant endeavor, (even preoccupation) to keep on thrusting more and more material between consciousness and the real deeper level of the unconscious, so that the latter became increasingly obscured. The result was

Chapter 2 - The Illusion Of Separation

a kind of bedlam, in which there was no order, no control, and no sense. This was exactly how he FELT about it.

46   The later theoretical switch to the primacy of anxiety was an interesting device intended to deny both the instinctive nature of destructiveness, and the force of the power of miscreation. By placing the emphasis on the RESULT, the generative nature of the power was minimized.

47   Destructive behavior IS instinctual. The instinct for creation is NOT obliterated in miscreation. That is why it is always invested with reality.

48   One of the chief ways in which man can correct his magic-miracle confusion is to remember that he did not create himself. He is apt to forget this when he becomes egocentric, and this places him in a position where belief in magic is virtually inevitable. His instincts for creation were given him by his own Creator, who was expressing the same instinct in His Creation. Since the creative ability rests solely in the mind, everything which man creates is necessarily instinctive. [103]

49   We have already said that the basic conflict is one between love and fear, [104] and that the proper organization of the psyche rests on a lack of level confusion. The section on psychic energy should be re-read very carefully, [105] because it is particularly likely to be misinterpreted until this section is complete.

50   It has already been said that man CANNOT control fear, because he himself created it. His belief in it renders it out of his control by definition.

> For this reason, any attempt to resolve the basic conflict through the concept of mastery of fear is meaningless. In fact, it asserts the power of fear by the simple assumption that it need be mastered at all.

51

> The essential resolution rests entirely on the mastery of love.

In the interim, conflict is inevitable. The reason for this is the strangely illogical position in which man had placed himself. Since we have frequently emphasized that correction must be applied within the level that error occurs, it should be clear that the miracle MUST be illogical because its purpose is to correct the illogical and restore order.

---

103 This p48 is repeated later in this section as p61 It was crossed out at this location in the ur text.
104 This section, p33
105 This section, p34-42

E. The Correction for Lack of Love

52   Two concepts which CANNOT coexist are nothing and everything. To whatever extent one is believed in, the other HAS BEEN abolished. In the conflict, fear is really nothing, and love is really everything. (This recognition is really the basis for the castration complex.) This is because whenever light penetrates darkness,[106] it DOES abolish it. The unwillingness to be seen, or submit error to light, is spuriously associated with active doing. In this incarnation, this can take the form of oedipal involvement and concomitant castration anxiety.

53   However, in more long range and meaningful terms, the oedipal complex is a miniature of the true Separation fear, and the castration complex is a way of denying that it ever occurred. Like all pseudo-solutions, this kind of distorted thinking is very creative, but false.

The Separation HAS occurred. To deny this is merely to misuse denial.

However, to concentrate on error is merely a further misuse of legitimate psychic mechanisms.

> The true corrective procedure, which has already been described as the proper use of the spiritual eye (or true vision), is to accept the error temporarily, BUT ONLY as an indication that IMMEDIATE correction is mandatory. This establishes a state of mind in which the Atonement can be accepted without delay.

54   It is worth repeating that ultimately there is no compromise possible between everything and nothing. The purpose of time is essentially a device by which all compromise in this respect can be abolished. It seems to be abolished by degrees precisely because time itself involves a concept of intervals which do not really exist. The faulty use of creation has made this necessary as a corrective device.

55   "And God so loved the world that He gave his only begotten Son so that whosoever believeth on Him shall not perish but have Eternal Life"[107] needs only one slight correction to be entirely meaningful in this context. It should read "And God so loved the world that he gave it TO His only begotten Son." It should be noted that God HAS begotten only ONE Son.

56   If you believe that all of the Souls that God created ARE His Sons, and if you also believe that the Sonship is One, then every Soul MUST be a Son of God , or an integral part of the Sonship. You do not find the concept that the whole is greater than its parts difficult to understand. You should therefore not have too great difficulty with this. The Sonship in its Oneness DOES transcend the sum of its parts. However, it loses this

---

106 1 John 1:5 This is the message which we have heard from Him and declare to you, that God is light and in Him is no darkness at all.

107 John 3:16 For God so loved the world that He gave His only begotten Son, that whoever believes in Him should not perish but have everlasting life.

Chapter 2 - The Illusion Of Separation

special state as long as any of its parts are missing. This is why the conflict cannot ultimately be resolved UNTIL all of the individual parts of the Sonship have returned. Only then, in the true sense, can the meaning of wholeness be understood.

57   The concept of minus numbers has always been regarded as a mathematical rather than an actual expedient. (This is a major limitation on mathematics as presently understood.) Any statement which implies degrees of difference in negation is essentially meaningless. What can replace this negative approach is a recognition of the fact that as long as one part (which is the same as a million or ten or eight thousand parts) of the Sonship is missing, it is NOT complete.

58   In the Divine psyche, the Father and the Holy Spirit are not incomplete at all. The Sonship has the unique faculty of believing in error, or incompleteness, if he so elects. However, it is quite apparent that so to elect IS to believe in the existence of nothingness. The correction of this error is the Atonement.

59   We have already briefly spoken about readiness. But there are some additional awarenesses which might be helpful.

Readiness is nothing more than the prerequisite for accomplishment. The two should not be confused. As soon as a state of readiness occurs, there is always some will to accomplish, but this is by no means undivided. The state does not imply more than the potential for a shift of will. Confidence cannot develop fully until mastery has been accomplished.

We began this section with an attempt to correct the fundamental human error that fear can be mastered. The Correction was that ONLY love can be mastered. When I told you that you were "ready for Revelation," I did not mean that you had in any way mastered this form of communication. However, you yourself attested to your readiness by insisting that I would not have said so if it had not been true. This IS an affirmation of readiness. Mastery of love necessarily involves a much more complete confidence in the ability than either of you has attained. But the readiness at least is an indication that you believe this is possible. This is only the beginning of confidence.

60   In case this be misunderstood as a statement that an enormous amount of time will be necessary between readiness and mastery, I would again remind you that time and space are under My control.

61   [108] One of the chief ways in which man can correct his magic-miracle confusion is to remember that he did not create himself. He is apt to forget this when he becomes egocentric, and this places him in a position where belief in magic is virtually inevitable. His instincts for creation were given him by his own Creator, who was expressing the

---

[108] This paragraph is a repeat of p48 from earlier in this section.

E. The Correction for Lack of Love

same instinct in His Creation. Since the creative ability rests solely in the mind, everything which man creates is necessarily instinctive.

62   It also follows that whatever he creates is real in his own eyes, but not necessarily in the sight of God. This basic distinction leads us directly into the real meaning of the Last Judgment.

S: I am aware of the fact that you would much rather continue with the parallels involved in other theories of basic conflict. However, this would merely be a delay which we will engage in only if you regard it as essential.

F. The Meaning of the Last Judgment

1   The Final Judgment is one of the greatest threat concepts in man's perception. This is only because he does not understand it. Judgment is not an essential attribute of God. Man brought judgment into being only because of the Separation. God Himself is still the God of mercy.

After the Separation, however, there WAS a place for justice in the schema, because it was one of the many learning devices which had to be built into the overall plan. Just as the Separation occurred over many millions of years, the Last Judgment will extend over a similarly long period, and perhaps even longer. Its length depends, however, on the effectiveness of the present speed-up.

We have frequently noted that the miracle is a device for shortening but not abolishing time. If a sufficient number of people become truly miracle-minded quickly, the shortening process can be almost immeasurable. But it is essential that these individuals free themselves from fear sooner than would ordinarily be the case, because they MUST emerge from basic conflict if they are to bring peace to the minds of others.

2   The Last Judgment is generally thought of as a procedure undertaken by God. Actually, it will be undertaken solely by man, with My help. It is a Final Healing, rather than a meting out of punishment, however much man may think punishment is deserved. Punishment as a concept is in total opposition to Right-Mindedness. The aim of the Final Judgment is to RESTORE Right-Mindedness TO man.

3   The Final Judgment might be called a process of Right-evaluation. It simply means that finally all men must come to understand what is worthy and what is not.

After this, their ability to choose can be reasonably directed. Unless this distinction has been made, the vacillations between free and imprisoned will cannot but continue. The first step toward freedom, then, MUST entail a sorting out of the false from the true. This is a process of division only in the constructive sense, and reflects the true meaning of the Apocalypse.

Chapter 2 - The Illusion Of Separation

Man will ultimately look upon his own creations, and will to preserve only what is good, just as God Himself once looked upon what he had created, and knew that it WAS good.[109] At this point, the mind Will will begin to look with love on its creations, because of their great worthiness. The mind will inevitably disown its miscreations, and having withdrawn belief from them, they will no longer exist.

4   The term Last Judgment is frightening, not only because it has been falsely projected onto God, but also because of the association of "Last" with death. This is an outstanding example of upside down perception. Actually, if it is examined objectively, it is quite apparent that it is really the doorway to life. No man who lives in fear is really alive.

5   His own final judgment cannot be directed toward himself, because he is not his own creation. He can apply it meaningfully, and at any time, to everything he has ever created, and retain in his real memory only what is good. This is what his own Right-Mindedness CANNOT BUT dictate.

The purpose of time is solely to "give him time" to achieve this judgment. It is his own perfect judgment of his own creation. When everything that he retains is lovable, there is no reason for any fear to remain in him. This IS his part in the Atonement.

---

[109] Genesis 1:31 Then God saw everything that He had made, and indeed it was very good. So the evening and the morning were the sixth day.

Chapter 3 - Retraining The Mind

A. Introduction

1   All learning involves attention and study at some level. This course is a MIND-TRAINING course. Good students assign study periods for themselves. However, since this obvious step has not occurred to you, and since we are cooperating in this, I will make the obvious assignment now.

2   B is better at understanding the need to study the notes than you are, but neither of you realizes that many of the problems you keep being faced with may ALREADY have been solved there. YOU do not think of the notes in this way at all. B DOES from time to time, but he generally says, "It's probably in the notes," and DOESN'T look it up. He believes that, although he reads them over, they cannot REALLY help him until they are complete.

3   First of all, he cannot be sure of this unless he tries. Second, they would BE completed if both of you so willed.

4   You vaguely know that the course is intended for some sort of preparation. I can only say that you are not prepared.

5   I was amused when you reminded B. that he, too, was being prepared for something quite unexpected, and he said, he was not at all curious about what it was. This disinterest is very characteristic of him when he is afraid. Interest and fear do NOT go together, as your respective behavior clearly shows.

6   Mental retardation is a defense which, like the others EXCEPT the Atonement, can be used on behalf of error or truth, as elected. When it occurs in REALITY, it is a temporary device, agreed on beforehand, to check the miscreative abilities of strong but misdirected wills.

7   It is necessary that this appropriate use of the defense BE considered real, because otherwise it cannot serve. The lesson involves not only the individual himself, but also his parents, siblings, and all of those who come in close relation with him.

    The VALUE of the experience depends on the need of each particular learner. The person himself is a POOR learner, by definition, only as a step toward changing from a bad to a good one.

8   Mental retardation can also be used as a maladaptive defense, if the wrong (or attack) side is employed. This produces the "pseudo-retardation syndrome" which is justly classified as a psychiatric (or disturbed-level) symptom.

Chapter 3 - Retraining The Mind

Both of you do this all the time. B. acts as if he does not understand even his OWN special language, let alone mine, and you cannot read at all.

9   This represents a joint attack on both yourselves AND me, because it renders YOUR mind weak, and mine incompetent. Remember, this puts you in a truly fearful position. If you cannot understand either your own mind OR mine, you do not KNOW what is really willed. It is thus IMPOSSIBLE to avoid conflict, as defined before, because even if you act ACCORDING TO will, you wouldn't know it.

10 The next part of this course rests too heavily on the earlier part not to REQUIRE its study. Without this, you will become much too fearful when the unexpected DOES occur to make constructive use of it.

However, as you study the notes, you will see some of the obvious implications, unless you still persist in misusing the defense of mental retardation. Please remember that its constructive use, described above, is hardly a REAL part of your own REAL proper equipment. It is a PARTICULARLY inappropriate defense as you use it, and I can only urge you to avoid it.

11 The reason why a solid foundation is necessary at this point is because of the highly likely confusion of "fearful" and "awesome," which most people do make. You will remember that we said once before [110] that awe is inappropriate in connection with the Sons of God, because you should not experience awe in the presence of your own equals.

But it WAS emphasized that awe IS a proper reaction of the Soul in the presence of its Creator.

12 So far, this course has had only indirect recourse to God, and rarely even refers to Him directly.

I have repeatedly emphasized that awe is not appropriate in connection with me, BECAUSE of our inherent equality. I have been careful to clarify my own role in the Atonement, without either over or understating it. I have tried to do exactly the same things in connection with yours.

13 The next step, however, DOES involve the direct approach to God Himself. It would be most unwise to start on this step at all without very careful preparation, or awe will surely be confused with fear, and the experience will be more traumatic than beatific.

14 Healing is of God in the end. The means are carefully explained in the notes. Revelation has occasionally SHOWN you the end, but to reach it the means are needed.

[Tim Note: The following section is very important. It uses specific examples with Bill and Helen, to demonstrate how to use self-awareness to correct error. Because of its

---

110 Chapter 1 B. Principles Of Miracles Principle 47, p1-3

A. Introduction

importance, I have left it all as the primary message, without marking the Bill/Helen/Jesus dialogs as separate.]

15   The following is the only detailed description which need be written down as to how error interferes with preparation. The events specifically referred to here could be any events, nor does their particular influence matter. It is the process which is to be noted here, and not its results. The kind of beliefs, and the fallacious premises involved in misthought are as well exemplified here as elsewhere. There is nothing of special interest about the events described below, EXCEPT their typical nature.

If this is a true course in mind-training, then the whole value of this section rests ONLY in showing you what NOT to do. The more constructive emphasis is, of course, on the positive approach. Mind-watching would have prevented any of this from occurring, and will do so any time you permit it to.

16   Tell B. that the reason why he was so strained yesterday is because he allowed himself a number of fear-producing attitudes. They were fleeting enough to be more will-of-the-wisps than serious will-errors, but unless he watches this kind of thing, he WILL find the notes fearful, and, knowing him well, will mis-distantiate. His unprovoked irritation was unpardonable EXCEPT by himself, and he did not choose to pardon it.

YOU did, but I am afraid you were under some strain in doing so. This was unfortunate, and weakened your own ability to behave healingly toward B. at the time, and later also toward Louis, both of whom DID act stupidly. But one stupidity at a time is usually enough. You are getting too close to the misuse of mental retardation when stupidity sets in all around.

17   B., having already weakened himself, was very un-miracle-minded, first by not asking Dora if she wanted a lift in the cab, which was going her way. Even if she didn't want it, she would have been able to use the thought well. There is probably no human error that is more fear-provoking (in the will/behavior conflict sense) than countering any form of error with error. The result can be highly inflammable. By reacting to Dora's stupidity with his own, all of the elements which are virtually certain to engender fear have been provided.

18   B should note that this is one of the few times that he had to wait for a cab. He thought he took care of it by holding the door of a cab which did come for that lady, but he was misguided in this belief. Beliefs are THOUGHTS, and thus come under Christ-guidance, NOT control. Actually, by giving this cab to her, he was very unkind to you. It was quite apparent that you were extremely cold, and also very late. The idea that giving her the cab would atone for his previous errors was singularly out of place, and well

Chapter 3 - Retraining The Mind

calculated to lead to further error. If, instead of attempting to atone on his own, he had asked for guidance, there would have been no difficulty whatever in the cab situation. It was not necessary that anyone wait at all.

19   B's original slight to Dora, because of his own need to get home as he perceived it, stopped him from benefiting from the time-saving device of the miracle. He would have gotten home MUCH quicker if he had taken time to use time properly.

20   YOU were still suffering from strain [111], and got quite irritated at the girl who stood next to the door on the side which blocked its opening. Her presence there made it necessary each time the door was opened to hold it for a much longer time than was necessary, and you were angry because this made you cold. Actually, the girl was taking care of the younger child who was standing outside, and both of them were really mentally retarded. If you will remember, the older girl asked you very uncertainly about the bus, and you were well aware at the time of her extreme uncertainty.

21   It would have been much wiser had you built up her confidence, instead of associating with her stupidity. This reduced your own efficiency, and the only thing that saved you then was that you DID remember, in the cab, to ask me about the notes, instead of assuming that you were necessarily to arrange to meet the next day and go over them. B. had already become so misguided that it did not occur to him that his own will, (which he justified by the contents of the recent notes —a misuse of truth only seemingly on its own behalf) might be questionable. (You took poor notes yourself here, because you got mad at him on remembering this. While you did try to will right in the cab, you did not quite succeed. The error is showing up now.)

22   B thus placed himself in a condition to experience a fear rather than a love reaction.

H notes that she was going to write "an excellent position," but did not do so.

S: Answer: You were right about the misuse of "excellent" here, and please do cross it out. You are STILL angry. An excellent position for miscreation is not a meaningful approach to the problem.

23   It was indeed discourteous ("indeed" is not necessary; it was your OWN error here; I am NOT saying this with any harsh overtones at all. I am just trying to create better learning conditions for the study periods. We want as little interference as possible, for VERY good reasons.)

24   Now, go back to B; he WAS discourteous when he told you that HE wanted to keep the original copy of the notes, having decided to have them Xeroxed on his OWN will, and then justifying it by a very slight misinterpretation of what I said about "useful for others." In fact, if he will re-read the actual quote, he will see that it REALLY means

---

111 This section: p16

A. Introduction

"useful for HIM." YOU had interpreted it that way, and frankly this was pretty clear to me at the time.

But this sort of thing happens all the time. It should, be noted, however, that the result was not only considerable and totally unnecessary planning on B's part, but also a failure to utilize what WAS intended for him as a help for HIMSELF. And before YOU get too self-satisfied, I would remind you that you do it all the time, too.

25   B. acted inappropriately toward YOU, by saying that he wanted to be SURE that the original was not lost or dirty. It is noticeable that, having already decided what HE wanted to do, it never occurred to him that it IS possible that HE might lose or dirty them himself, especially as he had not entrusted them to me. This is a form of arrogance that he would be much happier without. He should also note that this would probably not have occurred had he not been ALREADY literally "off the beam." Be SURE to tell him that this pun is to reassure him that I am not angry. If he does not get it, or does not like it, I KNOW it is not very good. The reason is that HE put me in a position where I can really give him very little at the moment.

26   But I want him to know that I am VERY well aware of the exceedingly few times he now makes errors of this kind. He has come a VERY long way in this respect. It seems a shame that he should allow himself even this much discomfort from it.

27   I suggest to YOU that we pray for him, and I pray for your full cooperation in this. This will correct YOUR errors, and help him react better to the work on the bookcase, which may otherwise lend itself for misuse by misprojection. There would have been no problem at all about the bookcase, and perhaps even no bookcase, if the solution of the storage problem had been left to me. I have promised to guide you OUT of problems, and will certainly not create them for you. But this means that you do not undertake to solve them yourselves. A storage problem is hardly more difficult for me to solve than a space problem, (see comments under special principles for miracle workers.) [112]

28   You started well in your attempt to pray with me for B., but ended badly. This is because you had already made a number of earlier errors. You were wrong to be pleased with Bill F's criticism of Rose, and should not have enjoyed Bill F's description of Zanvil's caricaturing of her. You could have laughed WITH Bill, but NOT AT Rose. Real courtesy NEVER does this. You should know that all God's children are fully worthy of COMPLETE courtesy. You should NEVER join with one at the EXPENSE of another.

29   When you called B about joining you, Gene, and Anne at lunch, YOU should have waited to ask ME. In fact, you should not even have told Anne that you would call. Then you could have asked B. FIRST if HE would want to come, and called ANNE back. It is true that it was better that he came, but this has nothing to do with the real issue. There

---

112 Forward reference: This Chapter B. Special Principles Of Miracle Workers, p2

Chapter 3 - Retraining The Mind

are ways of treating others in which ONLY consistent courtesy, even in very little things, is offered. This is a VERY HEALING habit to acquire.

30 B's answer to your call was a clear statement of his own sadly conflicted state. He said, "I don't want to join you, but that's ungracious, so I'll go." Whenever ANY invitation to join others in a gracious way is offered, it should ALWAYS be met with respect, although it need not always be accepted. However, if it is MET ungraciously the resulting feeling may well be one of coercion. This is ALWAYS a split-will reaction.

31 B. did not solve this by ACTING graciously. The lunch need not have entailed either mental or physical strain for him, and no "need to escape" should have arisen. This was a regression of the unprofitable kind. B. will continue to experience this need from time to time, until he is willing to realize that there is nothing he needs or wants to escape from.

32 It is very hard to get out of the chain of miscreation which can arise out of even the simplest mis-thought. To borrow one of your own phrases, "This kind of human tragedy is far easier to avert than to undo."

33 You must both learn not to let this kind of chain reaction START. You will NOT be able to control it once it has started, because everything and everyone will be pulled into the misprojection, and misinterpreted accordingly. NOTHING is lovely to the unloving. This is because they are CREATING ugliness.

34 You, Helen, were definitely not acting right-mindedly by writing these notes right in front of Jonathan. (Note that you wrote his name as "Jonathan" this time, although previously in these same notes you referred to him as "Louis," intentionally using his real name. Actually, of course, it does not matter what you call him, but NOTE that you FELT FREE at that time to CHOOSE the name YOU preferred to use. This time, you were FORCED to call him "Jonathan" because you were ATTACKING him when you took the notes in front of him, and are now falling back on the magical device of "protecting his name."

35 H: I had been considering calling B rather ambivalently, and had gotten up to do so, but remembered to ask. The answer was to call him at 8:30. It would be better if HE called, but he may not decide to do so. If he does not, you should try to get through, and if he has decided NOT to be there, just leave a message that it is not important. This is still a kindly gesture, and the message should be put in a gentle way. (B. did call H.)

36 Without going into further elaboration, and we could devote many hours to this, lets consider all the time that we had to waste today. AND all the notes that could have been devoted to a better purpose than undoing the waste, and thus creating further waste. There IS a better use for time, too. I would have liked to have spent some time on corrections of the past notes, as an important step before reviewing them. A major point

A. Introduction

of clarification is necessary in connection with the phrase "replacing hatred (or fear) with love."

37   S: No, Helen, do NOT check this against the prayer that B. very kindly typed for you on the card. That WAS a gracious offering on his part, and YOU also accepted it with grace at the time. Why should you deprive yourself of the value of the offering by referring this correction first to HIM?

38   These notes did not continue at this time, due to the obvious fact that H. was still clearly not in her right mind. However, B later suggested that "correct" or "correct for" should be used instead of "replace." At the time, he was quite sure about this, and he was perfectly right. The reason why it was essential that HE make this correction was that the word "replace" was his choice originally, and reflected a temporary misunderstanding of his own. It was, however, both courteous and necessary that he change this himself, both as a sign of his own better understanding, and of an avoidance of correction by someone else, which would have been discourteous.

B. Special Principles for Miracle Workers

1   The miracle abolishes the need for lower order concerns. Since it is an illogical, or out-of-pattern time interval, by definition, the ordinary considerations of time and space do not apply.

2   For example, I do NOT regard time as you and B. do, and Kolb's space problem is NOT mine.

    When YOU perform a miracle, I will arrange both time and space to adjust to it.

3   Clear distinction between what HAS BEEN Created and what IS BEING created is essential. ALL forms of correction (or healing) rest on this FUNDAMENTAL correction in level perception. [113]

4   Another way of stating this is: NEVER confuse right with wrong-mindedness. Responding to ANY form of miscreation with anything EXCEPT a DESIRE TO HEAL (or a miracle) is an expression of this confusion.

5   The miracle is ALWAYS a DENIAL of this error, and an affirmation of the truth. Only Right-Mindedness CAN create in a way that has any real effect. Pragmatically, what has no real effect, has no real existence. Its REAL effect, then, is emptiness. Being without substantial content, it lends itself to projection.

---

[113] Chapter 1 B. Principles Of Miracles, b. The Concept Of Lack, p9
    Chapter 2 A. Introduction, p4

Chapter 3 - Retraining The Mind

6   The level-adjustment power of the miracle creates the right perception for healing. Until this has occurred, healing cannot be understood. Forgiveness is an empty gesture, unless it entails correction. Without this, it is essentially judgmental, rather than healing.

7

    Miraculous forgiveness is ONLY correction. It has no element of judgment at all. "Father forgive them for they know not what they do"[114] in NO way EVALUATES what they do. It is strictly limited to an appeal to God to HEAL their minds. There is no reference to the outcome of their misthought. THIS does not matter.

8   The Biblical injunction "Be of one mind"[115] is the statement for REVELATION readiness. My OWN injunction "Do this in remembrance of me" [116] is the request for cooperation in miracle-workers. It should be noted that the two statements are not in the same order of reality, because the latter involves a time awareness, since memory implies recalling the PAST in the present.

9   Time is under MY direction, but Timelessness belongs to God alone. In time, we exist for and with each other. In Timelessness, we coexist with God.

C. Atonement without Sacrifice

1   There is one more point which must be perfectly clear before any residual fear which may still be associated with miracles becomes entirely groundless. The Crucifixion did NOT establish the Atonement. The Resurrection did. This is a point which many very sincere Christians have misunderstood. Nobody who was free of the scarcity-fallacy could POSSIBLY have made this mistake.

---

114 Luke 23:34 And Jesus said, Father, forgive them; for they know not what they do. And parting his garments among them, they cast lots.

115 2 Corinthians 13:11 Finally, brethren, farewell. Become complete. Be of good comfort, be of one mind, live in peace; and the God of love and peace will be with you.
Also Philippians 2:1-8 If there is therefore any comfort in Christ, if any consolation of love, if any fellowship of the Spirit, if any tender mercies and compassions, fulfill ye my joy, that ye be of the same mind, having the same love, being of one accord, of one mind; doing nothing through faction or through vainglory, but in lowliness of mind each counting other better than himself; not looking each of you to his own things, but each of you also to the things of others. Have this mind in you, which was also in Christ Jesus: who, being in the form of God, counted it not a prize to be on an equality with God, but emptied himself, taking the form of a servant, being made in the likeness of men; and being found in fashion as a man, he humbled himself, becoming obedient even unto death, yea, the death of the cross.

116 Luke 22:19 And he took bread, and gave thanks, and brake it, and gave unto them, saying, This is my body which is given for you: this do in remembrance of me.

C. Atonement without Sacrifice

2   If the Crucifixion is seen from an upside down point of view, it certainly does appear AS IF God permitted, and even encouraged, one of his Sons to suffer BECAUSE he was good. Many very devoted ministers preach this every day. This particularly unfortunate interpretation, which actually arose out of the combined misprojection of a large number of my own would-be followers, has led many people to be bitterly afraid of God.

3   This particularly anti-religious concept happens to enter into many religions, and this is neither by chance nor coincidence.

4   The real Christian would have to pause and ask "how could this be?" Is it likely that God Himself would be capable of the kind of thinking which His own Words have clearly stated is unworthy of man?

5   (There are times when) The best defense, as always, is NOT to attack another's position, but rather to protect the truth. It is not necessary to consider anything acceptable, if you have to turn a whole frame of reference around in order to justify it. This procedure is painful in its minor applications, and genuinely tragic on a mass basis. Persecution is a frequent result, justified by the terrible misprojection that God Himself persecuted His own Son on behalf of salvation. The very words are meaningless.

6   It has always been particularly difficult to overcome this because, although the error itself is no harder to overcome than any other error, men were unwilling to give it up because of its prominent escape value. In milder forms, a parent says "This hurts me more than it hurts you," and feels exonerated in beating a child. Can you believe that the Father REALLY thinks this way?

7

> It is so essential that all such thinking be dispelled that we must be VERY sure that NOTHING of this kind remains in your mind. I was NOT punished because YOU were bad. The wholly benign lesson which the Atonement teaches is wholly lost if it is tainted with this kind of distortion in ANY form.

8   "Vengeance is Mine sayeth the Lord [117]" is strictly a karmic viewpoint. It is a real misperception of truth, by which man assigns his own evil past to God. The "evil conscience" from the past has nothing to do with God. He did not create it, and He does not maintain it. God does NOT believe in karmic retribution at all. His Divine mind does not create that way. HE does not hold the evil deeds of a man even against HIMSELF. Is it likely, then, that He would hold against any man the evil that ANOTHER did?

---

[117] Deuteronomy 32:35 Vengeance is Mine, and recompense; Their foot shall slip in due time; For the day of their calamity is at hand, And the things to come hasten upon them.
    Also, Romans 12:19 Beloved, do not avenge yourselves, but rather give place to wrath; for it is written, "Vengeance is Mine, I will repay," says the Lord.

Chapter 3 - Retraining The Mind

9   Be very sure that you recognize how impossible this assumption really is, and how ENTIRELY it arises from misprojection. This kind of error is responsible for a host of related fallacies, including the misbelief that God rejected man and forced him out of the Garden of Eden,[118] or that I am misdirecting you. I have made every effort to use words which are ALMOST impossible to distort, but man is very inventive when it comes to twisting symbols around.

10   God Himself is not symbolic; He is FACT. The Atonement, too, is totally without symbolism. It is perfectly clear, because it exists in light. Only man's attempts to shroud it in darkness have made it inaccessible to the unwilling, and ambiguous to the partly willing. The Atonement itself radiates nothing but truth. It therefore epitomizes harmlessness, and sheds ONLY blessing. It could not do this if it arose from anything other than perfect innocence! Innocence is wisdom, because it is unaware of evil, which does not exist. It is, however, PERFECTLY aware of EVERYTHING, that is true.

11   The Resurrection demonstrated that NOTHING can destroy truth. Good can withstand ANY form of evil, because light abolishes ALL forms of darkness.[119] The Atonement is thus the perfect lesson. It is the final demonstration that all of the other lessons which I taught are true.

12   Man is released from ALL errors if he believes in this. The deductive approach to teaching accepts the generalization which is applicable to ALL single instances, rather than building up the generalization after analyzing numerous single instances separately. If you can accept the ONE GENERALIZATION NOW, there will be no need to learn from many smaller lessons.

13   NOTHING can prevail against a Son of God who commends his Spirit into the hands of His Father.[120] By doing this, the mind awakens from its sleep, and the Soul remembers its Creator. All sense of Separation disappears, and level confusion vanishes. The Son of God IS part of the holy Trinity, but the Trinity Itself is One. There is no confusion within ITS levels, because they are of One Mind and One Will. This Single Purpose creates perfect integration, and establishes the reign of the Peace of God.

14   But this vision can be perceived only by the truly innocent. Because their hearts are pure, they defend true perception, instead of defending themselves AGAINST it. Understanding the lesson of the Atonement, they are without the will to attack, and

---

118 Genesis 3:23-24 Therefore the LORD God sent him out of the garden of Eden to till the ground from which he was taken. So He drove out the man; and He placed cherubim at the east of the garden of Eden, and a flaming sword which turned every way, to guard the way to the tree of life.

119 1 John 1:5 This is the message which we have heard from Him and declare to you, that God is light and in Him is no darkness at all.

120 Luke 23:46 And when Jesus had cried out with a loud voice, He said, "Father, "into Your hands I commit My spirit." Having said this, He breathed His last.

C. Atonement without Sacrifice

therefore they see truly. This is what the Bible means when it says "(and) when He shall appear (or be perceived) we shall be like Him, for we shall see Him AS HE IS. [121]"

15   Sacrifice is a notion totally unknown to God. It arises solely from fear of the Records. [122] This is particularly unfortunate, because frightened people are apt to be vicious. Sacrificing others in any way is a clear-cut violation of God's own injunction that man should be merciful even as His Father in Heaven is merciful. [123]

16   It has been harder for many Christians to realize that this commandment (or assignment) also applies to THEMSELVES. Good teachers never terrorize their students. To terrorize is to attack, and this results in rejection of what the teacher offers. This results in learning failures.

17   I have been correctly referred to in the Bible as "The Lamb of God who taketh away the sins of the world. [124] " Those who represent the lamb as blood-stained (an all too widespread conceptual error) do NOT understand the meaning of the symbol.

18   Correctly understood, the symbol is a very simple parable, or teaching device, which merely depicts my innocence. The lion and the lamb lying down together [125] refers to the fact that strength and innocence are NOT in conflict, but naturally live in peace. "Blessed are the pure in heart for they shall see God [126]" is another way of saying the same thing. Only the innocent CAN see God.

19   There has been some controversy (in human terms) as to whether seeing is an attribute of the eyes, or an expression of the integrative powers of the brain. Correctly understood, the issue revolves around the question of whether the body or the mind can see (or understand). This is not really open to question at all.

---

121 1 John 3:2 Beloved, now we are children of God; and it has not yet been revealed what we shall be, but we know that when He is revealed, we shall be like Him, for we shall see Him as He is.

122 Chapter 2   C. Healing As Release From Fear, p22
     Chapter 22   E. The Correction For Lack Of Love, p26
         Akashic Record. A term Edgar Cayce used, referring to the accumulated collective experience in separated consciousness in the One Mind or Sonship. It is also used by other groups and people, but Helen was familiar with Edgar Cayce.

123 Luke 6:36 Be ye merciful, even as your Father is merciful.

124 John 1:29 On the morrow he seeth Jesus coming unto him, and saith, Behold, the Lamb of God, which taketh away the sin of the world!

125 Isaiah 11:6 "The wolf also shall dwell with the lamb, The leopard shall lie down with the young goat, The calf and the young lion and the fatling together; And a little child shall lead them.

126 Matthew 5:8 Blessed are the pure in heart: for they shall see God.
     Also: Psalm 24:3 Who shall ascend into the hill of the Lord? or who shall stand in his holy place? 4 He that hath clean hands, and a pure heart; who hath not lifted up his soul unto vanity, nor sworn deceitfully. He shall receive the blessing from the Lord, and righteousness from the God of his salvation.

Chapter 3 - Retraining The Mind

20   The body is not capable of understanding. Only the mind KNOWS anything. A pure mind knows the truth, and this IS its strength. It cannot attack the body, because it knows EXACTLY what the body IS. This is what "a sane mind in a sane body" really means.

21   A sane mind is NOT out for blood. It does not confuse destruction with innocence, because it associates innocence with strength, NOT with weakness. Innocence is INCAPABLE of sacrificing anything, because the innocent mind HAS everything and strives only to PROTECT its Wholeness. This is why it CANNOT misproject. It can only honor man, because honor is the NATURAL greeting of the truly loved to others who are LIKE them.

22   The lamb taketh away the sins of the world only in the sense that the state of innocence or Grace, is one in which the meaning of the Atonement is perfectly apparent. The innocence of God is the true state of the mind of His Son. In this state, man's mind DOES see God, and because he sees Him as he Is, he knows that the Atonement, NOT sacrifice, is the ONLY appropriate gift to His OWN altar, where nothing except perfection truly belongs. [127] The understanding of the innocent is TRUTH. That is why their altars are truly radiant.

23   Though Christians generally (but by no means universally) recognize the contradiction involved in victimizing others, they are less adept at ensuring their own inability to victimize themselves. Although this appears to be a much more benign error from the viewpoint of society, it is nevertheless inherently dangerous because once a two-edged defense is used, its direction cannot be self-controlled.

24   B. recently observed how many ideas were condensed into relatively few pages here. This is because we have not been forced to dispel miscreations throughout. (There is one set of notes not yet transcribed which is devoted to this. These emphasize only the enormous waste of time that is involved.) Cayce's notes, too, could have been much shortened. Their excessive length is due to two factors. The first involves a fundamental error which Cayce himself made, and which required constant undoing. The second is more related to the attitude of his followers. They are unwilling to omit anything he said. This is respectful enough, but not overly-judicious. I would be a far better editor, if they would allow me this position on their staff.

25   It is obvious that Cayce himself was not able to transcend the misperceptions of the need for sacrifice, or he could not possibly have been willing to sacrifice himself.

Anyone who is unable to leave the requests of others unanswered has not entirely transcended egocentricity.

I never "gave of myself" in this inappropriate way, nor would I ever have encouraged Cayce to do so.

---

[127] Matthew 9:13 For I desire mercy and not sacrifice, And the knowledge of God more than burnt offerings

C. Atonement without Sacrifice

26   Cayce could not see the Atonement as totally lacking in sacrifice at ANY level. It WAS obvious to him that the mind cannot be so limited. It was equally apparent to him that the Soul is merely unaffected by such an idea. This left him only the body with which to invest his misperception. This is also why he used his own mind at the "EXPENSE of his body."

27   Because Cayce was a somewhat erratic listener, he was compelled to correct his own errors at very great length, and not always adequately. Consider the basis from which he started, when he began with "yes, we have the body." It is noteworthy that in all these readings, a large section was actually devoted to the body, even though he usually concluded with the caution that the body cannot be healed by itself. It would have saved an enormous number of words if he had always begun with this.

28   Cayce and his devotion to me are in no way underestimated by the realization that he worked under very great strain, which is ALWAYS a sign that something is wrong. One of the difficulties inherent in trance states is that it is very difficult to overcome the split which the trance itself induces through the medium of communications made while in the trance state.

29   Cayce's whole approach put him in a real double-bind, from which he did not recover. When he spoke of a dream in which he saw his own rather immanent reincarnation, he was perfectly accurate. He was sufficiently attuned to real communication to make it easy to correct his errors, and free him to communicate without strain. It is noticeable throughout his notes that he frequently engaged in a fallacy that we have already noted in some detail: namely, the tendency to endow the physical with nonphysical properties. [128] Cayce suffered greatly from this error. He did not make either of the other three. [129] However, you will remember that it is this one which is particularly vulnerable to magical associations. Cayce's accuracy was so great that, even when he did this, he was able to apply it constructively. But it does not follow that this was a genuinely constructive approach.

30   It should also be noted that, when Cayce attempted to "see" the body in proper perspective, he saw physically discernible auras surrounding it. This is a curious compromise, in which the nonphysical attributes of the self are approached AS IF they could be seen with the physical eye.

31   Cayce's illiteracy never stood in his way. This is because illiteracy does not necessarily imply any lack of love, and in Cayce's case very definitely did not. He therefore had no difficulty at all in overcoming this seeming limitation.

---

[128] Chapter 1 B. Principles Of Miracles C. Distortions of Miracle Impulses, p14
[129] Chapter 1 B. Principles Of Miracles b. The Concept Of Lack, p9 - 27

Chapter 3 - Retraining The Mind

What DID hamper him was a profound sense of personal unworthiness, which, characteristically enough, was sometimes over-compensated for in what might be called a Christian form of grandiosity. Cayce was essentially uncharitable to himself. This made him very erratic in his own miracles, and, because he was genuinely anxious to help others, left himself in a highly vulnerable position.

32   His son comments both on the rather erratic nature of the Cayce household, and also on the rather uneven nature of Cayce's temper. Both of these observations are true, and clearly point to the fact that Cayce did not apply the Peace of God to himself. Once this had occurred, particularly in a man whose communication channels were open, it was virtually impossible for him to escape external solutions. Cayce was a very religious man, who should have been able to escape fear through religion. Being unable to apply his religion wholeheartedly to himself, he was forced to accept certain magical beliefs which were alien to his own Christianity. This is why he was so different when he was asleep, and even disowned what he said in this state.

33   The lack of integration which this split state implies is clearly shown in certain off-the-mark detours into areas such as the effects of stones on the mind, and some curious symbolic attempt to integrate churches and glands. (This is hardly more peculiar than some of your own confusion.)

34   Cayce's mind was imprisoned to some extent by an error against which you have been cautioned several times. He looked to the past for an EXPLANATION of the present, but he never succeeded in separating the past FROM the present. When he said "mind is the builder," he did not realize that it is only what it is building NOW that really creates the future. The past, in itself, does not have the ability to do this. Whenever we move from one instant to the next, the previous one no longer exists. In considering the body as the focus for healing, Cayce was expressing his own failure to accept this AS ACCOMPLISHED. He did not fail to recognize the value of the Atonement for others, but he did fail to accept its corrective merit for himself.

35   As we have frequently emphasized, man CANNOT control his own errors. Having created them, he does believe in them. Because of his failure to accept his own perfect freedom FROM the past, Cayce could not really perceive others as similarly free. This is why I have not wholly endorsed the Cayce documents for widespread use.

36   I am heartily supportive of the ARE's endeavor to make Cayce's singular contributions immortal, but it would be most unwise to have them promulgated as a faith until they have been purged of their essential errors. This is why there have been a number of unexplained set backs in their explication. It is also one of the many reasons why the Cayce material, a major step in the speedup, must be properly understood before it can be meaningfully validated.

C. Atonement without Sacrifice

37   Cayce's son has been wise in attempting to deal with reliability, which in Cayce's case is very high. There is a way of validating the material, and Hugh Lynn is perfectly aware that this must be done eventually. He is also aware of the fact that he is unable to do it. In the present state of the material, it would be most unwise even to attempt it. There is too much that IS invalid. When the time comes that this can be corrected to the point of real safety, I assure you it will be accomplished. In tribute to Cayce, I remind you that no effort is wasted, and Cayce's effort was very great.

38   It would be most ungrateful of me if I allowed his work to produce a generation of witch doctors. I am sorry that Cayce himself could not rid himself of a slight tendency in this direction. But fortunately I have a fuller appreciation of him than he had.

39   I am repeating here a Biblical injunction of my own, already mentioned elsewhere, that if my followers eat any deadly thing it shall not hurt them. This is what Cayce could NOT believe, because he could not see that, as a Son of God, he WAS invulnerable.

D. Miracles as Accurate Perception

1   We have repeatedly stated that the basic concepts referred to throughout the notes are NOT matters of degree. Certain fundamental concepts CANNOT be meaningfully understood in terms of co-existing polarities. It is impossible to conceive of light and darkness, or, everything and nothing, as joint possibilities. They are all true OR all false. It is absolutely essential that you understand completely that behavior is erratic until a firm commitment to one or the other is made.

2   A firm commitment to darkness or nothingness is impossible. Nobody has ever lived who has not experienced some light and some of everything. This has made everybody really unable to deny truth totally, even if he deceives himself in this connection most of the time. That is why those who live largely in darkness and emptiness never find any lasting solace. (This really answers B's question about whether people return voluntarily.)

3   Innocence is also not a partial attribute. It is not a real defense UNTIL it is total. When it is partial, it is characterized by the same erratic nature that holds for other two-edged defenses. The partly innocent are apt to be quite stupid at times. It is not until their innocence is a genuine viewpoint which is universal in its application that it becomes wisdom.

4   Innocent (or true) perception means that you NEVER misperceive, and ALWAYS see truly. More simply, this means that you never see what does not exist in reality. Whenever you lack confidence in what someone else will do, you are attesting to your belief that he is not in his Right Mind. This is hardly a miracle-based frame of reference. It also has the disastrous effect of denying (incorrect use) the essentially creative power of the miracle. The miracle perceives everything AS IT IS. If nothing but the truth exists

Chapter 3 - Retraining The Mind

(and this is really redundant in statement, because what is not true CANNOT exist) Right-Minded seeing cannot see ANYTHING BUT perfection. We have said many times that ONLY what God creates, or what man creates with the same will, has any real existence. This, then, is all that the innocent can see. They do not suffer from the delusions of the Separated ones.

5   The way to correct all such delusions is to withdraw your faith from them, and invest it ONLY in what is true. To whatever extent you side with false perception in yourself or others, you are validating a basic misperception. You CANNOT validate the invalid. I would suggest that you voluntarily give up all attempts to do so, because they can be only frantic. If you are willing to validate what is true in everything you perceive, you will make it true for you.

6   Remember that we said that truth overcomes ALL error. This means that if you perceive truly, you are canceling out misperceptions in yourself AND others simultaneously. Because you see them as they were really created and can really create, you offer them your own validation of THEIR truth. This is the real healing which the miracle actively creates.

7   S: Reply to H's question: 'Is this all?' The reason why this is so short, despite its extreme importance, is because it is not symbolic. This means that it is not open to more than one interpretation. This means that it is unequivocal. It also explains the quotation which you have never gotten correctly in complete form before:

> "But this we know, that when He shall appear (or be perceived) we shall be like Him for we shall see Him as He is. And every man that hath this hope in him purifieth himself even as He is pure. [130]"

Every man DOES have the hope that he can see correctly, because the ability to do so is IN him. Man's ONLY hope IS to see things as they are.

E. Perception versus Knowledge

1   On Wed. evening, Nov. 24, H. had sudden flash of illumination and very much wanted to offer prayer for B., which she did as follows: "Jesus, help me see my brother (B.) as he really is, and thus release both him and me." H. also thought later: Every time there is anything unlovable that crosses one's mind (re sex, possession, etc.) you should immediately recognize that you do not want to hurt your brother. On Thurs. morning, the prayer for the miracle occurred as follows stated above.

---

[130] 1 John 3:2-3 Beloved, now are we children of God, and it is not yet made manifest what we shall be. We know that, if he shall be manifested, we shall be like him; for we shall see him even as he is. And every one that hath this hope set on him purifieth himself, even as he is pure.

E. Perception versus Knowledge

2   You had a lot of trouble afterwards with the words (which are essentially irrelevant) partly because you were dissatisfied with yourself at the time, but also because you ARE confused about the difference between perception and cognition. You will note that we have said very little about cognition as yet. (Aside: One of the exceptions is in the correction formula for fear, which begins with KNOW first) The reason is because you must get your perceptions straightened out before you can KNOW anything.

3   To know is to be certain. Uncertainty merely means that you DON'T know. Knowledge is power BECAUSE it is certain, and certainty is strength. Perception is temporary. It is an attribute of the space-time belief, and is therefore subject to fear or love. Misperception produces fear, and true perception produces love. NEITHER produces certainty because all perception varies. That is why it is NOT knowledge. True perception is the BASIS for knowledge, but KNOWING is the affirmation of truth.

4   All of your difficulties ultimately stem from the fact that you do not recognize, or KNOW, yourselves, each other, or God. "Recognize" means "know again." This means that you knew before. (Note that it does not mean SAW before.) You can see in many ways, because perception involves different interpretations, and this means it is not whole. The miracle is a way of PERCEIVING, not a way of knowing. It is the right answer to a question, but you do not ask questions at all when you know.

5   Questioning delusions is the first step in undoing them. The miracle, or the right answer, corrects them. Since perceptions CHANGE, their dependence on time is obvious. They are subject to transitory states, and this implies variability by definition. How you perceive at any given time determines what you DO, and action MUST occur in time. Knowledge is timeless because certainty is not questionable. You KNOW when you have ceased to ask questions.

6   The "questioning mind" perceives itself in time, and therefore looks for FUTURE answers. The unquestioning mind is closed merely because it believes the future and the present will be the same. This establishes an unchanged state, or stasis. This is usually an attempt to counteract an underlying fear that the future will be WORSE than the present, and this fear inhibits the tendency to question at all.

7   Visions are the natural perception of the spiritual eye, but they are still corrections. B's question about the "spiritual eye" was a very legitimate one. The "spiritual eye" is symbolic, and therefore NOT a device for knowing. It IS, however, a means of right perception, which brings it into the proper domain of the miracle, but NOT of revelation. PROPERLY speaking, a "vision of God" is a miracle rather than a revelation. The fact that perception is involved at all removes the experience from the realm of knowledge. That is why these visions do not last.

Chapter 3 - Retraining The Mind

8   The Bible instructs you to "KNOW thyself," or BE CERTAIN. Certainty is always of God. When you love someone, you have PERCEIVED him as he is, and this makes it possible for you to KNOW him. But it is not until you RECOGNIZE him that you KNOW him. Only then are you ABLE to stop asking questions about him.

9   While you ask questions about God, you are clearly implying that you do NOT know Him. Certainty does not require action. When you say you are ACTING on the basis of sure knowledge, you are really confusing perception and cognition. Knowledge brings MENTAL strength for creative THINKING, but not for right doing.

10   Perception, miracles and doing are closely related. Knowledge is a result of revelation, and induces only thought (thinking). Perception involves the body even in its most spiritualized form. Knowledge comes from the altar within, and is timeless because it is certain. To perceive the truth is not the same as KNOWING it.

     This is why B. is having so much trouble in what he calls "integrating" the notes. His tentative perception is too uncertain for knowledge, because knowledge is SURE. Your perception is so variable that you swing from sudden but real knowledge to complete cognitive disorganization. This is why B. is more prone to irritation, while you are more vulnerable to rage. He is consistently BELOW his potential, while you achieve it at times and then swing very wide of the mark.

11   Actually, these differences do not matter. But I thought you might be glad to learn that you are much better off with DIFFERENT perceptual problems than you would be if you suffered from similar ones. This enables each of you to RECOGNIZE (and this is the right word here) that the misperceptions of the other are unnecessary. It is because you do not KNOW what to do about it that B. reacts to yours with irritation, and you respond to his with fury.

12   I repeat again that if you ATTACK error, you will hurt yourself. You do not RECOGNIZE each other when you attack. Attack is ALWAYS made on a stranger. You are MAKING him a stranger by misperceiving him, so that you CANNOT know him. It is BECAUSE you have made him into a stranger that you are afraid of him. PERCEIVE him correctly, so that your Soul can KNOW him.

13   Right perception is necessary before God can communicate DIRECTLY to his own altars, which he has established in His Sons. There he can communicate His certainty, and His KNOWLEDGE will bring the peace WITHOUT question.

14   God is not a stranger to His Own Sons, and His Sons are not strangers to each other. Knowledge preceded both perception and time, and will also ultimately replace (or correct for) them. This is the real meaning of the Biblical account of God as "Alpha and Omega, the Beginning and the End." [131] It also explains the quotation "Before Abraham

---

131 Revelation 1:8 I am Alpha and Omega, the beginning and the ending, saith the Lord, which is, and which

E. Perception versus Knowledge

WAS, I AM." [132] Perception can and must be stabilized, but knowledge IS stable. "Fear God and keep His Commandments" [133] is a real scribal error. It should read, "KNOW God and accept His certainty." (This error is why the commandments are all negative, in contrast to Christ's statement about "Thou shalt love," etc.) There are no strangers in His Creation. To create as He Created, you can create only what you KNOW and accept as yours.

15   God knows His Children with perfect certainty. He Created them by knowing them.

He recognizes them perfectly. When they do not recognize each other, they do not recognize Him. Brothers can misperceive one another, but they rarely maintain that they do not KNOW each other. This is possible only if they maintain that they are NOT really brothers. The Bible is VERY specific on this point. [134]

F. Conflict and the Ego

1   Most of the abilities man now possesses are only shadows of his real strengths. The Soul knows, loves, and creates. These are its unequivocal functions. All of the functions of man are equivocal, or open to question or doubt. This is because he can no longer be certain how he will USE them. He is therefore incapable of knowledge, because he is uncertain. He is also incapable of true loving, because he can perceive lovelessly. He cannot create surely, because perception deceives, and illusions are not pure.

2   Perception did not exist until the Separation had introduced degrees, aspects and intervals. The Soul has no levels, and ALL conflict arises from the concept of levels. Wars arise when some regard others as if they were on a different level. All interpersonal conflicts arise from this fallacy. Only the levels of the Trinity are capable of Unity.

The levels which man created by the Separation are disastrous. They cannot BUT conflict. This is because one is essentially meaningless to another. Freud realized this perfectly, and that is why he conceived as forever irreconcilable the different levels of his

---

was, and which is to come, the Almighty.
Revelation 21:6 And he said unto me, It is done. I am Alpha and Omega, the beginning and the end. I will give unto him that is athirst of the fountain of the water of life freely.
Revelation 22:13 I am Alpha and Omega, the beginning and the end, the first and the last.
132 John 8:58 Jesus said to them, "Most assuredly, I say to you, before Abraham was, I AM.";
133 Deuteronomy 6:2 That thou mightest fear the Lord thy God, to keep all his statutes and his commandments,
134 Matthew 22:36 Master, which is the great commandment in the law?
37 Jesus said unto him, Thou shalt love the Lord thy God with all thy heart, and with all thy soul, and with all thy mind. 38 This is the first and great commandment.
39 And the second is like unto it, Thou shalt love thy neighbour as thyself.
40 On these two commandments hang all the law and the prophets.

Chapter 3 - Retraining The Mind

psyche. They were conflict-prone by definition, because they wanted different things and obeyed different principles.

3 In our picture of the psyche, there is an unconscious level, which properly consists ONLY of the miracle ability and should be under MY direction; and a conscious level, which perceives or is aware of impulses from both the unconscious and the superconscious. These are the sources of the impulses it receives. Consciousness is thus the level of perception, but NOT of knowledge. Again, to PERCEIVE is NOT to know. (In this connection, Cayce is more accurate than Freud.)

4 Consciousness was the first split that man introduced into himself. He became a PERCEIVER rather than a creator in the true sense.

5 Consciousness is correctly identified as the domain of the ego.

Jung was right indeed in insisting that the ego is NOT the self, and that the self should be regarded as an achievement. He did not RECOGNIZE (a term we now understand) that the Achievement was God's. In a sense, the ego was a man-made attempt to perceive himself as he wished, rather than as he IS. This is an example of the created/creator confusion we spoke of before. [135] He can only KNOW himself as he IS, because that is all he can be SURE of. Everything else IS open to question.

6 The ego is the questioning compartment in the post-Separation psyche which man created for himself. It is capable of asking valid questions, but not of perceiving wholly valid answers, because these are cognitive, and cannot BE perceived. The endless speculation about the meaning of mind has led to considerable confusion because the mind IS confused. Only One-Mindedness is without confusion. A separate, or divided, mind MUST be confused. A divided mind is uncertain by definition. It HAS to be in conflict because it is out of accord with itself.

7 Intrapersonal conflict arises from the same basis as interpersonal. One part of the psyche perceives another part as on a different LEVEL, and does not understand it. This makes the parts strangers to each other, WITHOUT RECOGNITION. This is the essence of the fear-prone condition, in which attack is ALWAYS possible.

8 Man has every reason to feel anxious, as he perceives himself. This is why he cannot escape fear until he KNOWS that he DID not and CAN not create himself. He can NEVER make this misperception valid, and when he at last PERCEIVES clearly, he is GLAD HE CAN'T. His Creation is beyond his own error variance, and this is why he MUST eventually choose to heal the Separation.

---

[135] Chapter 1 B. Principles Of Miracles, b. The Concept Of Lack, p9
   Chapter 2 A. Introduction, p4
   This chapter: B. Special Principles Of Miracle Workers, p3

F. Conflict and the Ego

9   Right-mindedness is not to be confused with the KNOWING mind, because it is applicable only to right perception. You can be right-minded or wrong-minded, and this is subject to degrees, a fact which clearly demonstrates a lack of association with knowledge.

     (No, Helen, this is PERFECTLY clear and DOES follow the previous section. Neither you nor I is at all confused, even in grammar.)

10   The term "right-mindedness" is properly used as the correction for wrong-mindedness, and applies to the state of mind which induces accurate perception. It is miraculous because it heals misperception, and healing is indeed a miracle, in view of how man perceives himself. Only the sick NEED healing. The Soul does not need healing, but the mind DOES.

11   Freud gave a very graphic but upside down account of how the divisions of the mind arose from the bottom UP. Actually, this is impossible, because the unconscious cannot create the conscious. You cannot create something you can't KNOW. Freud was greatly worried about this, being VERY bright, though misguided, and attempted to get around it by introducing a number of "borderline" areas which merely resulted in fuzziness. This was particularly unfortunate, because he was capable of going much higher, if he had not been so afraid. This is why he kept pulling the mind DOWN.

12   The ego did NOT arise out of the unconscious. A lower-order perception cannot create a higher-order one, (which is the way you perceive the structure of the psyche if you look at it from the bottom UP) because it doesn't understand it. But a higher-order perception CAN create a lower-order one by understanding it in terms of MISperception.

13   Perception ALWAYS involves some misuse of will, because it involves the mind in areas of uncertainty. The mind is very active because it has will-power. When it willed the Separation it willed to perceive. Until it chose to do this, it willed only to know. Afterwards, it had to will ambiguously, and the only way out of ambiguity IS clear perception.

14   The ego is as frail as Freud perceived it. The later theorists have tried to introduce a less pessimistic view, but have looked in the wrong direction for their hope. Any attempt to endow the ego with the attributes of the Soul, is merely confused thinking. Freud was more clear-sighted about this, because he knew a BAD thing when he perceived it, but he failed to recognize that a bad thing cannot exist. It is therefore wholly unnecessary to try to get out of it. As you very rightly observed yourself, the thing to do with a desert is to LEAVE. [136]

15   The mind returns itself to its proper function only when it WILLS TO KNOW. This places it in the Soul's service, where perception is meaningless. The superconscious is

---

[136] Chapter 1 B. Principles Of Miracles Principle 42, p35

Chapter 3 - Retraining The Mind

the level of the mind which wills to do this. (Freud was particularly distorted on this point, because he was getting too far UP for comfort according to his own perception.) But he WAS right in maintaining that the "parts" of the psyche cannot be correctly perceived either as THINGS or as entirely separate. (He would have thought better if he had said "entirely separated.")

16   The mind DID divide itself when it willed to create its own levels AND the ability to perceive them. But it could NOT entirely separate itself from the Soul, because it is FROM the Soul that it derives its whole power to create. Even in miscreating, will is affirming its source, or it would merely cease to be. This is impossible, because it IS part of the Soul, which God created, and which is therefore eternal.

17   The ability to perceive made the body possible, because you must perceive SOMETHING, and WITH something. This is why perception involves an exchange, or a translation, which knowledge does NOT need. The interpretive function of perception, actually, a distorted form of creation, then permitted man to interpret the body as HIMSELF, which, although depressing, was a way out of the conflict he induced. (This has already been covered in some detail. [137])

18   The superconscious, which KNOWS, could not be reconciled with this loss of power, because it was incapable of darkness. This is why it became almost inaccessible to the mind, and entirely inaccessible to the body. It was PERCEIVED as a threat, because light does abolish darkness by establishing the clear fact that it ISN'T THERE. The truth will ALWAYS destroy error in this sense. This is not an ACTIVE process of destruction at all. We have already emphasized the fact that knowing does not DO anything. [138] It can be PERCEIVED as an attacker, but it CANNOT attack.

19   What man perceives as its attack is his own recognition of the fact that it can always be REMEMBERED, because it has never been destroyed. This is not a literal remembering as much as a re-membering.

(That is largely for B. I wish he would decide to use that talent of his constructively. He has no idea of how powerful it could be. Actually, it does come from the unconscious, and is really a distorted form of miraculous perception which he has reduced to word twisting. Although this can be quite funny, it is still a real waste. Maybe he'd care to let me control it, and still use it humorously himself. He doesn't have to decide it is one OR the other.)

20   The unconscious should never have been reduced to a "container" for the waste products of conflict. Even as HE perceives his psyche, every level has a creative potential, because nothing man creates can wholly lose this.

---

137 Chapter 1 C. Distortions of Miracle Impulses p15
138 This Chapter E. Perception Versus Knowledge, p9

F. Conflict and the Ego

21 God and the Souls He created remain in surety, and therefore KNOW that no miscreation exists. Truth cannot deal with unwilling error, because it does not will to be blocked out. But I was a man who remembered the Soul and its knowledge. Tell B. that when he refused to misperceive he was indeed behaving as I behaved. And as a man, I did not attempt to counteract error with knowledge, so much as to CORRECT error from the bottom up. I demonstrated both the powerlessness of the body AND the power of the mind. By uniting MY will with that of my Creator, I brought His Light back into the mind. I naturally remembered the Soul and its own real purpose.

22 I cannot unite your will with God's for you. But I CAN erase all misperceptions from your mind, if you will bring it under my guidance. ONLY your misperceptions stand in your own way. Without them, your own choice is certain. Sane perception INDUCES sane choosing. The Atonement was an act based on true perception. I cannot choose for you, but I CAN help you make your own right choice.

23 "Many are called but few are chosen [139] " SHOULD read, "ALL are called but few choose to listen. Therefore, they do not choose RIGHT." The "chosen ones" are merely those who choose right SOONER. This is the real meaning of the celestial speed-up. Strong wills can do this NOW. And you WILL find rest for your Souls. [140] God knows you only in peace, and this IS your reality.

24 Note that the term "insight," though referring to lofty perception, is not an attribute of knowledge. This is why terms like "lofty" are meaningless in this context. Insight is not the way TO knowledge, but it IS a prerequisite FOR knowledge. Being of God, knowledge has nothing to do with your perceptions at all. That is why it can only be a gift of God TO you.

G. The Loss of Certainty

1 We said before that the abilities which man possesses are only shadows of his true abilities. The Soul's true functions are knowing, loving, and creating. The intrusion of the ability to perceive, which is inherently judgmental, was introduced only after the Separation. No one has been sure of anything since then. You will also remember that I made it very clear that the Resurrection was the return to knowledge, which was accomplished by the union of my will with the Father's.

2 Since the Separation, the words "create" and "make" are inevitably confused. When you make something, you make it first out of a sense of lack or need, and second, out of

---

[139] Matthew 22:14 So the last will be first, and the first last. For many are called, but few chosen.
    Also, Matthew 20:16 "For many are called, but few are chosen."
[140] Jeremiah 6:16 Thus says the LORD: "Stand in the ways and see, And ask for the old paths, where the good way is, And walk in it; Then you will find rest for your souls. But they said, "We will not walk in it.';

Chapter 3 - Retraining The Mind

a something that already exists. Anything that is made is made for a specific purpose. It has no true generalizability. When you make something to fill a perceived lack, which is obviously why you would make anything, you are tacitly implying that you believe in the Separation. Knowing does not lead to doing, as we have frequently observed already.

3   What appears to be contradictory about the difference between knowing and perceiving, and Revelation and miracles, is again the fallacy that is the root cause of all subsequent errors. The miracle was associated with perception, and not with knowing. However, we also noted that prayer is the medium of miracles, and also the natural communication of the Creator and the Created. Prayer is always an affirmation of knowledge, not of accurate perception. That is why unless perception has entered into it, it calls on Revelation.

4   The confusion between your own creation and what you create is so profound that it has literally become impossible to know anything, because knowledge is always stable. It is quite evident that human beings are not. Nevertheless, they are perfectly stable as God created them. In this sense, when their behavior is unstable, they are obviously disagreeing with God's idea of the Creation. This is a fundamental right of man, although not one he would care to exercise if he were in his Right Mind.

5   The problem that is bothering you most is the fundamental question which man continually asks of himself, but which cannot properly be directed to himself at all. He keeps on asking "himself" what he is. This implies that the answer is not only one which he knows, but one which is up to him. The first part of this statement is perfectly true, but the second part is not. We have frequently commented on the absolute necessity of correcting all fallacious thinking which associates man in any way with his own Creation.

Man CANNOT perceive himself correctly. He has no image at all. The word "image" is always perception related, and is not a product of knowing. Images are symbolic, and stand for something else. The current emphasis on "changing your image" is a good description of the power of perception, but it implies that there is nothing to KNOW.

6   Prayer is the medium of miracles, not because God created perceptions, but because God created YOU. At the beginning of this course, we said that YOU are a miracle. [141] Therefore, the miracle worker is a miracle NOT of his own creation. Unless perception rests on some knowing basis, it is so unstable that it doesn't mean anything.

Knowing is not open to interpretation, because its meaning is its own. It is possible to interpret meaning, but this is always open to error because it involves the perception of meaning. All of these wholly needless complexities are the result of man's attempt to

---

141 Chapter 1 B. Principles Of Miracles Principle 25, p2

G. The Loss of Certainty

regard himself both as separated and unseparated at the same time. It is impossible to undertake a confusion as fundamental as this without engaging in further confusion.

7   Methodologically, man's mind has been very creative. But, as always occurs when method and content are separated, it has not been utilized for anything but an attempt to escape a fundamental and entirely inescapable impasse. This kind of thinking cannot result in a creative outcome, though it has resulted in considerable ingenuity. It is noteworthy, however, that this ingenuity has almost totally divorced him from knowledge.

8   Knowledge does not require ingenuity at all. When we say "the truth shall set you free," [142] we mean that all this kind of thinking is a waste of time, but that you are free of the need of engaging in it.

9   Note again that the functions of the Soul were not referred to as abilities. This point requires clarification, because abilities are beliefs which are BASED on the scarcity fallacy, since they do not mean anything apart from within-group comparisons. As you yourself never fail to point out, "nobody has none of an ability, and nobody has all of it." That is, of course, why the curve never rests on the line. The clearest implications of relativity, which properly inheres in this statement, DEMONSTRATE that abilities are not functions of the Soul. The Soul's functions are NOT relative. They are ABSOLUTE. They are OF God and FROM God, and therefore God-like.

10 Prayer is a way of asking for something. When we said that prayer is the medium of miracles, we also said that the only meaningful prayer is for forgiveness, because those who have been forgiven HAVE everything. Once forgiveness has been accepted, prayer in the usual sense becomes utterly without meaning. Essentially, a prayer for forgiveness is nothing more than a request that we may be able to recognize something we already have.

11 In electing the ability to perceive instead of the will to know, man placed himself in a position where he could resemble his Father ONLY by perceiving miraculously. But he lost the knowledge that he HIMSELF is a miracle. MIRACULOUS CREATION was his own Source, and also his own real function. "God created man in his own image and likeness [143] " is correct in meaning, but the words are open to considerable misinterpretation. This is avoided, however, if "image" is understood to mean "thought," and "likeness" is taken as "of a like quality." God DID create the Son in His own Thought, and of a quality like to His own. There IS nothing else.

---

142 John 8:32 and ye shall know the truth, and the truth shall make you free.
143 Genesis 1:26-27 Then God said, "Let Us make man in Our image, according to Our likeness; let them have dominion over the fish of the sea, over the birds of the air, and over the cattle, over all the earth and over every creeping thing that creeps on the earth." So God created man in His own image; in the image of God He created him; male and female He created them.

Chapter 3 - Retraining The Mind

12   Perception is impossible WITHOUT a belief in "more" and "less." Unless perception, at every level, involves selectivity, it is incapable of organization. In all types of perception, there is a continual process of accepting and rejecting, of organizing and reorganizing, and of shifting and changing focus. Evaluation is an essential aspect of perception, because judgment MUST be made for selection. "Lack of lack" is a concept which is meaningless to a perceiver, because the ability to perceive at all RESTS ON lack.

13   What happens to perceptions if there ARE no judgments, and there is nothing BUT perfect equality? Perception is automatically useless. Truth can only be KNOWN. All of it is equally true, and knowing any part of it IS to know all of it.

14   Only perception involves partial awareness. Knowledge transcends ALL of the laws which govern perception. Partial KNOWLEDGE is impossible. It is all One, and has no separate parts i.e. the parts have NOT separated. This IS the real knowledge. You who are really one with it need but know YOURSELF and your knowledge is complete. To know God's miracle is to know Him.

15   Forgiveness is the healing of the perception of separation. Correct perception of EACH OTHER is necessary ONLY because minds have willed to see themselves AS separate beings. Each Soul knows God completely. This IS the miraculous power of the Soul. The fact that each Soul has this power completely is a fact that is entirely alien to human thinking, in which if any ONE has everything, there is nothing LEFT.

16   God's miracles are as total as His Thought, because they ARE His thoughts. God shines in them all with perfect light. If they recognize this light anywhere, they know it universally. Revelation cannot be explained, because it IS knowledge. Revelation HAPPENS. It is the only REALLY natural happening, because it reflects the nature of God.

17   As long as perception lasts, prayer has a place. Since perception rests on lack, those who perceive have not totally accepted the Atonement and given over themselves to truth. Perception IS a separated state, and the perceiver DOES need healing. Communion, not prayer, is the natural state of those who know. God and HIS miracles are inseparable.

18   All words, at best, are preparatory. THE word is really a thought. No one WORD is universally meaningful, because a word is a symbol, but thought is not divisible by creation. The original name for "thought" and "word" was the same. The quotation should read "In the beginning was the thought, and the thought was with God, and the

G. The Loss of Certainty

thought WAS God." [144] How beautiful indeed are the thoughts of God, who live in His light. Your worth is beyond perception because it is beyond doubt.

19   Do not perceive yourself in different lights. KNOW yourself in the One Light, where the miracle which is you is perfectly clear.

20   The prerequisites for therapy must include the following conditions:
21
   1. The procedure must involve the recognition rather than the denial of the importance of thought.

22
   2. The exact equality of everyone who is involved. This must include Me.

23
   3. No one is either therapist or patient. (B. should add "teacher or pupil.")

24
   4. Above all EVERYONE involved must want to give up everything that is NOT true. The reason for the negative emphasis here is that therapy implies something HAS gone wrong. Even though the purpose is to correct, those who are ill ARE negative.

25
   5. Therapy is EXACTLY the same as all other forms of miracle-working. It has no separate laws of its own. All of the points that were given for miracles apply to therapy because, UNLESS therapy proceeds from miracle-mindedness, it CANNOT heal.

26
   6. The therapist (hopefully) does have the role of being the better perceiver. (This is also, again hopefully, true of the teacher.) It does not follow that he is the better knower. Temporarily, the therapist or teacher can help in straightening out twisted perceptions, which is also the only role that I would ever contribute myself. All therapy should do is try to place EVERYONE involved in the right frame of mind to help one another. It is essentially a process of true courtesy, including courtesy to Me.

---

144 John 1:1 In the beginning was the Word, and the Word was with God, and the Word was God.
   2 The same was in the beginning with God.
   3 All things were made by him; and without him was not any thing made that was made.
   4 In him was life; and the life was the light of men.

Chapter 3 - Retraining The Mind

27   Any form of mental illness can truthfully be described as an expression of viciousness. We said before that those who are afraid are apt to be vicious. If we were willing to forgive other people's misperceptions of us, they could not possibly affect us at all. There is little doubt that you can explain your present attitudes in terms of how people used to look at you, but there is no wisdom in doing so. In fact, the whole historical approach can justifiably be called doubtful.

28   As you have so often said, no one has adopted ALL of his parents' attitudes as his own. In every case, there has been a long process of choice, in which the individual has escaped from those he himself vetoed, while retaining those he voted FOR. B. has not retained his parents political beliefs, in spite of the particular kind of newspapers that constituted their own reading matter in this area. The reason why he could do this was because he believed he was free in this area.

29   There must be some acute problem OF HIS OWN that would make him so eager to accept their misperception of his own worth. This tendency can ALWAYS be regarded as punitive. It cannot be justified by the inequality of the strengths of parents and children. This is never more than temporary, and is largely a matter of maturational and thus physical difference. It does not last unless it is held onto.

30   When B's father came to his new office and "destroyed" it, it is quite apparent that B. MUST have been willing to let it be destroyed. The many times that he has commented on this event alone would suggest that the extreme importance of this misperception in his own distorted thinking. Why should anyone accord an obvious misperception so much power? There cannot be any real justification for it, because even B. himself recognized the real problem by saying "How could he do this to me?" The answer is HE didn't.

31   B. has a very serious question to ask himself in this connection. We said before that the purpose of the Resurrection was to "demonstrate that no amount of misperception has any influence at all on a Son of God." This demonstration EXONERATES those who misperceive, by establishing beyond doubt that they have NOT hurt anyone. B's question, which he must ask himself very honestly, is whether he is willing to demonstrate that his parents have NOT hurt him. Unless he is willing to do this, he has not forgiven them.

32   The essential goal of therapy is the same as that of knowledge. No one can survive independently as long as he is willing to see himself through the eyes of others. This will always put him in a position where he MUST see himself in different lights. Parents do not create the image of their children, though they may perceive images which they do create. However, as we have already said, you are not an image. If you SIDE WITH image-makers, you are merely being idolatrous.

G. The Loss of Certainty

33   B. has no justification whatever for perpetuating ANY image of himself at all. He is NOT an image. Whatever is true of him is wholly benign. It is essential that he KNOW this about himself, but he cannot know it while he chooses to interpret himself as vulnerable enough to BE hurt. This is a peculiar kind of arrogance, whose narcissistic component is perfectly obvious. It endows the perceiver with sufficient unreal strength to make him over, and then acknowledges the perceiver's miscreation. There are times when this strange lack of real courtesy appears to be a form of humility. Actually, it is never more than simple spite.

34   Bill, your parents did misperceive you in many ways, but their ability to perceive was quite warped, and their misperceptions stood in the way of their own knowledge. There is no reason why it should stand in the way of yours. It is still true that you believe they DID something to you. This belief is extremely dangerous to your perception, and wholly destructive of your knowledge. This is not only true of your attitudes toward your parents, but also of your misuse of your friends. You still think that you MUST respond to their errors AS IF they were true. By reacting self-destructively, you are GIVING them approval for their misperceptions.

35   No one has the right to change himself according to different circumstances. Only his actions are capable of appropriate variation. His belief in himself is a constant, unless it rests on perceptual acuity rather than knowledge of what he is.

36   It is your DUTY to establish beyond doubt that you are totally unwilling to side with (identify with) anyone's misperceptions of you, including your own. If you become concerned with totally irrelevant factors, such as the physical condition of a classroom, the number of students, the hour of the course, and the many elements which you may choose to select for emphasis as a basis for misperception, you have lost the knowledge of what ANY interpersonal relationship is for. It is NOT true that the difference between pupil and teacher is lasting. They meet IN ORDER to abolish the difference. At the beginning, since we are still in time, they come together on the basis of inequality of ability and experience. The aim of the teacher is to give them more of what is temporarily his. This process has all of the miracle conditions we referred to at the beginning. The teacher (or miracle worker) gives more to those who have less, bringing them closer to equality with him, at the same time gaining for himself.

37   The confusion here is only because they do not gain the same things, because they do not NEED the same things. If they did, their respective, though temporary roles would not be conducive to mutual profit. Freedom from fear can be achieved by BOTH teacher and pupil ONLY if they do not compare either their needs or their positions in regard to each other in terms of higher and lower.

Chapter 3 - Retraining The Mind

38   Presumably, children must learn from parents. What parents learn from children is merely of a different order. Ultimately, there is no difference in order, but this involves only knowledge. Neither parents nor children can be said to HAVE knowledge, or their relationships would not exist AS IF they were on different levels. The same is true of the teacher and the pupil. Children have an authority problem ONLY if they believe that their image is influenced BY the authority. This is an act of will on their part, because they are electing to misperceive the authority and GIVE him this power.

39   A TEACHER with an authority problem is merely a pupil who refuses to teach others. He wants to maintain HIMSELF in a position where he can be misused and misperceived. This makes him resentful of teaching, because of what he insists it has done to him.

40   The ONLY way out of this particular aspect of the desert is still to leave. The way this is left is to release EVERYONE involved, by ABSOLUTELY REFUSING to engage in any form of honoring error. Neither teacher nor pupil is imprisoned by learning unless he uses it as an attack. If he does this, he will be imprisoned whether he actually teaches or learns, or refuses to be 144 engaged in the process at all.

41   The role of a teacher, properly conceived, is one of leading himself and others out of the desert. The value of this role can hardly be underestimated, if only because it was one to which I very gladly dedicated my own life. I have repeatedly asked MY pupils to follow me. This means that, to be effective teachers, they MUST interpret teaching as I do. I have made EVERY effort to teach you ENTIRELY without fear. If you do not listen, you will be unable to avoid the VERY obvious error of perceiving teaching as a threat.

42   It is hardly necessary to say that teaching is a process whose purpose is to produce learning. The ultimate purpose of ALL learning is to abolish fear. This is necessary so that knowledge can happen. The role of the teacher is NOT the role of God. This confusion is all too frequently made, by parents, teachers, therapists, and the clergy. It is a real misunderstanding of both God and His miracles. Any teacher who believes that teaching is fearful CANNOT learn because he is paralyzed. He also cannot really teach.

43   B. was quite right in maintaining that this course is a prerequisite for his. However, he was really saying much more than that.

The purpose of this course IS to prepare you for knowledge. So is the only real purpose of ANY legitimate course. All that is required of you as a teacher is to follow Me.

44   Whenever anyone decides that he can function only in SOME roles but not in others, he cannot BUT be attempting to make a compromise which will not work.

G. The Loss of Certainty

If B. is under the misbelief that he is coping with the fear problem by functioning as an administrator and as a teacher of interns, but NOT as a teacher of students, he is merely deceiving himself. He owes himself greater respect.

There is nothing as tragic as the attempt to deceive one's self, because it implies that you perceive yourself as so unworthy that deception is more fitting for you than truth. Either you can function in all of the roles you have properly undertaken to fill, or you cannot function effectively in any of them. This IS an all or none decision. You CANNOT make inappropriate level distinctions within this choice. You are either capable or not. This does not mean that you can DO everything, but it DOES mean that you are either totally miracle-minded or not. This decision is open to NO compromise whatever.

When B. says that he cannot teach, he is making the same mistake that we spoke of before, when he acted as if universal laws applied to everyone except him. This is not only arrogant, but patently untrue. Universal laws MUST apply to him, unless he does not exist. We will not bother to argue about this.

45 Descartes engaged in a very interesting teaching procedure, and one from which he himself learned a great deal. He began with doubting the existence of everything, except himself. He insisted that his own existence was not open to doubt, and rebuilt his entire thought system on the one premise "I think, therefore I am." It is noteworthy that he arrived at accepting the entire system he originally doubted, solely on the basis of this ONE piece of knowledge. There was, however, a distinct shift in his own perception. He no longer really questioned the reality of what he perceived, because he KNEW he was there.

46 We mentioned before that B. is not too sure of this, and that is why we suggested that he concentrate on "Lord, here I am."

47 A teacher is unlikely to be effective unless he begins with BEING THERE. (B,) This is not really open to question. You will lose all your fear of teaching and relating in any form once you know who you are. There is no point whatever in remaining in the prison of believing that this is up to you. You do NOT exist in different lights. It is this belief which has confused you about your own reality. Why would you want to remain so obscure to yourself?

H. Judgment and the Authority Problem.

1 We have already discussed the Last Judgment in some though insufficient detail. [145] After the Last Judgment, there isn't any more. This is symbolic only in the sense that everybody is much better off WITHOUT judgment. When the Bible says "Judge not that

---

145 Chapter 2 Section F. The Meaning Of The Last Judgment

Chapter 3 - Retraining The Mind

ye be not judged [146] " it merely means that if you judge the reality of others at all, you will be unable to avoid judging your own. The choice to judge rather than know has been the cause of the loss of peace. Judgment is the process on which perception but not cognition rests. We covered this before [147] in terms of selectivity. Evaluation was said at that time to be its obvious prerequisite.

2   Judgment ALWAYS involves rejection. It is not an ability which emphasizes ONLY the positive aspects of what is judged, whether it be in or out of the self.

> However, what has been perceived and rejected, or judged and found wanting, remains in the unconscious because it HAS been perceived.

Watson had a very relevant notion of the unconscious in this connection. In fact, it was so relevant that he dropped it as officially out of accord with Behaviorism. He was right on both counts.

3   One of the illusions from which human perception suffers is that what it perceives and judges against has no effect. This cannot be true, unless man also believes that what his judgment vetoes does not exist. He evidently does not believe this, or he would not have judged against it.

> It does not really matter, in the end, whether you judge right or wrong. Either way, you are placing your belief in the unreal. This cannot be avoided in any type of judgment, because it IMPLIES the belief that reality is yours to choose FROM.

4   You have no idea of the tremendous release and deep peace that comes from meeting yourselves and your brothers totally without judgment. If you will look back at the earlier notes about what you and your brothers ARE, [148] you will realize that judging them in any way is really without meaning. In fact, their meaning is lost to you precisely BECAUSE you ARE judging them. All uncertainty comes from a totally fallacious belief that you are under the coercion of judgment. You do not need it to organize your life, and you certainly do not need it to organize yourselves.

5   When you look upon knowledge, all judgment is automatically suspended, and this is the process that enables recognition to REPLACE perception. Man is very fearful of everything he has perceived and refused to accept. He believes that because he has refused to accept it, he has lost control over it. This is why he sees it in nightmares, or in pleasant disguise in what seems to be happier dreams. Nothing that you have refused to

---

146 Matthew 7:1 Judge not, that ye be not judged.
147 This Chapter G. The Loss Of Certainty, p12
148 This Chapter E. Perception Versus Knowledge, p12 – 15 (among others)

H. Judgment and the Authority Problem.

accept can be brought into awareness. It does NOT follow that it is dangerous. But it DOES follow that you have made it dangerous.

6   When you feel tired, it is merely because you have judged yourself as capable of being tired. When you laugh at someone it is because you have judged him as debased. When you laugh at yourself, you are singularly likely to laugh at others, if only because you cannot tolerate being more debased THAN others. All of this does make you tired, because it is essentially disheartening. You are not really capable of being tired, but you are very capable of wearying yourselves.

7   The strain of constant judgment is virtually intolerable. It is a curious thing that any ability which is so debilitating should be so deeply cherished. But there is a very good reason for this. (This, however, depends upon what you mean by good.)

8   If you wish to be the author of reality, which is totally impossible anyway, then you will insist on holding on to judgment. You will also use the term with considerable fear and believe that judgment will someday be used against you. To whatever extent it IS used against you, it is due ONLY to your belief in its efficacy as a weapon of defense for your own authority.

9

> The issue of authority is really a question of authorship. When an individual has an "authority problem," it is ALWAYS because he believes he is the author of himself, and resents his own projection that you share his delusion in this respect. He then perceives the situation as one in which two people are literally fighting for his own authorship. This is the fundamental error of all those who believe they have usurped the power of God.

10   The belief is very frightening to them, but hardly troubles God at all. He is, however, eager to undo it, not to punish His children, but ONLY because He knows that it makes them unhappy. Souls were given their own true authorship, and men preferred to remain anonymous when they chose to separate themselves FROM their Author. The word "authority" has been one of their most fearful symbols ever since. Authority has been used for great cruelty, because, being uncertain of their true Authorship, men believe that their creation was anonymous. This has left them in a position where it SOUNDS meaningful to consider the possibility that they must have created themselves.

11   The dispute over authorship has left such uncertainty in the minds of man that some people have gone so far as to doubt whether they were ever created at all. Despite the apparent contradiction in this position, it is in one sense more tenable than the view that they created themselves. At least, it acknowledged the fact some TRUE authorship is necessary for existence.

Chapter 3 - Retraining The Mind

12   Only those who give over all desire to reject can KNOW that their own rejection is impossible.

You have not usurped the power of God, but you HAVE lost it. Fortunately, when you lose something, this does not mean that the something has gone. It merely means that YOU do not know where it is. Existence does not depend on your ability to identify it, or even to place it. It is perfectly possible to look on reality without judgment, and merely KNOW it is there. By knowing this, you are not doubting its reality at all.

13   Peace is a natural heritage of the Soul. Everyone is free to refuse to accept his inheritance, but he is NOT free to establish what his inheritance IS. [149] The problem which everyone MUST decide is the fundamental question of his own authorship. All fear comes ultimately, and sometimes by way of very devious routes, from the denial of Authorship. The offense is never to God, but only to the denier himself. He has thrown away the reason for his own peace, and sees himself only in pieces. This strange perception IS an authority problem. It is also the basis for castration anxiety, since both forms of error are fundamentally the same.

14   Neither you nor B. can find peace while this authority problem continues.

But the truth is still that there IS no problem about this. There is no man who does not feel that he is imprisoned in some way. If this has been the result of his own free will, he must regard his will as if it were NOT free, or the obviously circular reasoning of his own position would be quite apparent.

15   Free will MUST lead to freedom. Judgment always imprisons, because it separates segments of reality according to highly unstable scales of desire. Wishes are not facts, by definition. To wish is to imply that willing is not sufficient. However, no one really believes that what is wished is as real as what is willed. Instead of "seek you first the Kingdom of Heaven [150] " say "Will ye first the Kingdom of Heaven," and you have said "I know what I am, and I will to accept my own inheritance."

16   It is ESSENTIAL that this whole authority problem be voluntarily dismissed at once and for all before B's course. Neither of you understands how important this is for your sanity. You are both quite insane on this point. (This is not a judgment. It is merely a fact. (No, Helen, you SHOULD use the word "fact." This is just as much a fact as God is. A fact is literally a "making" or a starting point. You DO start from this point, and your thinking is inverted because of it.)

---

149 Luke 15:11-24 And he said, A certain man had two sons: 12 And the younger of them said to his father, Father, give me the portion of goods that falleth to me (inheritance). And he divided unto them his living. 13 And not many days after the younger son gathered all together, and took his journey into a far country, and there wasted his substance with riotous living. ...

150 Matthew 6:33 But seek ye first his kingdom, and his righteousness; and all these things shall be added unto you.

I. Creating versus the Self-Image

1 Every system of thought MUST have a starting point. It begins with either a making or a creating, a difference which we have already covered. Both are acts of will, except that making involves doing, and creating involves active willing. Their resemblance lies in their power as FOUNDATIONS. Their difference lies in what rests upon them. Both are cornerstones for systems of belief by which men live.

2 It is a mistake to believe that a thought-system which is based on lies is weak. NOTHING made by a child of God is without power. It is absolutely essential that you realize this, because otherwise you will not understand why you have so much trouble with this course, and will be unable to escape from the prisons you have (made) created for yourselves. (The use of creative here was an error. You should have said 'made' for yourself.)

3 You have both made the error of the psychotherapist we described in some detail before, [151] and it is particularly serious at this time. You cannot resolve your authority problem by depreciating the power of your minds. It CAN hurt you if you misuse it, because you KNOW its strength. You also know that you CANNOT weaken it any more than you can weaken God.

4 The devil [152] is a frightening concept ONLY because he is thought of as extremely powerful and extremely active. He is perceived as a force in combat with God, battling Him for possession of Souls. He deceives by lies, and builds kingdoms of his own, in which everything is in direct opposition to God. Yet, he ATTRACTS men rather than repels them, and they are perceived as willing to "sell" him their Souls in return for gifts they KNOW are of no real worth at all.

5 This makes absolutely no sense. The whole picture is one in which man acts in a way he HIMSELF realizes is self destructive, but which he does NOT WILL to correct, and therefore perceives the cause as beyond his control.

6 We have discussed the fall or Separation before, but its meaning must be clearly understood, without symbols. The Separation is NOT symbolic. It is an order of reality, or a system of thought that is PERFECTLY real in time, though not in Eternity. All beliefs are real to the believer.

---

151 Chapter 2 E. The Correction For Lack Of Love, p11 - 12

152 Revelation 12:7-10 And war broke out in heaven: Michael and his angels fought with the dragon; and the dragon and his angels fought, but they did not prevail, nor was a place found for them in heaven any longer. So the great dragon was cast out, that serpent of old, called the Devil and Satan, who deceives the whole world; he was cast to the earth, and his angels were cast out with him. Then I heard a loud voice saying in heaven, "Now salvation, and strength, and the kingdom of our God, and the power of His Christ have come, for the accuser of our brethren, who accused them before our God day and night, has been cast down."

Chapter 3 - Retraining The Mind

7   The fruit of only ONE tree was "forbidden" to man in his symbolic garden.[153] But God could not have forbidden it, or it could not have BEEN eaten. If God knows His children, and I assure you he does, would he have put them in a position where their own destruction was possible? The "tree" which was forbidden was correctly named "tree of knowledge." Yet God created knowledge, and gave it freely to His Creations. The symbolism here is open to many interpretations, but you may be SURE that any interpretation which perceives either God OR His creations as if they were capable of destroying their own Purpose is wrong.

8   Eating of the tree of knowledge is a symbolic expression for incorporating into the self the ability for self-creation. This is the ONLY sense in which God and His souls are NOT co-creators. The belief that they ARE is implicit in the "self concept," a concept now made acceptable by its WEAKNESS, and explained by a tendency of the self to create an IMAGE of itself. Its fear aspect is usually ascribed to the "father figure," a particularly interesting idea, in view of the fact that nobody means the physical father by the term. It refers to an IMAGE of a father in relation to an IMAGE of the self.

9   Once again, images are perceived, NOT known. Knowledge cannot deceive, but perception CAN. Man can perceive himself as self-creating, but he CANNOT do more than BELIEVE it. He CANNOT make it true. I told you before that when you finally perceive correctly, you can only be GLAD YOU CAN'T.

But until then, the belief that you CAN is the central foundation-stone in your thought-system, and all your defenses are used to attack ideas which would bring it to light.

10   You still believe you are images of your own creation. You are split with your own Souls on this point, and there is NO resolution, because you believe the one thing that is literally INCONCEIVABLE. That is why you CANNOT create, and are afraid to make or produce.

11   You, Helen, are CONSTANTLY arguing about the authorship of this course. This is NOT humility; it is a REAL authority problem. You, Bill, really believe that by teaching you are assuming a dominant or father role, and that the "father figure" will kill you. This is not humility either. Castration fears are a particularly distorted reflection of the real basic anxiety, or Separation fear.

12   The mind can make the belief in Separation VERY real and VERY fearful.

        And this belief IS the devil.

---

153 Genesis 2:16-17 And the LORD God commanded the man, saying, "Of every tree of the garden you may freely eat; but of the tree of the knowledge of good and evil you shall not eat, for in the day that you eat of it you shall surely die."

I. Creating versus the Self-Image

It is powerful, active, destructive, and clearly in opposition to God, because it literally denies His Fatherhood. Never underestimate the power of this denial. Look at your lives and see what the devil has made. But KNOW that this making will surely dissolve in the light of truth, because its foundation IS a lie.

13   Your creation by God is the only foundation which cannot be shaken, because the light is IN it. Your starting point IS truth, and you MUST return to this Beginning. Much has been perceived since then, but nothing else has happened. That is why your Souls are still in peace, even though your minds are in conflict.

14   You have not yet gone back far ENOUGH and that is why you become so fearful. As you approach the beginning, you feel the fear of the destruction of your thought-systems upon you, as if it were the fear of death. There IS no death,[154] but there IS a belief in death.

15   The Bible says that the tree that bears no fruit will be cut off and will wither away.[155] Be glad! The light WILL shine from the true Foundation of Life, and your own thought-systems WILL stand corrected. They CANNOT stand otherwise.

16   You who fear salvation are WILLING death. Life and death, light and darkness, knowledge and perception are irreconcilable. To believe that THEY can be reconciled is to believe that God and man can NOT. Only the Oneness of Knowledge is conflictless. Your Kingdom is not of this world[156] because it was given you from BEYOND this world. Only IN this world is the idea of an authority problem meaningful. The world is not left by death but by truth, and truth CAN be known by all those for whom the Kingdom was created, and for whom it waits.

---

154 2 Timothy 1:10 But has now been revealed by the appearing of our Savior Jesus Christ, who has abolished death and brought life and immortality to light through the gospel,

155 John 15:2 Every branch in Me that does not bear fruit He takes away; and every branch that bears fruit He prunes, that it may bear more fruit.
3 Now ye are clean through the word which I have spoken unto you. 4 Abide in me, and I in you. As the branch cannot bear fruit of itself, except it abide in the vine; no more can ye, except ye abide in me.
5 I am the vine, ye are the branches: He that abideth in me, and I in him, the same bringeth forth much fruit: for without me ye can do nothing. 6 If a man abide not in me, he is cast forth as a branch, and is withered; and men gather them, and cast them into the fire, and they are burned.

156 John 18:36 Jesus answered, "My kingdom is not of this world. If My kingdom were of this world, My servants would fight, so that I should not be delivered to the Jews; but now My kingdom is not from here."

Chapter 4 – The Root Of All Evil

A. Introduction

1   (Aside to H. You were both wise and devoted (two words which are literally interchangeable in the sense that they truly bring on the exchange of one another.) in claiming your scribal functions and working so late. You HAD committed a serious error against your brother, and one who had asked for your help. A devoted priestess does not do this.

    The Bible says you should go WITH a brother twice as far as he asks. [157] It certainly DOES NOT suggest that you set him BACK on his journey.

2   Devotion to a brother CANNOT set YOU back either. It can ONLY lead to mutual progress. The result of genuine devotion is inspiration, a word which, properly understood is the OPPOSITE of fatigue. To be fatigued is to be DIS-spirited, but to be inspired is to be IN the spirit. To be egocentric IS to be dispirited. But to be self-centered in the RIGHT sense is to be inspired, or in the Soul. The truly inspired are enlightened, and cannot abide in darkness.

3   Do not attempt to break God's copyright, because His Authorship alone CAN copy right. Your own right authorship does NOT lie in remaking His copies, but in creating LIKE Him.

4   Embarrassment is ALWAYS an expression of egocentricity, an association which has been made before. [158] (Made, NOT created. This kind of association is ALWAYS man-made). Both of you have completed the SCT stem: When I was called on to speak—with —"I became embarrassed and COULD NOT SPEAK."

5   Tell B. that he cannot be embarrassed by his own words unless he believes that HE is responsible for them. We have already corrected "word" to "thought," [159] and he IS free to allocate the authorship for his thoughts as he elects. He can speak from his Soul or from his ego, precisely as he chooses. If he speaks from his Soul, he has chosen to "be still and know that I am God." [160] These words are inspired, because they come from

---

157 Matthew 5:41 And whoever compels you to go one mile, go with him two.
    [Under the law of Roman occupation, a Roman soldier could ask any Jew to carry their load for one mile. The teaching is to do whatever the world (seems to) ask of us, joyfully; not in a grievance – be kind, be helpful, no matter what.]
158 Chapter 1 B. Principles of Miracles, Principle 3, p2
159 Chapter 3 G. The Loss of Certainty, G. The Loss Of Certainty, p18
160 Psalms 46:10 Be still, and know that I am God: I will be exalted among the nations, I will be exalted in the earth.

A. Introduction

KNOWLEDGE. If he speaks from his ego, he is DISCLAIMING knowledge instead of AFFIRMING it, and is thus dis-spiriting himself.

6   The dis-spirited have no choice BUT to be narcissistic, and to be narcissistic IS to place your faith in the unworthy. Your real worth IS your divine authorship, and your Soul is its acknowledgment. I cannot guide your egos EXCEPT as you associate them with your Souls.

7   Attacking misidentification errors is neither MY function nor YOURS. Destroying the devil is a meaningless undertaking.

Cervantes [161] wrote an excellent symbolic account of this procedure, though he did not understand his own symbolism. The REAL point of his writing was that his "hero" was a man who perceived himself as unworthy because he identified with his ego and perceived its weakness. He then set about to alter his perception, NOT by correcting his misidentification, but by behaving egotistically.

8   Chesterton wrote an excellent description of Cervantes and his perception of his "unheroic hero," a view of man which the ego tolerates all too frequently, but the Soul NEVER countenances:

> "And he sees across a weary land a straggling road in Spain
> Up which a lean and foolish knight forever rides in vain." [162]

9   Do not embark on foolish journeys because they are indeed in vain. The ego may will them because the ego IS both lean and foolish. But the Soul CANNOT embark on them because it is forever Unwilling to depart from its Foundation.

> The journey to the cross should be the LAST foolish journey for every mind. Do not dwell upon it, but dismiss it as accomplished. If you can accept that as YOUR OWN last foolish journey, you are free also to join My Resurrection.

Human living has indeed been needlessly wasted in repetition compulsion. It re-enacts the Separation, the loss of power, the foolish journey of the ego in its attempt at reparation, and finally the crucifixion of the body, or death. Repetition compulsions can be endless, unless they are given up by an act of will, or, more properly as active creation. Do not make the pathetic human error of "clinging to the old rugged cross." The only message of the crucifixion is in respect for man's ability to OVERCOME the cross. Unless he does so, he is free to crucify himself as often as he chooses. But this was NOT the gospel I intended to offer him.

---

161 Cervante's novel "Don Quixote" and its "unhero" Don Juan tilting at windmills is referred to here.
162 From "Lepando" by G.K. Chesterton

Chapter 4 – The Root Of All Evil

10	We have another journey to undertake, and I hope that, (if both of) [163] you will read these notes carefully, they will help to prepare you to undertake it.

B. Right Teaching and Right Learning

1	We have spoken of many different human symptoms, and at this level there IS almost endless variation. But there is only one cause for all of them. The authority problem [164] IS "the root of all evil." [165] Money is but one of its many reflections, and is a reasonably representative example of the kind of thinking which stems from it. The idea of buying and selling implies precisely the kind of exchange that the Souls cannot understand at all, because their own Supply is always abundant, and all their demands are fully met.

2	Every symptom which the ego has made involves a contradiction in terms. This is because the mind is split between the ego and the Soul, so that WHATEVER the ego makes is incomplete and contradictory. Consider what a "speechless professor" means as a concept. It literally means a "nonprofessing professor," or a "nonspeaking speaker."

3	Untenable positions such as this are the result of the authority problem, which, because it accepts the one inconceivable thought as its premise, can only produce ideas which are inconceivable.

B. may claim (and has certainly done so in the past) that the PROFESSORSHIP was thrust upon him. This is not true. He wanted it very much, and also worked hard to get it. He would not have had to work so hard either, if he had not misunderstood it.

4	The term "profess" [166] is used quite frequently in the Bible, but in a somewhat different context. To profess is to identify with an idea and offer the idea to others to be

---

163 This is a good example of 'personal' being the same as 'all.' The separated mind will feel this kind of personal address to Helen and Bill 'is talking to them, not to me.' It will question if the same personal availability of Jesus or The Source is available to myself personally. Through out the remainder of the Course, as well as in the Gospel of John, Jesus makes it explicitly clear – that he is speaking to any one, totally personally – who will listen. It is all One Mind; and 'I' am NOT different than Bill, Helen, - or anyone. Note this discomfort of the separated mind to be unsure, or uncomfortable about this – and ask it to be undone. There is much to be gained in 'hearing' for yourself 'as them;' this is a powerful practice for letting go of our separated sense of self.

164 Chapter 3 H. Judgment and the Authority Problem, p9
	Chapter 3 I. Creating Versus the Self-Image, p3
	In general: Chapter 3 G. - I.

165 1 Timothy 6:10 For the love of money is a root of all kinds of evil, for which some have strayed from the faith in their greediness, and pierced themselves through with many sorrows.

166 1 Timothy 6:12 Fight the good fight of faith, lay hold on eternal life, whereunto thou art also called, and hast professed a good profession before many witnesses. (one example)

B. Right Teaching and Right Learning

THEIR own. The idea does NOT lessen; it becomes STRONGER. The teacher clarifies his own ideas and strengthens them BY teaching them.

5 Teacher and pupil, therapist and patient, are all alike in the learning process. They are in the SAME order of learning, and unless they SHARE their lessons they will lack conviction. If a salesman must believe in the product he sells, how much more must a teacher believe in the ideas which he professes. But he needs another condition; he must also believe in the students to whom he offers his ideas.

6 (B.) He could not be afraid to teach unless he still believes that interaction means loss, and that learning means separation. He stands guard over his own ideas, because he wants to protect his thought-system as it is, and learning MEANS change.

> Change is always fearful to the separated, because they cannot conceive of it as a change toward HEALING the separation. They ALWAYS perceive it as a change for further separation, because separation WAS their first experience of change.

7 Bill, your whole fear of teaching is nothing but an example of your own intense separation anxiety, which you have handled with the usual series of mixed defenses in the combined pattern of attack on truth and defense of error, which characterizes ALL ego-thinking.

8 You insist that if you allow no change to enter into your EGO, your SOUL will find peace. This profound confusion is possible only if one maintains that the SAME thought-system can stand on two foundations.

9 NOTHING can reach the Soul from the ego, and nothing FROM the Soul can strengthen the ego, or reduce the conflict within it. The ego IS a contradiction. Man's self and God's Self ARE in opposition. They are opposed in creation, in will, and in outcome. They are fundamentally irreconcilable because the Soul cannot perceive, and the ego cannot know. They are therefore NOT IN COMMUNICATION, and can never BE in communication.

10 Nevertheless the ego can learn, because its maker can be misguided, but CANNOT make the totally lifeless out of the life-given. The Soul need not be taught, but the ego MUST. The ultimate reason why learning or teaching is perceived as frightening is because true learning DOES lead to the relinquishment (NOT destruction) of the ego to the light of the Soul. This is the change the ego MUST fear, because it does not share my charity.

11 My lesson was like yours, and because I learned it I can teach it. I never attack your egos (in spite of H's strange beliefs to the contrary), but I DO try to teach them how their thought-systems have arisen. When I remind you of your TRUE Creation, your egos cannot BUT respond with fear.

Chapter 4 – The Root Of All Evil

12   (Bill,) Teaching and learning are your greatest strengths now, because you MUST change your mind and help others change theirs. It is pointless to refuse to tolerate change or changing because you believe that you can demonstrate by doing so that the Separation never occurred. The dreamer who doubts the reality of his dream while he is still dreaming it is not really healing the level-split.

13   You HAVE dreamed of a separated ego, and you HAVE believed in a world which rested upon it. This is very real to you. You cannot undo this by doing nothing and not changing.

14   If you are willing to renounce the role of guardians of your thought-systems and open them to me, I will correct them very gently, and lead you home. Every good teacher hopes to give his students so much of his own thinking that they will one day no longer need him. This is the one real goal of the parent, teacher, and therapist. This goal will not be achieved by those who believe that they will LOSE their child or pupil or patient if they succeed.

15   It is IMPOSSIBLE to convince the ego of this, because it goes against all of its own laws. But remember that laws are set up to protect the continuity of the system in which the law-maker believes. It is natural enough for the ego to try to protect itself, once YOU have made it. But it is NOT natural for YOU to want to obey its laws unless YOU believe in them.

16   The ego cannot make this choice because of the nature of its origin. But YOU can, because of the nature of YOURS. Egos can clash in any situation, but Souls cannot clash at all. If you perceive a teacher as merely a "larger ego," you WILL be afraid, because to ENLARGE an ego IS to increase separation anxiety. Do not engage in this foolishness (Bill.) I will teach with you and live with you, if you will think with me.

17   But my goal will always be to absolve you finally from the need for a teacher. This is the OPPOSITE of the ego-oriented teacher's goal. He is concerned with the effect of HIS ego on OTHER egos, and he therefore interprets their interaction as a means of ego preservation. This is no less true if he is afraid to teach than if he is frankly out to dominate through teaching. The form of the symptom is only a reflection of his particular way of handling the separation anxiety.

18   ALL separation anxiety is a symptom of a continuing will to remain separated. This cannot be repeated too often because you have NOT learned it. (Bill,) You are afraid to teach ONLY because you are afraid of the impression your image of yourself will make ON OTHER IMAGES. You believe that their APPROVAL of your image will exalt it, but also that your separation anxiety will be increased. You also believe that their DISAPPROVAL of it will lessen the separation anxiety, but at the cost of depression.

B. Right Teaching and Right Learning

19   I would not be able to devote myself to teaching if I believed either of these ideas, and YOU will not be a devoted teacher yourself as long as you maintain them. I am constantly being perceived as a teacher either to be exalted or rejected, but I do not accept either perception for myself.

20   Your own worth is NOT established by your teaching. Your worth was established by God. As long as you dispute this, EVERYTHING you do will be fearful, and particularly any situation which lends itself easily to the superior-inferior fallacy. Teachers must be patient, and repeat their lessons until they are learned. I am willing to do so, because I have no right to set your learning limits for you.

21

Once again, - NOTHING you do, or think, or will, or make is necessary to establish your worth. This point IS NOT DEBATABLE except in delusions. Your ego is NEVER at stake because God did not create it. Your Soul is never at stake because He DID. Any confusion on this point IS a delusion, and no form of devotion is possible as long as this delusion lasts.

22   (Bill,) If you will to be a devoted teacher rather than an egocentric one, you will not be afraid. The teaching situation IS fearful if it is misused as an ego involvement. If you become afraid, it is BECAUSE you are using it this way. But the devoted teacher perceives the situation AS IT IS, and NOT as HE wills it. He does not see it as dangerous because HE is not exploiting it.

23   The ego tries to exploit ALL situations into forms of praise for itself in order to overcome its doubts. It will be doubtful forever, or better, as long as you believe in it. You who made it CANNOT trust it, because you KNOW it is not real. The ONLY sane solution is not to try to change reality, which is indeed a fearful attempt, but to see it as it is. YOU are part of reality, which stands unchanged beyond the reach of your ego, but within easy reach of your Soul.

24   (Bill,) again I tell you that when you are afraid, be still and KNOW that God is real and YOU are His beloved son in whom he is well pleased. [167] Do not let your ego dispute this, because the ego cannot know what is as far beyond its reach as you are. God is NOT the author of fear. YOU are. You have willed, therefore, to create unlike Him, and you have made fear for yourselves.

25   You are not at peace, because you are not fulfilling your function. God gave you a very lofty responsibility which you are not meeting. You KNOW this, and you are afraid.

---

[167] Matthew 17:5 While he was still speaking, behold, a bright cloud overshadowed them; and suddenly a voice came out of the cloud, saying, "This is My beloved Son, in whom I am well pleased. Hear Him!"

Chapter 4 – The Root Of All Evil

But your egos have chosen to be afraid INSTEAD of meeting it. When you awaken you will not be able to understand this, because it is literally incredible.

26   DO NOT BELIEVE THE INCREDIBLE NOW. Any attempt to increase its believableness is merely to postpone the inevitable. The word "inevitable" is fearful to the ego, but joyous to the Soul. God IS inevitable and you CANNOT avoid Him any more than He can avoid YOU.

27   The ego is afraid of the Soul's joy, because once you have experienced this, you will withdraw all protection from your ego and become totally without investment in fear. Your investment is great now, because fear is a witness to the Separation, and your ego rejoices when you witness to it.

28   Leave it behind. Do not listen to it, and do not preserve it. Listen only to God, who is as incapable of deception as are the Souls he created. As teachers and therapists, release yourselves and release others. Do not present a false and unworthy picture of yourselves TO others, or accept such a picture OF them yourselves.

29   The ego has built a shabby and unsheltering home for you, because it cannot build otherwise. Do not try to make this impoverished house stand. ITS weakness IS your strength. Only God could make a home that was worthy of His Creations, who have chosen to leave it empty by their own dispossession.

30   His Home will stand forever, and is ready for you when you choose to enter. Of this you can be wholly certain. God is as incapable of creating the perishable as your ego is of making the eternal.

31   Of your egos you can do nothing to save yourselves or others. But of your Souls you can do everything for the salvation of both. Humility is a lesson for the ego, not for the Soul. The Soul is beyond humility, because it recognizes its radiance, and gladly sheds its light everywhere.

32   The meek shall inherit the earth [168] because their egos are humble, and this gives them better perception. The Kingdom of Heaven is the right of the Soul, whose beauty and dignity are beyond doubt, beyond perception, and stand forever as the mark of the love of God for His Creations, who are wholly worthy of Him and ONLY of Him. Nothing else is sufficiently worthy to be a gift for a creation of God Himself.

---

[168] Psalm 37:11 But the meek shall inherit the earth, And shall delight themselves in the abundance of peace. Matthew 5:5 Blessed are the meek, For they shall inherit the earth.

B. Right Teaching and Right Learning

33 I will substitute for your ego if you will, but NEVER for your Soul. [169] A father can safely leave a child with an elder brother who has shown himself responsible, but this involves no confusion about the child's origin. The brother can protect the child's body and his ego, which are very closely associated, but he does not confuse HIMSELF with the father because he does this, although the child may.

34 The reason why I can be entrusted with YOUR body and YOUR egos is simply because this enables YOU not to be concerned with them, and ME to teach you their unimportance. I could not understand their importance to YOU if I had not once been tempted to believe them myself. Let us undertake to learn this lesson together, so we can also be free of them together.

35 I need devoted teachers as much as I need devoted priestesses. They both heal the mind, and that is always my own aim. The Soul is far beyond the need of your protection OR mine.

36 The Biblical quotation should read "In this world you need NOT have tribulation BECAUSE I have overcome the world." [170] THAT is why you should "be of good cheer."

37 B's course was very carefully chosen, because "abnormal psychology" IS ego psychology. This is precisely the kind of content which should never be taught FROM the ego whose abnormality should be lessened by teaching, not increased. You, Bill, are particularly well suited to perceive this difference, and can therefore teach this course as it should be taught. Most teachers have an unfortunate tendency to teach the COURSE abnormally, and many of the students are apt to suffer considerable perceptual distortion because of their own authority problem.

38 Your teaching assignment (and I assure you it IS an assignment) will be to present perceptual distortions without either engaging in them yourself, or encouraging your students to do so. This interpretation of your role and theirs is too charitable to induce fear.

If you adhere to this role, you will both engender and experience hope, and you will inspire rather than dispirit the future teachers and therapists I am entrusting to you.

---

169 [It took me a long time to both get and accept this statement. 'Getting this' depends on our knowing our Being in stillness. When, in any interaction, with any person, in any situation, we choose to become totally still, with no (paying no attention to) thought or reaction of our own – then Our Source will give us a thought of what to say or what to do, and even of what to decide, as seems necessary. This 'openness and acceptance' replaces our ego reactivity.]

170 John 16:33 These things I have spoken unto you, that in me ye might have peace. In the world ye shall have tribulation: but be of good cheer ; I have overcome the world.

Chapter 4 – The Root Of All Evil

39   I promise to attend myself, and you should at least credit with me with some dependability in keeping my own promises. I never make them lightly, because I know the need my brothers have for trust. [171]

C. The Ego and False Autonomy

1   (Bill has) You have asked lately how the mind could ever have made the ego. This is a perfectly reasonable question; in fact, the best question either of you could ask. There is no point in giving an historical answer, because the past does not matter in human terms, and history would not exist if the same errors were not being repeated in the present.

B. has often told you that your thinking is too abstract at times, and he is right.

Abstraction DOES apply to knowledge, because knowledge is completely impersonal, and examples are irrelevant to its understanding. Perception, however, is always specific, and therefore quite concrete.

2   Perceptual distortions are not abstractions. They are merely confusions. Each man makes one ego for himself, although it is subject to enormous variation because of its instability, and one for everyone he perceives, which is equally variable. Their interaction IS a process which literally alters both, because they were not made either BY or WITH the unalterable.

3   It is particularly important to realize that this alteration can and does occur as readily when the interaction takes place IN THE MIND as when it involves physical presence. THINKING about another ego is as effective in changing relative perception as is their physical interaction. There could be no better example of the fact that the ego is an idea, though not a reality-based thought.

Your own present state is the best concrete example B. could have of how the mind could have made the ego. You DO have real knowledge at times, but when you throw it away it is as if you never had it. This willfullness is so apparent that B. need only perceive it to see that is DOES happen. If it can occur that way in the present, why should he be surprised that it occurred that way in the past? All psychology rests on the principle of continuity of behavior. Surprise is a reasonable response to the unfamiliar, but hardly to something that has occurred with such persistence.

4   An extreme example is a good teaching aid, not because it is typical, but because it is clear. The more complex the material, the clearer the examples should be for teaching purposes. (Bill, remember that for your own course, and do not avoid the dramatic. It

---

171 [Tim Note: Each of us 'is teaching' in any encounter. Either we are teaching truth is true – who and what we really are, or we are teaching separation is real. Jesus, The Source, IS always 'attending' when we are teaching. We can, and should, take his promise here – very personally.

C. The Ego and False Autonomy

holds the student's interest precisely because it is so apparent that it CAN be readily perceived.) But, as we have said before, all teaching devices in the hands of good teachers are aimed at rendering themselves unnecessary. I would therefore like to use your present state as an example of how the mind can work, provided you both fully recognize that it need not work that way.

I NEVER forget this myself, and a good teacher shares his own ideas, which he himself believes. Otherwise, he cannot really "profess" them, as we used the term before.[172]

5   With full recognition of its transitory nature, a recognition which I hope you both share, H. offers a very good teaching example of alternations between Soul and ego, with concomitant variation between peace and frenzy. In answer to B's question, it is perfectly apparent that when she is ego-dominated, she DOES NOT KNOW her Soul. Her abstract ability, which is perfectly genuine and does stem from knowledge, cannot help her because she has turned to the concrete which she cannot handle abstractly. Being incapable of appropriate concreteness perceptually, because her ego is not her natural home, she suffers from its intrusions, but NOT from complete lack of knowledge.

6   The result is a kind of "double vision," which would have produced an actual diplopia, if she had not settled for nearsightedness. This was an attempt to see the concrete more clearly through the ego's eyes, without the "interference" of the longer range. Her virtual lack of astigmatism is due to her real efforts at objectivity and fairness. She has not attained them, or she would not be nearsighted. But she HAS tried to be fair with what she permitted herself to see.

7   Why are you surprised that something happened in the dim past, when it is so clearly happening right now? You forget the love that even animals have for their own offspring, and the need they feel to protect them. This is because they regard them as part of themselves. No one disowns something he regards as a very real part of himself. Man reacts to his ego much as God does to His Souls, - with love, protection, and great charity. The reaction of man to the self he made is not at all surprising. In fact, it duplicates in many ways the way he will one day react to his real creations, which are as timeless as he is.

8   The question is not HOW man responds toward his ego, but only what he believes he IS. Again, belief is an ego-function, and as long as your origin is open to belief at all, you ARE regarding it from an ego viewpoint. That is why the Bible quotes me as saying, "Ye believe in God, believe also in me."[173] Belief DOES apply to me, because I am the teacher of the ego. When teaching is no longer necessary, you will merely know God.

---

172 This Chapter B. Right Teaching And Right Learning, p4
173 John 14:1 "Let not your heart be troubled: ye believe in God, believe also in me."

Chapter 4 – The Root Of All Evil

9   Belief that there IS another way is the loftiest idea of which ego-thinking is capable. This is because it contains a hint of recognition that the ego is NOT the self.

Helen always had this idea, but it merely confused her. B., you were more capable of a long-range view, and that is why your eyesight is good. But you were willing to see because you utilized judgment against what you saw. This gave you clearer perception than Helen's, but cut off the cognitive level more deeply. That is why you believe that you never had knowledge.

10   Repression HAS been a stronger mechanism in your own ego defense, and that is why you find her shifts so hard to tolerate. Willfullness is more characteristic of her, and that is why she has less sense than you do. It is extremely fortunate, temporarily, that the particular strengths you will both develop and use are precisely those which the other must supply now. You who will be the strength of God are quite weak, and you who will be God's help are clearly in need of help. What better plan could have been devised to prevent the intrusion of the ego's arrogance on the outcome?

11   Undermining the foundation of an ego's thought-system MUST be perceived as painful, even though this is anything but true. Babies scream in rage if you take away a knife or a scissors, even though they may well harm themselves if you do not. The speedup has placed you (both) in the same position.

12   You are NOT by any means prepared, and in this sense you ARE babies. You have no sense of real self-preservation and are very likely to decide that you need precisely what would hurt you most. Whether you know it now or not, however, you (both) HAVE willed to cooperate in a concerted and very commendable effort to become both harmLESS and helpFUL, two attributes which MUST go together. Your attitudes, even toward this, are necessarily conflicted, because ALL attitudes are ego-based.

13   This will not last. Be patient awhile, and remember what we have said once before; the outcome is as certain as God! [174] Helen used to perceive the quotation "To him that hath shall be given" [175] as a paradox that bordered on the ironic. She also had a similar reaction to another related one: "Faith is the gift of God." [176] We have re-interpreted both of these statements before, but perhaps we can make them even clearer now.

14   Only those who have a real and lasting sense of abundance can be truly charitable. This is quite obvious when you consider the concepts involved. To be able to give anything implies that you can do without it. Even if you associate giving with sacrifice,

---

174 Chapter 2 B. The Re-interpretation of Defenses, b. The Atonement As Defense, p31
175 Matthew 13:12 "For whosoever hath, to him shall be given, and he shall have more abundance: but whosoever hath not, from him shall be taken away even that he hath.
176 1 Corinthians 12:9 "To another faith by the same Spirit; to another the gifts of healing by the same Spirit;"

C. The Ego and False Autonomy

you still give only because you believe you are somehow getting something better so that you can do without the thing you give.

15   "Giving to get" is an inescapable law of the ego, which ALWAYS evaluates itself in relation to others' egos, and is therefore continually preoccupied with the scarcity principle which gave rise to it.

This IS the meaning of Freud's "pleasure principle." Freud was the most accurate "ego psychologist" we ever had, although he would not have preferred this description himself. His ego was a very weak and deprived concept, which could function ONLY as a thing in need.

16   The "reality principle" of the ego is not real at all. It is forced to perceive the "reality" of other egos, because it CANNOT establish the reality of itself. In fact, its whole perception of other egos AS real is ONLY an attempt to convince itself that IT is real.

17   "Self esteem," in ego terms, means nothing more than that the ego has deluded itself into accepting its reality and is therefore temporarily less predatory. This "self esteem" is ALWAYS vulnerable to stress, a term which really means that a condition has arisen in which the delusion of reality of the ego is threatened. This produces either ego-deflation or ego-inflation, resulting in either withdrawal or attack. The ego literally lives by comparisons. This means that equality is beyond its grasp, and charity becomes impossible.

18   The ego NEVER gives out of abundance, because it was made as a SUBSTITUTE for it. This is why the concept of GETTING arose in the ego's thought-system. All appetites are "getting" mechanisms representing ego needs to confirm itself. This is as true of bodily appetites as it is of the so-called "higher" ego needs. Bodily appetites are NOT physical in origin, because the ego regards the body as its home, and DOES try to satisfy itself through the body. But the IDEA that this is possible is a decision of the ego, which is completely confused about what is really possible. This accounts for its essential erraticness.

19   Consider the inevitable confusion which MUST arise from a perception of the self which responds: When I was completely on my own I "had no idea what was possible."

The ego DOES believe it is completely on its own, which is merely another way of describing how it originated. This is such a fearful state that it can only turn to other egos, and unite with them in a feeble attempt at identification, or attack them in an equally feeble show of strength. The ego is free to complete the stem: "When I was completely on my own" in any way it chooses, but it is NOT free to consider the validity of the premise itself, because this premise is its FOUNDATION.

Chapter 4 – The Root Of All Evil

> The ego IS the belief of the mind that it is completely on its own.

20   The ego's ceaseless attempts to gain the Soul's acknowledgement and thus establish its own existence are utterly useless. The Soul in its knowledge is unaware of the ego. It does NOT attack the ego. It merely cannot conceive of it at all. While the ego is equally unaware of the Soul, it DOES perceive itself as rejected by something which is greater than itself. This is why self-esteem in ego terms MUST be a delusion.

21   The creations of God do not create myths, but the creative efforts of man can turn to mythology, but only under one condition: What man then makes is no longer creative. Myths are entirely perceptions and are so ambivalent in form, and so characteristically good and evil in nature that the most benevolent of them is not without fearful components, if only in innuendo.

Myths and magic are closely associated, in that myths are usually related to the ego origins, and magic to the powers which the ego ascribes to itself. Every mythological system includes an account of "the creation," and associates this with its particular perception of magic.

22   The "battle for survival" is nothing more than the ego's struggle to preserve itself and its interpretation of its own beginning. This beginning is always associated with physical birth, because nobody maintains that the ego existed before that point in time. The religiously ego-oriented tend to believe that the Soul existed before, and will continue to exist afterwards, after a temporary lapse into ego-life. Some actually believe that the Soul will be punished for this lapse, even though in reality it could not possibly know anything about it.

23   The term "salvation" does NOT apply to the Soul, which is not in danger and does not need to be salvaged. Salvation is nothing more that "right-mindedness" which is NOT the one-mindedness of the Soul, but which must be accomplished before one-mindedness can be restored. Right-mindedness dictates the next step automatically, because right perception is uniformly without attack, so that wrong-mindedness is obliterated. The ego cannot survive without judgment, and is laid aside accordingly. The mind then has only ONE direction in which it can move.

24   The directions which the mind will take are always automatic, because they cannot BUT be dictated by the thought-system to which it adheres. Every thought-system has INTERNAL consistency, and this does provide a basis for the continuity of behavior. However, this is still reliability and NOT validity. Reliable behavior is a meaningful perception, as far as ego thinking goes. However, VALID behavior is an expression which is inherently contradictory, because validity is an END, and behavior is a

C. The Ego and False Autonomy

MEANS. These cannot be combined logically, because when an end has been attained, the means for its attainment are no longer meaningful.

25   Test constructors recognize that there are different kinds of validity, and also that they are of different orders. This means that they do not mean truth and do not pretend to mean it. Test validity can be judged by logic, by theory, and by practice, each being regarded as a different dimension. In each case, the amount of confidence is expressed in some form of percentage, either quantitatively, or merely in terms of "high," moderate, and low. But a hypothesis is tested as either true or false, to be accepted or rejected accordingly. If it is shown to be true it becomes a fact, after which no one attempts to evaluate it unless its status AS fact is questioned.

26   EVERY idea which the ego has accorded the status of fact is questionable, because facts are in the realm of knowledge. Confusing realms of discourse is a thinking error which philosophers have recognized for centuries. Psychologists are generally quite deficient in this respect, as are many theologians. Data from one realm of discourse do not mean anything in another, because they can be understood only WITHIN the thought-systems of which they are a part. This is why psychologists are concentrating increasingly on the ego, in an attempt to unify their clearly unrelated data. It need hardly be said that an attempt to relate the unrelated cannot succeed.

27   The recent ecological emphasis is but a more ingenious way of trying to impose order on chaos. We have already credited the ego with considerable ingenuity, though not with creativeness. But it should always be remembered that inventiveness is really wasted effort, even in its most ingenious forms. We do not have to EXPLAIN anything. This is why we need not trouble ourselves with inventiveness. The highly specific nature of invention is not worthy of the abstract creativity of God's Creations.

D. Love without Conflict

1   When H. reads this to you, Bill, try to listen very carefully.

You have never understood what "The Kingdom of Heaven is within you" [177] means. The reason you cannot understand it is because it is NOT understandable to the ego, which interprets it as if something outside is inside, which does not mean anything. The word "within" does not belong. The Kingdom of Heaven IS you.

2   What else BUT you did the Creator create, and what else but you IS His Kingdom? This is the whole message of the Atonement, a message which in its totality transcends

---

[177] Luke 17:20 20 And when he was demanded of the Pharisees, when the kingdom of God should come, he answered them and said, "The kingdom of God cometh not with observation: 21 Neither shall they say, Lo here! or, lo there! for, behold, the kingdom of God is within you."

Chapter 4 – The Root Of All Evil

the sum of its parts which we have covered before. [178] Christmas is not a time; it is a state of mind. The Christ Mind wills from the Soul, not from the Ego, and the Christ Mind IS yours.

3 You, too, have a Kingdom which your Soul has created. It has not ceased to create because your ego has set you on the road of perception. Your Soul's creations are no more fatherless than you are. Your ego and your Soul will never be co-creators, but your Soul and YOUR Creator will ALWAYS be. Be confident that your creations are as safe as you are.

> The Kingdom is perfectly united and perfectly protected,
> and the ego will not prevail against it.
> Amen.

4 That was written in that form because it is a good thing to use as a kind of prayer in moments of temptation. It is a declaration of independence. You will both find it very helpful if you understand it fully.

5 In its characteristic upside down way, the ego has taken the impulses from the superconscious and perceives them as if they arise in the unconscious. The ego judges what is to be accepted, and the impulses from the superconscious are unacceptable to it, because they clearly point to the unexistence of the ego itself.

The ego therefore experiences threat, and not only censors but also re-interprets the data. However, as Freud very correctly pointed out, what you do not perceive you still know, and it can retain a very active life BEYOND your awareness.

6 Repression thus operates to conceal not only the baser impulses, but also the most lofty ones from the ego's awareness, because BOTH are threatening to the ego and, being concerned primarily with its preservation in the face of threat, it perceives them as the same. The threat value of the lofty is really much greater to the ego, because the pull of God Himself can hardly be equated with the pull of human appetites.

7 By perceiving them as the same, the ego attempts to save itself from being swept away, as it would surely be in the presence of knowledge. The upper level of the unconscious thus contains the call of God as well as the call of the body. That is why the basic conflict between love and fear is unconscious. The ego cannot tolerate either and represses both by resorting to inhibition. Society depends on inhibiting the former, but SALVATION depends on disinhibiting the latter.

8 The reason you need my help is because you have repressed your own guide, and therefore need guidance. My role is to separate the true from the false in your own

---

178 Chapter 2 E. The Correction for Lack of Love, p56

D. Love without Conflict

unconscious, so it can break through the barriers the ego has set up and shine into your minds. Against our united strength, the ego CANNOT prevail.

9   It should be quite apparent to you by now why the ego regards the Soul as its "enemy." The ego arose from the Separation, and its continued existence depends on your continuing belief in the Separation. Reducing the Soul impulses to the unconscious, the ego has to offer you some sort of reward for maintaining this belief. All it CAN offer is a sense of temporary existence, which begins with its own beginning and ends with its own ending. It tells you that this life is YOUR existence because it IS its own.

10   Against this sense of temporary existence, the Soul offers the knowledge of permanence and unshakeable BEING. No one who has experienced the revelation of this can ever fully believe in the ego again. How can its meager offering to you prevail against the glorious gift of God?

11   You who identify with your egos cannot believe that God loves you. YOU do not love what you have made, and what you have made does not love you. Being made out of the denial of the Father, the ego has no allegiance to its own Maker. You cannot conceive of the real relationship that exists between God and His Souls, because of the hatred you have for the Self you have made. You project onto your own idea of yourself the will to separate, which conflicts with the love you also feel for what you have made because you made it.

12   No human love is without this ambivalence, and since no ego has experienced love WITHOUT ambivalence, the concept is beyond its understanding. Love will enter immediately into any mind which truly wants it, but it MUST want it truly. This means that it wants it WITHOUT ambivalence, and this kind of wanting is wholly without the ego's "drive to get."

13   There is a kind of experience that is so different from anything the ego can offer that you will never recover. The word is used quite literally here, - you will never be able to hide again. It is necessary to repeat that your belief in darkness and in hiding IS why the light cannot enter.

14   The Bible has many references to the immeasurable gifts which are for you, but for which YOU must ask. [179] This is not the condition as the ego sets conditions. It is the

---

[179] Matthew 6:7 But when ye pray, use not vain repetitions, as the heathen do: for they think that they shall be heard for their much speaking. 8 Be not ye therefore like unto them: for your Father knoweth what things ye have need of, before ye ask him. 9 After this manner therefore pray ye:

    Our Father which art in heaven, Hallowed be thy name.
10   Thy kingdom come, Thy will be done in earth, as it is in heaven.
11   Give us this day our daily bread.
12   And forgive us our debts, as we forgive our debtors.
13   And lead us not into temptation, but deliver us from evil:

Chapter 4 – The Root Of All Evil

glorious condition of what you ARE. No force except your own will is strong enough or worthy enough to guide you. In this you are as free as God, and must remain so forever.

15   You can never be bound except in honor, and that is always voluntary.

> Let us ask the Father in my name to keep you mindful of His love for you and yours for Him.

He has never failed to answer this request, because it asks only for what He has already willed. Those who call truly are ALWAYS answered.

16   Note: H. became very fearful here, and rather vaguely thought the answer was: "Thou shalt have no other Gods before me, because there ARE none. You still think there are."

17   It has never really entered your minds to give up every idea you have ever had that OPPOSES knowledge. You retain thousands of little scraps of meanness which prevent the Holy One from entering. Light cannot penetrate through the walls you make to block it, and it is forever UNwilling to destroy what you have made. No one can see THROUGH a wall, but I can step around it.

18   Watch your minds for the scraps of meanness, or you will be unable to ask me to do so. I can help you only as our Father Created us. I will love you and honor you and maintain complete respect for what you have made. But I will neither love nor honor it unless it is true. I will never forsake you, any more than God will. But I MUST wait as long as you will to forsake yourselves.

19   Because I wait in love and not in impatience, you will surely ask me truly. I will come gladly in response to a single unequivocal call. Watch carefully, and see what it is you are truly asking for. Be very honest with yourselves about this, for you we must hide nothing from each other.

20   If you will REALLY try to do this, you have taken the first step toward preparing your minds for the Holy One to enter. We will prepare for this together, and once He has come, you will be ready to help me make other minds ready for Him. How long will you deny Him His Kingdom?

21   In your own unconscious, deeply repressed by the ego, is the declaration of your release. GOD HAS GIVEN YOU EVERYTHING. This is the one fact which MEANS that the ego does not exist, and which therefore makes it profoundly afraid. In the ego's language, to have and to be are different, but they are identical to the Soul. It knows that you both HAVE everything and ARE everything. Any distinction in this respect is meaningful only when the idea of getting, which implies a lack, has already BEEN

For thine is the kingdom, and the power, and the glory, for ever.
Amen.

D. Love without Conflict

accepted. That is why we made no distinction before between HAVING the Kingdom of God and BEING the Kingdom of God.

22 The calm being of God's Kingdom, which in your sane mind is perfectly conscious, is ruthlessly banished from the part of the mind which the ego rules. The ego is desperate because it opposes literally invincible odds whether you are asleep or awake. Consider how much vigilance you have been willing to exert to protect your ego, and how little you have been willing to exert to protect your higher mind. Who but the insane would undertake to believe what is not true, and then protect this belief at the cost of Truth?

E. The Escape from Fear

1 If you cannot hear the voice of God, it is because you do not choose to listen. The fact that you DO listen to the voice of your ego is demonstrated by your attitudes, your feelings, and your behavior. Your attitudes are obviously conflicted; your feelings have a narrow range on the negative side, but are never purely joyous; and your behavior is either strained or unpredictable.

Yet this IS what you want. This is what you are fighting to keep, and what you are vigilant to save. Your minds are filled with schemes to save the face of your egos, and you do not seek the Face of God.

2 The glass in which the ego seeks to see its face is dark indeed. [180] How can it maintain the trick of its existence except with mirrors? But where you look to find yourself is up to you. We have said that you cannot change your mind by changing your behavior, [181] but we have also said, and many times before, that you CAN change your mind.

a. This Need Not Be

1 When your mood tells you that you have willed wrongly, and this is so whenever you are not joyous, then KNOW this need not be.

2 In every case you have thought wrongly about some Soul that God created, and are perceiving images your ego makes in a darkened glass. Think honestly what you have thought that God would NOT have thought, and what you have NOT thought that God would have you think. Search sincerely for what you have done and left undone accordingly. And then change your minds to THINK WITH GOD'S.

3 This may seem hard to you, but it is MUCH easier than trying to think AGAINST it. Your mind IS one with God's. Denying this and thinking otherwise has held your ego

---

[180] 1 Corinthians 1312 For now we see through a glass, darkly; but then face to face: now I know in part; but then shall I know even as also I am known.
[181] Chapter 2 D. Fear as Lack of Love, p7

Chapter 4 – The Root Of All Evil

4   When you are sad, KNOW that this NEED NOT BE. Depression ALWAYS arises ultimately from a sense of being deprived of something you want and do not have. KNOW you are deprived of nothing, except by your own decisions, and then decide otherwise.

5   When you are anxious, KNOW that all anxiety comes from the capriciousness of the ego, and NEED NOT BE. You can be as vigilant AGAINST the ego's dictates as FOR them.

6   When you feel guilty, KNOW that your ego has indeed violated the laws of God, but YOU have not. Leave the sins of the ego to me. That is what the Atonement is for. But until you change your mind about those your ego has hurt, the Atonement cannot release you. As long as you feel guilty, your ego is in command, because only the ego CAN experience guilt. THIS NEED NOT BE.

7   You, Helen, have been more honest that B. in really trying to see whom your ego has hurt, and also in trying to change your mind about them. (H. doubtful whether this is accurate-written at a time when she was very angry.)

I am not unmindful of your efforts, but you still have much too much energy invested in your ego. THIS NEED NOT BE. Watch your minds for the temptations of the ego, and do not be deceived by it. KNOW it offers you nothing.

8   You, B, have not made consistent efforts to change your mind except through applying old habit patterns to new ideas. But you have learned, and learned it better than H., (H. doubtful about accuracy here) that your mind gains control over ITSELF when you direct it genuinely toward perceiving someone ELSE truly. Your lack of vitality is due to your former marked effort at solving your needless depression and anxiety through disinterest. Because your ego WAS protected by this unfortunate negative attribute, you are afraid to abandon it.

9   When you have given up voluntary dis-spiriting, you have already seen how your mind can focus, and rise above fatigue, and heal. But you are not sufficiently vigilant against the demands of your ego that you disengage yourself. THIS NEED NOT BE. The habit of engaging WITH God and His Creations is easily made if you refuse actively to let your minds slip away. Your problem is not concentration: it is a belief that nobody, including yourself, is WORTH consistent effort.

10   Side with me CONSISTENTLY against this deception, as we have sided against it briefly already. Do not permit this shabby belief to pull you back. The disheartened are useless to themselves and to me, but only the ego can be disheartened.

E. The Escape from Fear

11   Have you REALLY considered how many opportunities you have to gladden yourselves, and how many of them you have refused? There is no limit to the power of a Son of God, but he himself can limit the expression of his power as much as he wills. Your mind and mine can unite in shining your ego away, and releasing the strength of God into everything you think and will and do.

Do no settle for ANYTHING less than this, and refuse to accept anything BUT this as your goal.

12   Watch your minds carefully for any beliefs that hinder its accomplishment, and step away from them.

Judge how well you have done this by your own feelings, *for this is the one RIGHT use of judgment.*

Judgment, like any other defense, can be used to attack or protect, to hurt or to heal. The ego SHOULD be brought to your own judgment and found wanting there. Without your own allegiance, protection, and love it cannot exist.

13   Judge your ego truly, and you MUST withdraw allegiance, protection, and love from it. You are mirrors of truth in which God Himself shines in perfect light. To the ego's dark glass you need but say, "I will not look there because I KNOW these images are not true."

14   Then through me, let the Holy One, shine upon you in peace, knowing that this and only this MUST be! His Mind shone on you in your creation, and brought YOUR mind into being. His Mind still shines on you and MUST shine THROUGH you.

Your ego cannot prevent HIM from shining on you, but it CAN prevent you from letting Him shine THROUGH you.

15   The first coming of Christ is just another name for the Creation, for Christ is the Son of God.

The SECOND coming of Christ means nothing more than the end of the ego's rule over part of the minds of men, and the healing of the mind.

I was created like you in the First, and I am reminding you that I have called you to join with me in the Second.

16   If you will think over your lives, you will see how carefully the preparations were made. I am in charge of the Second Coming as I have already told you, [182] and my

---

[182] Chapter 1 B. Principles Of Miracles Principle 26, p4; Principle 47, p5

judgment, which is used only for its protection, cannot be wrong because it NEVER attacks. YOURS is so distorted that you believe that I was mistaken in choosing you. I assure you this is a mistake of your own egos. Do NOT mistake it for humility.

17   Your egos are trying to convince you that THEY are real, and I am not, because if I AM real, I am no more real than YOU are. That knowledge, and I assure you that it IS knowledge, means that Christ must come into your minds and heal them.

18   While I am not attacking your egos, I AM working with your higher mind whether you are asleep or awake, just as your ego does with your lower mind. I am your vigilance in this, because you are too confused to recognize your own hope.

19   I was not mistaken. Your minds WILL elect to join with mine, and together we are invincible. You (two) will yet come together in my name and your sanity will be restored. I raised the dead by KNOWING that life is an eternal attribute of everything that the living God Created. Why do you believe that it is harder for me to inspire the dis-spirited or to stabilize the unstable? I do not believe that there is an order of difficulty in miracles: YOU do. I have called and you will answer. I KNOW that miracles are natural, because they are expressions of love. My calling you is as natural as your answer and as inevitable.

F. The Ego-Body Illusion

1   ALL things work together for good.

There are NO exceptions except in the ego's judgment. Control is a central factor in what the ego permits into consciousness, and one to which it devotes its maximum vigilance. This is NOT the way a balanced mind holds together. ITS control is unconscious.

2   The ego is further off balance by keeping its primary motivation UNconscious, and raising control rather than sensible judgment to predominance. It has every reason to do this, according to the thought-system which both gave rise to it and which it serves. Sane judgment would inevitably judge AGAINST it, and MUST be obliterated by the ego in the interest of its self-preservation.

3   A crucial source of the ego's off-balance state is its lack of discrimination between impulses from God and from the body. Any thought-system which makes THIS confusion MUST be insane. Yet this demented state is ESSENTIAL to the ego, which judges ONLY in terms of threat or nonthreat TO ITSELF.

4   In one sense, the ego's fear of the idea of God is at least logical, because this idea DOES dispel it. Fear of dissolution from the higher source, then, makes SOME sense in ego terms. But fear of the body, with which the ego identifies so closely, is more blatantly senseless. The body is the ego's home by its own election. It is the only

F. The Ego-Body Illusion

identification with which it feels safe, because the body's vulnerability is its own best argument that you CANNOT be of God.

5 This is the belief that it sponsors eagerly. Yet the ego hates the body, because it does not accept the idea that the body is good enough as its home. Here is where the mind becomes actually dazed. Being told by the ego that it is really part of the body, and that the body is its protector, it is also constantly informed that the body can NOT protect it. This, of course, is not only true, but perfectly obvious.

6 Therefore, the mind asks, "Where can I go for protection?," to which the ego replies, "Turn to me." The mind, and not without cause, reminds the ego that it has itself insisted that it IS identified with the body, so there is no point in turning to it for protection. The ego has no real answer to this because there ISN'T any. But it DOES have a typical solution. It obliterates the question from the mind's awareness. Once unconscious, it can and does produce uneasiness, but it cannot be answered because it cannot be asked.

7 This is the question which MUST be asked:

"Where am I to go for protection?"

Only an insane mind FAILS to ask it. Even the insane ask it unconsciously, but it requires real sanity to ask it consciously.

8 If you will remember your dream about the recorder, which was remarkably accurate in some ways because it came partly from ego-repressed knowledge, the real problem was correctly stated as "What is the question?" because, as you very well knew, the answer COULD be found if the question were recognized. If you remember, there were a number of solutions you attempted, all ego-based, not because you thought they would really work, but because the question ITSELF was obscure.

9 When the Bible says "Seek and ye shall find,"[183] it does NOT mean that you should seek blindly and desperately for something you wouldn't recognize. Meaningful seeking is consciously undertaken, consciously organized, and consciously directed.

B's chief contribution to your joint venture is his insistence that the goal be formulated clearly, and KEPT IN MIND.

10 You, Helen, are not good at doing this. You still search for many goals simultaneously, and this goal confusion, given a strong will, MUST produce chaotic behavior. B's behavior is not chaotic, because he is not so much goal-divided as not goal-ORIENTED. Where Helen has over invested in many goals, B has under invested in ALL goals. He has the advantage of POTENTIALLY greater freedom from

---

[183] Luke 11:9 And I say unto you, Ask, and it shall be given you; seek, and ye shall find; knock, and it shall be opened unto you.
Also, Jeremiah 29:13 And ye shall seek me, and find me, when ye shall search for me with all your heart.

Chapter 4 – The Root Of All Evil

distractibility, but he does not care enough to use it. Helen has the advantage of great effort, but she keeps losing sight of the goal.

11   B has very intelligently suggested that you both should set yourself the goal of really studying for this course. There can be no doubt of the wisdom of this decision, for any student who wants to pass it. But, knowing your individual weaknesses as learners and being a teacher with some experience, I must remind you that learning and wanting to learn are inseparable.

12   All learners learn best when they believe that what they are trying to learn is of value to them. But values in this world are hierarchical, and not everything you may WANT to learn has lasting value. Indeed, many of the things you want to learn are chosen BECAUSE their value will not last. The ego thinks it is an advantage not to commit itself to ANYTHING that is eternal, because the eternal MUST come from God.

13   Eternalness is the one function that the ego has tried to develop, but has systematically failed. It may surprise you to learn that had the ego willed to do so, it COULD have made the eternal, because, as a product of the mind, it IS endowed with the power of its own creator. But the DECISION to do this, rather than the ABILITY to do it is what the ego cannot tolerate. That is because the decision, from which the ability would naturally develop, would necessarily involve true perception, a state of clarity which the ego, fearful of being judged truly, MUST avoid.

14   The results of this dilemma are peculiar, but no more so than the dilemma itself. The ego has reacted characteristically here as elsewhere, because mental illness, which is ALWAYS a form of ego-involvement, is not a problem of reliability as much as of validity. The ego compromises with the issue of the eternal, just as it does with all issues that touch on the real question in ANY way. By compromising in connection with all TANGENTIAL questions, it hopes to hide the REAL question and keep it OUT OF MIND. Its characteristic "business" with non-essentials is precisely for that purpose.

15   Consider the alchemist's age-old attempts to turn base metal into gold. The one question which the alchemist did not permit himself to ask was "What For?" He COULD not ask this, because it would immediately become apparent that there was no sense in his efforts, even if he succeeded. The ego has also countenanced some strange compromises with the idea of the eternal, making odd attempts to relate the concept to the unimportant in an effort to satisfy the mind without jeopardizing itself. Thus, it has permitted many good minds to devote themselves to perpetual MOTION, but NOT to perpetual THOUGHTS.

16   Ideational preoccupations with conceptual problems set up to be incapable of solution are another favorite ego device for impeding the strong-willed from real progress in learning. The problems of squaring the circle, and carrying pi to infinity are

F. The Ego-Body Illusion

good examples. A more recent ego-attempt is particularly noteworthy. The idea of preserving the body by suspension, thus giving it the kind of limited immortality which the ego can tolerate, is among its more recent appeals to the mind.

17   It is noticeable that in all these diversionary tactics, the ONE question which is NEVER asked by those who pursue them is "What for?" This is the question which YOU must learn to ask in connection with everything your mind wills to undertake. What is your purpose? Whatever it is, you cannot doubt that it will channelize your efforts automatically. When you make a decision of purpose, then, you HAVE made a decision about future effort, a decision which will remain in effect UNLESS you change the DECISION.

18   Psychologists are in a good position to realize that the ego is capable of making and accepting as real some very distorted associations which are not true. The confusion of sex with aggression, and resulting behavior which is the same for BOTH, is a good example. This is understandable to the psychologist, and does not produce surprise. The lack of surprise, however, is NOT a sign of understanding. It is a symptom of the psychologist's ability to accept as reasonable a compromise which is clearly senseless, to attribute it to the mental illness of the patient rather than his own, and to limit his questions about both the patient AND himself to the trivial.

19   These relatively minor confusions of the ego are not among its more profound misassociations, although they DO reflect them. Your own egos have been blocking the more important questions which your minds should ask. You do NOT understand a patient while you yourselves are willing to limit the questions you raise about HIS mind, because you are also accepting these limits for YOURS. This makes you unable to heal him AND yourselves. Be ALWAYS unwilling to adapt to ANY situation in which miracle-mindedness is unthinkable. That state in ITSELF is enough to demonstrate that perception is wrong.

G. The Constant State

1   It cannot be emphasized too often that CORRECTING perception is merely a temporary expedient. [184] It is necessary ONLY because Misperception is a BLOCK to knowledge, while ACCURATE perception is a stepping-stone TOWARDS it. The whole value of right perception lies in the inevitable judgment which it necessarily entails that it is UNNECESSARY. This removes the block entirely.

2   You may ask how this is possible as long as you appear to be living in this world. And since this is a sensible question, it has a sensible answer. But you must be careful that you really understand the question. What IS the you who are living in this world?

---

184 This Chapter C. The Ego and False Autonomy, p23

Chapter 4 – The Root Of All Evil

Bill will probably have more trouble with this than you, but if he will try not to close his mind, he may decide that we are NOT engaging in denial after all.

3   To help him, it might be wise to review a number of the concepts with which he does not appear to have trouble, except at times. He liked the idea of invisibility, and was particularly open to the concept of different orders of reality. He also found the notion of varying densities of energy appealing. While he may yet agree that these are merely teaching aids, this is a good time to employ them.

4   Immortality is a constant state. It is as true now as it ever was or will be, because it implies NO CHANGE AT ALL. It is not a continuum, and it is NOT understood by comparing it with any opposite. Knowledge NEVER involves comparisons. That is its essential difference from everything else the mind can grasp.

5   "A little knowledge" is not dangerous except to the ego. Vaguely the ego senses threat, and, being unable to realize that "a little knowledge" is a meaningless phrase because "all" and "a little" in this context are the same, decides that since "all" is impossible, the fear does not lie in this. "A little," however, is a scarcity concept, and this the ego understands well. Regarding "all" as impossible, "a little" is perceived as the real threat.

6   The essential thing to remember always is that the ego DOES NOT RECOGNIZE the real source of its perceived threat. And if YOU associate yourself WITH the ego, YOU do not perceive the whole situation as it really is.

Only your allegiance to it gives the ego ANY power over you.

We have spoken of the ego as if it were a separate thing, acting on its own. This was necessary to persuade you that you cannot dismiss it lightly, and MUST realize how much of your thinking is ego-directed.

But we cannot safely leave it at that, or you will regard yourselves as necessarily conflicted as long as you are here, or more properly, BELIEVE that you are here.

7   The ego is nothing more than *a PART of your belief* about yourselves.

Your other life has continued without interruption, and has been and always will be totally unaffected by your attempts to dissociate. The ratio of repression and dissociation

G. The Constant State

of truth varies with the individual ego-illusion (tell Bill that phrase is VERY good), but dissociation is always involved, or you would not believe that you ARE here.

8   When I told Bill to concentrate on the phrase "here I am, Lord," [185] I did not mean "in this world" by "here." I wanted him to think of himself as a separate consciousness, capable of direct communication with the Creator of that consciousness. He, too, MUST begin to think of himself as a very powerful receiving and sending channel, a description I once gave you symbolically. Remember that HE understood it before you did, because you are more dissociative and less repressed.

9   Your great debt to each other is something you should never forget. It is exactly the same debt that you owe to me. Whenever you react egotistically towards each other, you are throwing away the graciousness of your indebtedness and the holy perception it would produce. The reason why the term "holy" can be used here is that, as you learn how much you ARE indebted to the whole Sonship which includes me, you come as close to knowledge as perception ever can. This gap is so small knowledge can easily flow across it and obliterate it forever.

10 You have very little trust in me as yet, but it will increase as you turn more and more often to me instead of to your egos for guidance.

The results will convince you increasingly that your choice in turning to me is the only sane one you can make.

No one who has learned from experience that one choice brings peace and joy while another brings chaos and disaster needs much conditioning.

The ego cannot withstand the conditioning process, because the process itself DEMONSTRATES that there is another way.

11 The classic conditioning by rewards model has always been most effective. Howard Hunt made a very good point in this connection, even though he did not understand that the real reason why conditioning through pain is not the most efficient method is because pain itself is an ego-illusion, and can never induce more than a temporary effect.

12 The rewards of God are immediately recognized as eternal. Since this recognition is made by YOU and NOT by your ego, the recognition ITSELF establishes that you and your ego CANNOT be identical. You may believe that you have already accepted the difference, but you are by no means convinced as yet. The very fact that you are preoccupied with the idea of escaping FROM the ego shows this.

13 You cannot escape from the ego by humbling it, or controlling it, or punishing it. The ego and the Soul DO NOT KNOW each other. The separated mind cannot maintain the separation EXCEPT by dissociating. Having done this, it utilizes repression against

---

185 Chapter 3 G. The Loss of Certainty, p46

Chapter 4 – The Root Of All Evil

all truly natural impulses, *not because the EGO is a separate thing, but because you want to believe that YOU are.*

> The ego is a device for maintaining this belief, but it is still only YOUR willingness to use the device that enables it to endure.

14   My trust in you is greater than yours in me at the moment, but it will not always be that way. Your mission is very simple. *You have been chosen to live so as to demonstrate that You are NOT an ego.* I repeat that I do not choose God's channels wrongly. [186] The Holy One shares my trust and always approves my Atonement decisions, because my will is never out of accord with His.

15   I have told you several times that I am in charge of the whole Atonement. [187] This is ONLY because I completed my part in it as a man, and can now complete it through other men. My chosen receiving and sending channels cannot fail, because I will lend them MY strength as long as theirs is wanting. I will go with you to the Holy One, and through MY perception HE can bridge the little gap. Your gratitude to each OTHER is the only gift I want. I will bring it to God for you, knowing that to know your brother IS to know God.

16   A little knowledge is an all-encompassing thing. If you are grateful to each other you are grateful to God for what He created. Through your gratitude you can come to know each other, and one moment of real recognition makes all men your brothers because they are all of your Father.

Love does not conquer all things, but it DOES set all things right.

17   Because you are all the Kingdom of God, I can lead you back to your own creations, which you do not yet know. God has kept them very safe in HIS knowing while your attention has wandered.

---

186 Chapter 3 F. Conflict and the Ego, p23 [Tim Note: Again, Jesus, the Source, is talking to each of us. As we each consciously begin to realize we are, and want to be about, awakening then we can be absolutely certain "we have been chosen" - because of our choosing to be about this.]

187 Chapter 1 B. Principles Of Miracles, Principle 26, p4; Principle 47, p5
[Tim Note: 'Jesus,' as when he says 'I' is a far greater awareness than an individual as we think of ourselves. Part of our mind may well rebel against the 'I am in charge' statement. However, that 'I' is the entire Christ Mind, or right-minded part of the One Mind of the Sonship, of which I, we, are also a part. That *part* of OUR Mind is in charge, not separated mind. It speaks to us, as in this channeled Course, as an Entity we can comprehend, i.e. Jesus.]

G. The Constant State

Bill gave you a very important idea when he told you that what has been dissociated IS STILL THERE. I am grateful to him for that, and I hope he will not decide that it is true only for you. Even though dissociation is much more apparent in you, and repression is much more evident in him, each of you utilizes both.

18   Wisdom always dictates that a therapist work through WEAKER defenses first.

That is why I suggested to Bill that he persuade you to deal with REPRESSION first. We have only just about reached the point where dissociation means much to you, because it is so important to your misbeliefs. Bill might do well, - and you could help him here, - to concentrate more on HIS dissociative tendencies and not try to deal with repression yet.

19   I hinted at this when I remarked on his habit of disengaging himself, and when I spoke to him about distantiation. These are all forms of dissociation, and these weaker forms were always more evident in him than in you. That is because dissociation was so extreme in your case that you did not have to hide it because you were not aware that it was there. Bill, on the other hand, DOES dissociate more than he thinks, and that is why he cannot listen. He does not need to go through the same course in repression that you did, because he will give up his major misdefense AFTER he has rid himself of the lesser ones.

20   Do not disturb yourself about repression, Bill, but DO train yourself to be alert to any tendency to withdraw from your brothers. Withdrawal is frightening, and you do not recognize all the forms it takes in you. Helen is right that she will experience things that will cut across all her perceptions because of their stunning knowledge. You were right that this will occur when she learns to recognize what she ALREADY knows and has dissociated.

21   You, Bill, will learn somewhat differently, because you are afraid of all complete involvements, and believe that they lessen YOU. You have learned to be so much more clear-sighted about this that you should be ready to oppose it in yourself RELATIVELY easily. As you come closer to a brother, you DO approach me, and as you withdraw from him I become distant to you.

22   Your giant step forward was to INSIST on a collaborative venture. This does NOT go against the true spirit of meditation at all. It is inherent IN it. Meditation is a collaborative venture with GOD. It CANNOT be undertaken successfully by those who disengage themselves from the Sonship, because they are disengaging themselves from me.

God will come to you only as you will give Him to your brothers. Learn first of them, and you will be ready to hear God as you hear them. That is because the function of love is One.

Chapter 4 – The Root Of All Evil

23 How can you teach someone the value of something he has thrown away deliberately? He must have thrown it away because he did NOT value it. You can only show him how miserable he is WITHOUT it, and bring it near very slowly, so he can learn how his misery lessens as he approaches it. This conditions him to associate his misery with its ABSENCE, and to associate the OPPOSITE of misery with its presence. It gradually becomes desirable, as he changes his mind about its worth.

24 I am conditioning you to associate misery with the ego, and joy with your Soul. You have conditioned yourself the other way around. But a far greater reward will break through any conditioning, if it is repeatedly offered when the old habit is broken. You are still free to choose. But can you really WANT the rewards of the ego in the presence of the rewards of God?

H. Creation and Communication

1 It should be clear that, while the content of any particular ego - illusion does not matter, it is usually more helpful to correct it in a specific context. Bill is right that you are too abstract in this matter. Ego-illusions are QUITE specific, although they frequently change, and although the mind is naturally abstract, it became concrete voluntarily as soon as it split. However, only PART of it splits, so only PART of it is concrete.

2 The concrete part is the same part that believes in the ego, because the ego DEPENDS on the specific. It is the part that believes your existence means you are SEPARATE. Everything the ego perceives is a separate whole, without the relationships that imply BEING. The ego is thus AGAINST communication, except in so far as it is utilized to ESTABLISH separateness, rather than to abolish it.

3 The communication system of the ego is based on its own thought-system, as is everything else it dictates. Its communication is controlled by its need to protect itself, and it will disrupt communication when it experiences threat. While this is always so, individual egos perceive different kinds of threat, which are quite specific in their own judgment. For example, although all forms of perceived demands may be classified, or judged, by the ego as coercive communication which must be disrupted, the response of breaking communication will nevertheless be to a SPECIFIC PERSON or persons.

4 The specificity of the ego's thinking, then, results in a spurious kind of generalization, which is really not abstract at all. It will respond in certain specific ways to all stimuli which it perceives as related. In contrast, the Soul reacts in the same way to everything it know is true, and does not respond at all to anything else. Nor does it make any attempt to ESTABLISH what is true. It knows that what is true is everything that

H. Creation and Communication

God created. It is in complete and direct communication with every aspect of Creation, because it is in complete and direct communication with its Creator.

5 THIS communication IS the will of God. Creation and communication are synonymous. God created every mind by communicating His Mind to it, thus establishing it forever as a channel for the reception of His Mind and Will. Since only beings of a like order can truly communicate. His Creations naturally communicate WITH Him and communicate LIKE Him. This communication is perfectly abstract, in that its quality is universal in application, and not subject to ANY judgment, ANY exception, or ANY alteration.

6 God made you BY this and FOR this. The mind can distort its functions, but it cannot endow itself with those it was not given. That is why the mind cannot totally lose the ability to communicate, even though it may refuse to utilize it on behalf of being. Existence as well as being rests on communication.

7 Existence is SPECIFIC in how, what, and with whom communication is worth undertaking. Being is completely without these distinctions. It is a state in which the mind IS in communication with everything that is real, including its own Soul. To whatever extent you permit this state to be curtailed, you are limiting your sense of your OWN reality, which becomes total only by recognizing ALL reality in the glorious context of its real relationship to YOU. This IS your reality. Do not desecrate it or recoil from it. It is your real home, your real temple, [188] and your real self.

8 God, who encompasses ALL Being, nevertheless created separate [189] beings who have everything individually, but who want to share it to increase their joy. Nothing that is real can be increased EXCEPT by sharing it. That is why God Himself created you. Divine Abstraction takes joy in application, and that is what creation MEANS. How, what, and to whom are irrelevant, because real creation gives everything since it can only create like itself. Remember that in being, there is no difference between having and being, as there is in existence. In the state of being, the mind gives everything always. [190]

9 The Bible repeatedly states that you should praise God. This hardly means that you should tell Him how wonderful He is. He has no ego with which to accept thanks, and no perceptions with which to judge your offerings. But unless you take your part in the creation, His joy is not complete because YOURS is incomplete. And THIS He does know. He knows it in his own Being and its experience of His Sons' experience. The

---

188 1 Corinthians 3:16 Do you not know that you are the temple of God and that the Spirit of God dwells in you?

189 Separate as in individual with self-awareness of Being; not as separated entities, which is the erroneous state of separation man is now in. There is a difference we grow in awareness of.

190 The 'meaning' of this paragraph can only be EXPERIENCED in deep stillness and awareness of Being. It cannot be 'understood' by the human mind, but we CAN experience it.

Chapter 4 – The Root Of All Evil

constant GOING OUT of His love is blocked when His Channels are closed, and He IS lonely when the minds He created do not communicate fully with Him.

10   God HAS kept your kingdom for you, but He cannot share His joy with you until you know it with your whole mind. Even revelation is not enough, because it is communication FROM God. But it is not enough until it is shared. God does not need revelation returned to Him, which would clearly be impossible, but He DOES want revelation brought to others. This cannot be done with the actual revelation, because its content cannot be expressed, and it is intensely personal to the mind which receives it. But it can still be returned BY that mind through its attitudes to other minds which the knowledge from the revelation brings.

11   God is praised whenever any mind learns to be wholly helpful. This is impossible without being wholly harmless, because the two beliefs cannot coexist. The truly helpful are invulnerable, because they are NOT protecting their egos, so that nothing CAN hurt them. Their helpfullness IS their praise of God, and He will return their praise of Him, because they are like Him and can rejoice together. God goes out to them and through them, and there is great joy throughout the Kingdom. Every mind that is changed adds to this joy with its own individual willingness to share in it.

12   The truly helpful are God's miracle-workers, whom I direct until we are all united in the joy of the kingdom. I will direct you to wherever you can be truly helpful, and to whoever can follow my guidance through you.

I arranged for Bill to attend the rehabilitation meetings for very good reasons, and I want him to know them so we can share our goal there.

I. True Rehabilitation

1   Properly speaking, every mind which is split needs rehabilitation. The medical orientation emphasizes the body, and the vocational orientation stresses the ego. The team approach generally leads more to confusion than anything else, because it is too often misused as an expedient for sharing the ego's dominion with other ego's rather than as a real experiment in cooperation of minds.

2   The reason why Bill needs this experience is because he needs rehabilitating himself. How often have I answered "help him" when you asked me to help you? He, too, has asked for help, and he has been helped whenever he was truly helpful to you. He has also gained to whatever extent he could give. He will help YOU more truly by going, if he can remember all the time he is there that his ONLY reason for being there is to REPRESENT ME.

I. True Rehabilitation

3   Rehabilitation, as a movement, has been an improvement over overt neglect, but it is often little more than a painful attempt on the part of the halt to lead the blind. Bill, you will see this at every meeting. But this is not why you were chosen to go.

    You have a fear of broken bodies, because your ego cannot tolerate them. Your ego cannot tolerate ego-weakness, either, without ambivalence, because it is afraid of its own weakness and the weakness of its chosen home.

4   That is really why you recoil from the demands of the dependent, and from the sight of a broken body. Your ego is threatened, and blocks your natural impulse to help, placing you under the strain of divided will. You withdraw to allow your ego to recover, and to regain enough strength to be helpful again on a basis limited enough NOT to threaten your ego, but also too limited to give YOU joy.

5   Those with broken bodies are often looked down on by the ego, because of its belief that nothing but a perfect body is worthy as its OWN temple. A mind that recoils from a hurt body is in great need of rehabilitation itself. A damaged brain is also hardly a danger. ALL symptoms of hurt need true helpfullness, and whenever they are met with this, the mind that so meets them heals ITSELF.

6   Rehabilitation is an attitude of praising God as He Himself knows praise. He offers praise to you, and you must offer it to others. The real limitations on clinical psychology, as it is evaluated by its followers at present, are not reflected by the attitudes of psychiatrists, or medical boards, or hospital administrators, even though most of them are sadly in need of rehabilitation themselves.

7   The real handicaps of the clinicians lie in their attitudes to those whom their egos perceive as weakened and damaged. By these evaluations, they have weakened and damaged their own helpfullness, and have thus set their own rehabilitation back. Rehabilitation is NOT concerned with the ego's fight for control, nor the ego's need to avoid and withdraw.

8   Bill, you can do much on behalf of your own rehabilitation AND Helen's, and much more universally as well, if you think of the Princeton meetings in this way:

> I am here ONLY to be truly helpful.
> I am here to represent Christ, who sent me.
> I do not have to worry about what to say or what to do, [191]
> because the one who sent me will direct me.
> I am content to be wherever He wishes,
> knowing he goes there with me.
> I will be healed as I let him teach me to heal.

---

[191] Matthew 10:19 But when they deliver you up, do not worry about how or what you should speak. For it will be given to you in that hour what you should speak;

Chapter 5 – Healing And Wholeness

A. Introduction

1   To heal is to make happy. I told you once to think how many opportunities you have to gladden yourselves, and how many you have refused. [192] This is exactly the same as telling you that you have refused to heal yourselves. The light that belongs in you is the light of joy. Radiance is not associated with sorrow. Depression is often contagious, but although it may affect those who come in contact with it, they do not yield to its influence wholeheartedly. But joy calls forth an integrated willingness to share in it, and thus promotes the mind's natural impulse to RESPOND AS ONE.

2   Those who attempt to heal without being wholly joyous themselves call forth different kinds of responses at the same time, and thus deprive others of the joy of responding wholeheartedly.

    To be wholehearted, you MUST be happy. If fear and love cannot coexist, and if it is impossible to be wholly fearful and remain alive, then the only possible whole state IS that of love. There is no difference between love and joy. Therefore, the only possible whole state IS the wholly joyous.

3   To heal, or to make joyous, is therefore the same as to integrate and MAKE ONE. That is why it makes no difference TO what part or BY what part of the Sonship the healing is done. EVERY part benefits, and benefits equally. YOU are being blessed by every beneficent thought of any of your brothers anywhere. You should want to bless them in return, out of gratitude.

4   You do not have to know them individually, or they you. The light of joy is so strong that it radiates throughout the Sonship and returns thanks to the Father for radiating HIS joy upon it. Only God's own holy children are worthy to be channels of his beautiful joy, because only they are beautiful enough to hold it by sharing it. It is impossible for a Child of God to love his neighbor EXCEPT as himself. [193]

    That is why the healer's prayer is,

        "Let me know this brother as I know myself."

---

192 Chapter 4 E. The Escape From Fear a. This Need Not Be, p11
193 Matthew 22:36 Master, which is the great commandment in the law?
    37 Jesus said unto him, "Thou shalt love the Lord thy God with all thy heart, and with all thy soul, and with all thy mind. 38 This is the first and great commandment.
    39 And the second is like unto it, Thou shalt love thy neighbour as thyself.
    40 On these two commandments hang all the law and the prophets."

B. Healing as Joining

1   *Healing is an act of thought by which two minds perceive their oneness, and become glad.* This gladness calls to every part of the Sonship to rejoice with them, and lets God Himself go out into them and through them. Only the healed mind can experience revelation with lasting effect, because revelation is an experience of pure joy. If you do not will to be wholly joyous, your mind cannot HAVE what it does not will to BE.

2   Remember that the Soul knows no difference between being and having. The higher mind thinks according to the laws which the Soul obeys, and therefore honors only the laws of God. To Him, getting is meaningless, and giving is all. Having everything, the Soul HOLDS everything by GIVING it, thus creating as the Father created.

3   If you think about it, you will see that, while this kind of thinking is totally alien to having THINGS, even to the lower mind it is quite comprehensible in connection with IDEAS. If you share a physical possession, you DO divide its ownership. But if you share an IDEA, you do NOT lessen it. ALL of it is still yours, although all of it has been given away. Further, if the person to whom you give it accepts it as HIS, he reinforces it in YOUR mind, and thus INCREASES it.

4   If you can accept the concept that the world IS one of ideas, the whole belief in the false association which the ego has made between giving and LOSING is gone. Let us start our process of re-awakening with just a few simple concepts:

> Thoughts INCREASE by being given away.
> The more who BELIEVE in them, the STRONGER they become.
> EVERYTHING is an idea.
> How, then, is it possible that giving and losing can be meaningfully associated?

5   This is the invitation to the Holy Spirit. I told you that I could reach up and bring the Holy Spirit down to you. [194] But I can bring Him to you only at your own invitation.

The Holy Spirit is nothing more than your own right mind.

He was also mine. The Bible says, "May the mind be in you that was also in Christ Jesus," [195] and uses this as a BLESSING. It is the blessing of miracle-mindedness. It asks that you may think as I thought, joining with me in Christ-thinking.

6   The Holy Spirit is the only part of the Holy Trinity which is symbolic. He is referred to in the Bible as the Healer, the Comforter, and the Guide. He is also described as

---

194 Chapter 1 B. Principles Of Miracles Principle 47, p7
195 Philippians 2:5 Let this mind be in you, which was also in Christ Jesus:

Chapter 5 – Healing And Wholeness

something separate, apart from the Father and from the Son. I myself said, "and if I go I will send you ANOTHER comforter, and he will abide with you." [196]

7   The Holy Spirit is a difficult concept to grasp, precisely because it IS symbolic, and therefore open to many different interpretations. As a man and as one of God's creations, my right thinking, which came from the Universal Inspiration which IS the Holy Spirit, taught me first and foremost that this Inspiration is for ALL. I could not have it myself without knowing that.

8   The word "know" is proper here, because the Holy Inspiration is so close to knowledge that it calls it forth, or better, allows it to come. We have spoken before of the higher or true perception, which is so close to truth that God Himself can flow across the little gap. [197] Knowledge is always ready to flow everywhere, but it cannot oppose. Therefore you can obstruct it, although you can never lose it.

9   The Holy Spirit is the Christ mind that senses the knowledge that lies beyond perception.

It came into being with the separation as a protection, and inspired the beginning of the Atonement at the same time. Before that, there was no need for healing and no-one was comfortless.

C. The Mind of the Atonement

1   God honored even the miscreations of His Children because they had made them. But he also blessed them with a way of thinking about them that could raise their perceptions until they became so lofty that they could reach almost back to Him.

2   The Holy Spirit is the mind of the Atonement. It represents a state of mind that comes close enough to one-mindedness that transfer is at last possible. As you well know, transfer depends on common elements in the old learning and the new situation to which it is transferred.

Perception is not knowledge, but it can be TRANSFERRED to knowledge, or CROSS OVER into it. It might even be more helpful here to use the literal meaning "carried over," for the last step is taken by God.

---

196 John 14:15 If ye love me, keep my commandments.
   16 And I will pray the Father, and he shall give you another Comforter, that he may abide with you for ever; 17 Even the Spirit of truth; whom the world cannot receive, because it seeth him not, neither knoweth him: but ye know him; for he dwelleth with you, and shall be in you.
   18 I will not leave you comfortless: I will come to you.
197 Chapter 4 G. The Constant State, p9

C. The Mind of the Atonement

3   The Holy Spirit, the shared Inspiration of all the Sonship, induces a kind of perception in which many elements are like those in the Kingdom of Heaven Itself:

4   First, its universality is perfectly clear, and no-one who receives it could ever believe for one instant that sharing it involves anything BUT gain.

5   Second, it is incapable of attack, and is therefore truly open. This means that although it does not engender knowledge, it does not obstruct it in any way.

Third, it is an unequivocal call to love.

6   There is a point at which sufficient quantitative changes produce real qualitative differences. The next point requires real understanding, because it is the point at which the shift occurs.

7   Finally, it points the way beyond the healing which it brings, and leads the mind beyond its own integration into the paths of creation.

8   Healing is not creating; it is reparation. The Holy Spirit promotes healing by looking beyond it, to what the children of God were before healing was needed, and will be when they have BEEN healed. This alteration of the time sequence should be quite familiar, because it is very similar to the shift in time perception which the miracle introduces. [198]

9   The Holy Spirit is the MOTIVATION for miracle-mindedness.
    It is the will to HEAL the separation by letting it go. It is IN you because God placed it in your mind, and although you can keep it asleep you cannot obliterate it. God Himself keeps it alive by transmitting it from His Mind to yours as long as there is time. It is partly His will and partly yours. The miracle itself is just this fusion or union of will between Father and Son.

10 The Holy Spirit is the Spirit of Joy.
    It is the call to return, with which God blessed the minds of the separated Sons. This the vocation of the mind. It had no calling until the separation, because before it had only BEING, and would not have understood the call to right thinking.

---

[198] Chapter 1 B. Principles Of Miracles Principle 14; Principle 49; Principle 50

Chapter 5 – Healing And Wholeness

The Holy Spirit was God's answer to the separation, the means by which the Atonement could repair until the whole mind returned to creating. The Atonement and the separation began at the same time. When man made the ego, God placed in him the call of joy. This call is so strong that the ego always dissolves at its sound.

11   That is why you can choose to listen to two voices within you. One you made yourself, and that one is not of God. But the other is given you by God, Who asks you only to listen to it.

The Holy Spirit IS in you in a very literal sense. It is the voice that calls you back to where you were before and will be again.

D. The Voice for God

1   It is possible even in this world to hear ONLY that voice and no other. It takes effort and great willingness to learn. It is the final lesson that I learned, and God's Sons are as equal as learners as they are as Souls. The voice of the Holy Spirit IS the call to Atonement, or the restoration of the integrity of the mind. When the Atonement is complete and the whole Sonship is healed, there will be no call to return, but what God creates is eternal. The Holy Spirit will remain with the Sons of God, to bless THEIR creations and keep them in the light of joy.

2   You ARE the Kingdom of Heaven, but you have let the belief in darkness enter your minds, and so you need a new light. The Holy Spirit is the radiance that you must let banish the idea of darkness. His is the glory before which dissociation falls away, and the Kingdom of Heaven breaks through into its own.

3   Before the separation you did not need guidance. You KNEW as you will know again, but you do not know now. God does not guide, because He can share only PERFECT KNOWLEDGE. Guidance is EVALUATIVE, because it implies that there is a RIGHT way and also a WRONG way, one to be chosen and the other avoided. By choosing one, you give up the other. This IS a conflict state. It MEANS that knowledge has been lost, because knowledge is SURE.

4   God is not in you; YOU are part of HIM. When you willed to leave Him, He gave you a voice to speak FOR Him, because He could no longer share His knowledge with you without hindrance. Direct communication was broken, because you had made another voice through another will. The Holy Spirit calls you both to remember and forget. You have chosen to be in a state of opposition, in which opposites are possible. As a result, there ARE choices which you must make. In the holy state, the will is free in the sense that its CREATIVE power is unlimited, but choice itself is meaningless.

D. The Voice for God

5 Freedom to choose is the same POWER as freedom to create, but its APPLICATION is different. Choosing MEANS divided will. The Holy Spirit is one way of choosing. This way is in you BECAUSE there is also another way. God did not leave His Children comfortless, even though they left Him. The voice they put in their minds was NOT the voice of His Will, for which the Holy Spirit speaks. The call to return is stronger than the call to depart, but it speaks in a different way.

6 The voice of the Holy Spirit does not command, because it is incapable of arrogance.

It does not demand, because it does not seek control.

It does not overcome, because it does not attack.

It merely REMINDS.

It is compelling only because of what it reminds you OF. It brings to your mind the OTHER way, remaining quiet even in the midst of the turmoil you have made for yourselves. The voice for God is always quiet, because it speaks of peace. Yet peace is stronger than war, because it heals. War is DIVISION, not increase. No-one gains from strife.

7 "What profiteth a man if he gain the whole world and lose his own Soul?" [199] This means that if he listens to the wrong voice, he has LOST SIGHT of his Soul. He CANNOT lose it, but he CAN not know it. It is therefore LOST TO HIM, until he chooses right. The Holy Spirit is your guide in choosing. He is the part of your mind which ALWAYS speaks for the right choice, because he speaks for God. He is your remaining communication with God, which you can interrupt, but cannot destroy.

8 The Holy Spirit is the way in which God's will can be done on earth as it is in Heaven. Both Heaven and Earth are in YOU, because the call of both are in your wills, and therefore in your minds. The voice for God comes from your own altars to Him. These altars are not THINGS. They are DEVOTIONS.

But you have other devotions now. Your divided devotion has given you the two voices, and you must choose at which altar you will to serve. The call you answer now IS an evaluation, because it is a DECISION. The decision itself is very simple. It is made on the basis of which call is worth more to you.

---

[199] Matthew 16:26 For what is a man profited, if he shall gain the whole world, and lose his own soul? or what shall a man give in exchange for his soul?
Mark 8:36 For what shall it profit a man, if he shall gain the whole world, and lose his own soul?

Chapter 5 – Healing And Wholeness

9 My mind will always be like yours, because we were created as equals. It was only my DECISION that gave me all power in Heaven and earth. My only gift to you is to help you make the same decision FOR YOURSELF. The will for this decision is the will to SHARE it, because the decision itself IS the decision to share. It is MADE BY GIVING, and is therefore the one act of mind that resembles true creation.

10 You understand the role of models in the learning process, and the importance of the models you value and choose to follow in determining what you will to learn. I am your model for decision. *By deciding for God, I showed you that this decision CAN be made, and that YOU can make it.* I promised you that the mind that made the decision for me is also in YOU, and that you can let it change you just as it changed me. This mind is unequivocal, because it hears only ONE VOICE, and answers in ONE WAY.

11 You are the light of the world with me. Rest does not come from sleeping, but from waking. The Holy Spirit is the call to awake and be glad. The world is very tired, because it is the IDEA of weariness. Our task is the joyous one of waking it to the call for God. Everyone will answer the call of the Holy Spirit, or the Sonship cannot be as one. What better vocation could there be for any part of the Kingdom than to restore it to the perfect integration that can make it whole?

12 Hear only this through the Holy Spirit within you, and teach your brothers to listen as I am teaching you. When you are tempted by the wrong voice, call on me to remind you how to heal by sharing my decision and MAKING IT STRONGER. As we share this goal, we increase its power to attract the whole Sonship, and to bring it back into the Oneness in which it was created.

13 Remember that "Yolk" means "join together," and "burden" means message. Let us reconsider the biblical statement "my yolk is easy and my burden light" [200] in this way. Let us join together, for my message is Light.

14 I came to your minds because you had grown vaguely aware of the fact that there is another way, or another voice. Having given this invitation to the Holy Spirit, I could come to provide the model for HOW TO THINK.

15 Psychology has become the study of BEHAVIOR, but no-one denies the basic law that behavior is a response to MOTIVATION, and motivation is will. I have enjoined you to behave as I behaved, but we must respond to the same mind to do this. This mind is the Holy Spirit, whose will is for God always. It teaches you how to keep me as the model for your thought, and behave like me as a result.

---

[200] Matthew 11:28 Come unto me, all ye that labour and are heavy laden, and I will give you rest.
29 Take my yoke upon you, and learn of me; for I am meek and lowly in heart: and ye shall find rest unto your souls. 30 For my yoke is easy, and my burden is light.

16   The power of our joint motivation is beyond belief, but NOT beyond accomplishment. What we can accomplish together has no limits, because the call for God IS the call to the unlimited. Child of God, my message is for YOU, to hear and give away as you answer the Holy Spirit within you.

E. The Guide to Salvation

1   The way to LEARN TO KNOW your brother is by perceiving the Holy Spirit in him. We have already said that the Holy Spirit is the bridge or thought-transfer of perception TO knowledge, [201] so we CAN use the terms as if they were related, because in HIS mind they are. This relationship MUST be in His mind, because unless it were, the separation between the two ways of thinking would not be open to healing. He is part of the Holy Trinity, because His Mind is partly YOURS and also PARTLY GOD'S. This needs clarification not in statement, since we have said this before, but in EXPERIENCE.

2   The Holy Spirit is the IDEA of healing. Being thought, the idea GAINS AS IT IS SHARED. Being the call FOR God, it is also the idea OF God. If you are part of God, it is also the idea of YOURSELF, as well as of all the parts of God. The idea of the Holy Spirit shares the property of other ideas, because it follows the laws of the universe of which IT is a part. Therefore, it is strengthened by being given away. It increases in YOU as you give it to your brothers.

3   *Since thoughts do not have to be conscious to exist, your brother does NOT have to be AWARE of the Holy Spirit, either in himself or in you for this miracle to occur.* He may have dissociated the call for God, just as YOU have. But the dissociation is healed in BOTH of you as you see it in him, and thus acknowledge its BEING.

    Bill, who has made a number of vital contributions to our joint venture, made a major one a while ago, which he himself did not appreciate or even understand. If we recognize its value together, we will be able to use it together, because it is an idea, and must therefore be shared to be held.

4   When Bill said that he was determined "NOT to see you that way," he was speaking negatively. If he will state the same idea POSITIVELY, he will see the POWER of what he said. He had realized that there are two ways of seeing you, and also that they are diametrically opposed to one another. These two ways must be in HIS mind, because he was referring to HIMSELF as the perceiver. They must also be in YOURS, because he was perceiving YOU.

---

201 Chapter 4 G. The Constant State, p15

Chapter 5 – Healing And Wholeness

5   What he was really saying was that he would NOT look at you through HIS ego, or perceive YOUR ego in you. Stated positively, he would see you through the Holy Spirit in HIS mind, and perceive it in YOURS.

What you acknowledge in your brother, you ARE acknowledging in yourself. What you share you STRENGTHEN. The voice of the Holy Spirit IS weak in you. That is why you MUST share it, because it must be INCREASED in strength before YOU can hear it. It is impossible to hear it in yourself while it is so weak in your OWN mind. It is NOT weak in itself; but it IS limited by your unwillingness to hear it.

6   Will itself is an idea, and is therefore strengthened by being shared. You have made the mistake of looking for the Holy Spirit in YOURSELVES, and that is why your meditations have frightened you. By adopting the ego's viewpoint, you undertook an ego-alien journey WITH THE EGO AS GUIDE. This was BOUND to produce fear.

Bill's better idea needs to be strengthened in BOTH of you. Since it was HIS, HE can increase it by giving it to you.

7   Delay is of the ego, because time is ITS concept. Delay is obviously a TIME idea. Both time AND delay are meaningless in eternity. We have said before that the Holy Spirit is God's answer to the ego. Everything of which the Holy Spirit reminds you is in direct opposition to the ego's notions, because true and false perceptions are THEMSELVES opposed. The Holy Spirit has the task of UNDOING what the ego has made. It must undo it in the same realm of discourse in which the ego itself operates, or the mind would be unable to understand the change. We have repeatedly emphasized the fact that one level of the mind is not understandable to another. So it is with the ego and the soul, and with time and eternity.

8   Eternity is an idea of God, so the soul understands it perfectly. Time is a belief of the ego, so the lower mind, which IS the ego's domain, accepts it without question. The only aspect of time which is really eternal is NOW. That is what we REALLY mean when we say that now is the only time. The literal nature of this statement does not mean anything to the ego. It interprets it, at best, to mean "don't worry about the future." This is NOT what it really means at all.

9   The Holy Spirit is the mediator between the interpretations of the ego and the knowledge of the Soul. Its ability to deal with symbols enables it to work AGAINST the ego's beliefs in its own language. Its equal ability to look BEYOND symbols into eternity also enables it to understand the laws of God, for which it speaks.

10 It can thus perform the function of RE-INTERPRETING what the ego makes, not by destruction, but by understanding. Understanding is light, and light leads to knowledge. The Holy Spirit is IN light, because it is IN YOU who ARE light. But you yourselves do

E. The Guide to Salvation

not know this. It is therefore the task of the Holy Spirit to re-interpret you on behalf of God.

11   You cannot understand yourselves alone. This is because you have no meaning apart from your rightful place in the Sonship, and the rightful place of the Sonship in God. This is your life, your eternity, and YOURSELF. It is of this that the Holy Spirit reminds you. It is this that the Holy Spirit SEES. This vision invariably frightens the ego, because it is so calm. Peace is the ego's greatest enemy, because according to ITS interpretation of reality, war is the guarantee of its survival. The ego becomes strong in strife because if you believe there is strife, you will react viciously because the idea of danger has entered your mind. This idea itself IS an appeal to the ego.

12   The Holy Spirit is as vigilant as the ego to the call of danger, opposing it with ITS strength just as the ego WELCOMES it with all its might. The Holy Spirit counters this welcome by welcoming peace. Peace and eternity are as closely related as are time and war. Perception as well as knowledge derive meaning from RELATIONSHIPS. Those which you accept are the foundations of your beliefs.

13   The Separation is merely another term for a split mind. It was not an act, but a thought. Therefore, the idea of Separation can be given away, just as the idea of unity can, and either way, it will be STRENGTHENED IN THE MIND OF THE GIVER. The ego is the symbol of the Separation, just as the Holy Spirit is the symbol of peace. What you perceive in others you are STRENGTHENING IN YOUR SELF.

You let your mind misperceive, but the Holy Spirit lets your mind re-interpret its own misperceptions. The Holy Spirit is the perfect teacher. It uses only what your minds ALREADY understand, to teach you that you do not understand it.

14   The Holy Spirit can deal with an unwilling learner without going counter to his will, because part of his will IS still for God. Despite the ego's attempts to conceal this part, it is still much stronger than the ego, even though the ego does not recognize it. The Holy Spirit recognizes it perfectly, because it is its own dwelling place, or the place in the mind where it is at home. YOU are at home there, too, because it is a place of peace, and peace is of God.

15   You who are part of God are not at home EXCEPT in His peace. If peace is eternal, you are at home only in eternity. The ego made the world as IT perceives it, but the Holy Spirit, the RE-INTERPRETER of what the ego made, sees it only as a teaching device for bringing you home. The Holy Spirit must perceive time and re-interpret it into the timeless. The mind must be led into eternity THROUGH time, because having made time it is capable of perceiving its opposite.

16   The Holy Spirit must work through opposites, because it must work with and for a mind that IS in opposition. Correct and learn, and be open to learning. You have NOT

Chapter 5 – Healing And Wholeness

made truth, but truth can still set you free. Look as the Holy Spirit looks, and understand as He understands. His understanding looks back to God, in remembrance of Me. He is in Holy Communion always, and He is part of YOU. He is your guide to salvation, because he holds the remembrance of things past and to come. He holds this gladness gently in your minds, asking only that you INCREASE it in His name by sharing it to increase His joy in YOU.

F. Therapy and Teaching

1   You must have noticed how often I have used your own ideas to help YOU.

B. is right is saying that you have learned to be a loving, wise, and very understanding therapist, except for yourself. That exception has given you more than perception for others because of what you saw in them, but less than knowledge of your real relationships TO them because you did NOT make them part OF you.

Understanding IS beyond perception, because it introduces meaning. But it is below knowledge, even though it can grow TOWARDS it. It is possible, with great effort, to understand someone else and to be helpful to him, but the effort is misdirected. The misdirection is quite apparent. It is directed AWAY from you.

2   This does NOT mean that it is lost to you, but it DOES mean that you are not aware of it. I have saved all of your kindnesses and every loving thought you have had, and I assure you, you have had many. I have purified them of errors which hid their light, and have kept them for you in their own perfect radiance. They are beyond destruction and beyond guilt. They came from the Holy Spirit within YOU, and we know that what God creates is eternal.

3   Bill once spoke of the Kingdom in this way, because he yearns for what he has repressed. You are much more afraid of it, because dissociation is more fearful. B's better contact has allowed him the strength to retain the fear in awareness, and to resort to displacement, which he is learning to overcome with YOUR help. That is because you do not perceive HIM as dissociated, and can help him with his repression, which does not frighten you. He, on the other hand, has no difficulty in seeing YOU dissociate, and does not have to deal with repression in you, which WOULD produce fear in him.

4   Joining in Atonement, which I have repeatedly asked you to do, is ALWAYS a way OUT of fear. This does not mean that you can safely fail to acknowledge anything that is true, but the Holy Spirit will not fail to help you re-interpret EVERYTHING that you perceive as fearful, and teach you ONLY what is loving IS true. It is beyond your ability to destroy, but entirely within your grasp. It BELONGS to you because YOU created it. It is yours because it is part of you, just as you are part of God, because He created you.

F. Therapy and Teaching

5 The Atonement is the GUARANTEE of the safety of the Kingdom. Nothing good is lost, because it comes from the Holy Spirit, the voice for Creation. Nothing that is not good was ever created, and therefore CANNOT be protected. What the ego makes it KEEPS TO ITSELF, and so it is without strength. Its unshared existence does not die. It was merely never born. Real birth is not a beginning; it is a CONTINUING. Everything that CAN continue has already BEEN born. But it can INCREASE as you are willing to return the part of your mind that needs healing to the higher part, and thus render your creating (creation) undivided.

6 You yourself always told your patients that the real difference between neurotic and 'healthy' guilt feelings was that neurotic guilt feelings DO NOT HELP ANYONE. This distinction was very wise, though incomplete. Let us make the distinction a little sharper now.

Neurotic guilt feelings are a device of the ego for "atoning" without sharing, and for asking for pardon without change. The ego NEVER calls for real atonement, and cannot tolerate real forgiveness, which IS change.

7 Your concept of "healthy guilt feelings" has great merit, but without the concept of the Atonement it lacked the healing potential it held. YOU make the distinction in terms of feelings which led to a decision not to REPEAT the error, which is only PART of healing. *Your concept therefore lacked the idea of UNDOING it.* What you were really advocating, then, was adopting a policy of sharing without a real FOUNDATION.

8 I have come to give you the foundation, so your own thoughts can make you REALLY free. You have carried the burden of the ideas you did NOT share, and which were therefore too weak to increase, but you did NOT recognize how to UNDO their existence because you HAD made them. *You CANNOT cancel out your past errors alone. They will NOT disappear from your mind without remedy. The remedy is NOT of your making, any more than YOU are.*

9 The Atonement cannot be understood except as a PURE ACT OF SHARING. That is what is meant when we said that it is possible even in this world to listen to ONE voice. If you are part of God, and the Sonship is one, you CANNOT be limited to the self the ego sees. Every loving thought held in ANY part of the Sonship belongs to every part.

It is shared BECAUSE it is loving. Sharing is God's way of creating, and also YOURS. Your ego can keep you in exile FROM the Kingdom but in the Kingdom itself it has no power.

10 You have become willing to receive my messages as I give them, without interference by the ego, so we can clarify an earlier point which was mentioned before.

Chapter 5 – Healing And Wholeness

We said that you will one day teach as much as you learn, and that will keep you in balance. [202] The time is now, because you have let it be now. You cannot learn EXCEPT by teaching. I heard one voice because I had learned that learning is attained BY teaching. I understood that I COULD NOT ATONE FOR MYSELF ALONE.

11 Listening to one voice MEANS the will to share the voice to hear it yourself. The mind that was in me is still irresistibly drawn to every mind created by God, because God's wholeness IS the wholeness of his Son.

> Turning the other cheek [203] does NOT mean that you should submit to violence without protest.
> It means that you cannot be hurt, and do not want to show your brother anything except your wholeness.

Show him that he CANNOT hurt you,
and hold nothing against him, or you hold it against yourself.

12 Teaching is done in many ways, by formal means, by guidance, and above all BY EXAMPLE. If you will to learn, you MUST will to teach. Teaching is therapy because it means the sharing of ideas, and the awareness that to share them is to strengthen them. The union of the Sonship IS its protection.

The ego cannot prevail against the Kingdom BECAUSE it is united, and the ego fades away and is undone in the presence of the attraction of the parts of the Sonship which hear the call of the Holy Spirit to be as One.

13 I cannot forget my need to teach what I have learned which arose in me BECAUSE I learned it. I call upon you to teach what you have learned, because by so doing YOU can depend on it. Make it dependable in my name, because my name is the name of God's Son. What I learned I give you freely, and the mind which was in me rejoices as YOU will to hear it. The Holy Spirit atones in all of us by UNDOING, and thus lifts the burden you have placed in your mind. By following Him, He leads you back to God where you belong. And how can you find this way except by taking your brother with you?

14 My part in the Atonement is not complete until YOU join it, and give it away. As you teach, so shall you learn. I will never leave you or forsake you, [204] because to forsake

---

202 Chapter 1 B. Principles Of Miracles Principle 24, p12
203 Matthew 5:38-40 Ye have heard that it hath been said, An eye for an eye, and a tooth for a tooth:
   But I say unto you, That ye resist not evil: but whosoever shall smite thee on thy right cheek, turn to him the other also. And if any man will sue thee at the law, and take away thy coat, let him have thy cloak also.
204 Hebrews 13:5 Let your conversation be without covetousness; and be content with such things as ye have: for he hath said, I will never leave thee, nor forsake thee.

F. Therapy and Teaching

you would be to forsake myself and God who created me. You will forsake yourselves and your God if you forsake any of YOUR brothers. You are more than your brother's keeper. [205] In fact, you do not WANT to keep him. You must learn to see him as he is, and KNOW that he belongs to God, as you do. How could you treat your brother better than by rendering unto God [206] the things which are God's?

15   Ideas do not LEAVE the mind which thought them in order to have separate being. Nor do separate thoughts conflict with one another in space, because they do not occupy space at all.

HUMAN ideas can conflict in content, because they occur at different levels, and include opposite thoughts at the SAME level. IT IS IMPOSSIBLE TO SHARE OPPOSING THOUGHTS. The Holy Spirit does not LET you forsake your brothers. Therefore, you can really share only the parts of your thoughts which are of Him, which He also keeps for YOU. And of such is the Kingdom of Heaven. All the rest remains with you until He has re-interpreted them in the light of the Kingdom, making them, too, worthy of being shared. When they have been sufficiently purified, He lets you give them away. The will to share them IS their purification.

16   The Atonement gives you the power of a healed mind, but the power to create is of God.

Therefore, those who have been forgiven must devote themselves first to healing, because having RECEIVED the idea of healing they MUST give it to hold it.

The full power of creation (creating) cannot be expressed as long as any of God's ideas are withholding it from the Kingdom. The joint will of ALL the Sonship is the only creator that can create like the Father. That is because only the complete can think completely, and the thinking of God lacks nothing. Everything YOU think that is not through the Holy Spirit IS lacking.

---

205 Genesis 4:9 And the Lord said unto Cain, Where is Abel thy brother? And he said, I know not: Am I my brother's keeper?

206 Mark 12:17 And Jesus answering said unto them, Render to Caesar the things that are Caesar's, and to God the things that are God's. And they marvelled at him.
Luke 20:25 And he said unto them, Render therefore unto Caesar the things which be Caesar's, and unto God the things which be God's.

Chapter 5 – Healing And Wholeness

17
> How can you who are so Holy suffer?
>
> All your past, except its beauty, is gone,
> and nothing is left except a blessing.
>
> You can indeed depart in peace,
> because I have loved you as I loved myself.
>
> You go WITH my blessing and FOR my blessing.
> Hold it and share it, that it may always be ours.
>
> I place the peace of God in your heart,
> and in your hands, to hold and share.
>
> The heart is pure to hold it,
> and the hands are strong to give it.

We cannot lose. My judgment is as strong as the wisdom of God, in whose Heart and Hands we have our being. His quiet children are His blessed sons. The Thoughts of God are with you.

G. The Two Decisions

1   Perhaps this will become clearer and more personally meaningful if the ego's use of guilt is clarified. The ego has a purpose, just as the Holy Spirit has. The ego's purpose is FEAR, because only the fearful can be egotistic. The ego's logic is as impeccable as that of the Holy Spirit, because your mind has all the means at its disposal to side with Heaven or earth, as it elects. But let us again remember that both are in you.

2   In Heaven there is no guilt, because the Kingdom is attained through the Atonement, which creates it in you. The word "create" is appropriate here, because once what YOU have made is undone by the Holy Spirit, the blessed residue IS restored, and therefore continues in creation. What is truly blessed is incapable of giving rise to guilt, and must give rise to joy. This makes it invulnerable to the ego, because its peace is unassailable. It is invulnerable to disruption BECAUSE it is whole.

3   Guilt is ALWAYS disruptive. Anything that engenders fear is divisive, because it obeys the law of division. If the ego is the symbol of the separation, it is also the symbol of guilt.

G. The Two Decisions

Guilt is more than merely not of God. It is the symbol of the ATTACK on God.

This is a totally meaningless concept EXCEPT to the ego, but do not underestimate the power of the ego's belief in it.

This is the belief from which ALL guilt really stems.

4   The ego IS the part of the mind which believes in division. But how can part of God detach itself WITHOUT believing it is attacking Him? We spoke before of the authority problem as involving the concept of USURPING His power. [207] The ego believes that this is what YOU did, because it believes it IS you. It follows, then, that if you identify WITH the ego, you MUST perceive yourself as guilty.

5   Whenever you respond to your ego, you WILL experience guilt, and you WILL fear punishment. The ego is quite literally a fearful thought. And however ridiculous the idea of attacking God may be to the sane mind, never forget that the ego is NOT SANE. It REPRESENTS a delusional system, and it speaks FOR it. Listening to the ego's voice MEANS that you believe it is possible to attack God. You believe that a part of Him has been torn away by YOU.

6   The classic picture of fear of retaliation from without then follows, because the severity of the guilt is so acute that it MUST be projected. Although Freud was wrong about the basic conflict itself, he was very accurate in describing its effects.

Whatever you accept INTO your mind has reality for you. It is, however, only the ACCEPTANCE which makes it real.

7   As an extreme example of dissociation yourself, You should have little trouble in understanding that it is perfectly possible not to ACCEPT what IS in your minds.

If you enthrone the ego in it, the fact that you have accepted it, or allowed it to enter, MAKES IT YOUR REALITY. This is because the mind as God created it IS capable of creating reality. We said before that you must learn to think WITH God. [208] To think WITH Him is to think LIKE Him. This engenders joy, not guilt, because it is natural. Guilt is a sure sign that your thinking is Unnatural. Perverted thinking will ALWAYS be attended with guilt, because it IS the belief in sin.

---

207 Chapter 2   A. Introduction, p13
  Chapter 3   H. Judgment and the Authority Problem, p9
208 Chapter 4   E. The Escape From Fear, a. This Need Not Be, p2-3
  This Chapter   F. Therapy And Teaching, p16

Chapter 5 – Healing And Wholeness

8   The ego does not perceive sin as a lack of love. It perceives it as a POSITIVE ACT OF ASSAULT. This is an interpretation which is necessary to its survival, because as soon as YOU regard it as a LACK, you will automatically attempt to remedy the situation. And you will also succeed. The ego regards this as doom, but YOU must learn to regard it as freedom.

9   The guiltless mind cannot suffer. Being sane, it heals the body because IT has been healed. The sane mind cannot conceive of illness, because it cannot conceive of attacking anything or anyone. We said before that illness is a form of magic. It might be better to say it is a form of magical SOLUTION.

The ego believes that by punishing ITSELF, it will mitigate the punishment of God. Yet even in this it is arrogant.

It attributes to God a punishing attempt, and then takes over this intent as its OWN prerogative.

It tries to usurp ALL the functions of God as it perceives them, because it recognizes that only total allegiance can be trusted.

10   The ego cannot OPPOSE the laws of God, any more than YOU can. But it can INTERPRET them according to what it wants, just as YOU can.

That is why the question "what DO you want" must be answered. You ARE answering it every minute and every second, and each moment of decision is a judgment which is anything BUT ineffectual. Its effects will follow automatically UNTIL THE DECISION IS CHANGED. This is a redundant statement, because you have NOT learned it. But again, any decision can be Unmade as well as made.

11   But remember that the ALTERNATIVES are unalterable. The Holy Spirit, like the ego, is a decision. Together they constitute all the alternatives which your mind CAN accept and obey.

>The ego and the Holy Spirit are the ONLY choices which are open to you.
>
>God created one, and so you cannot eradicate it.
>YOU made the other, so you CAN.

Only what God creates is irreversible and unchangeable. What YOU have made can always be changed, because when you do not think LIKE God, you have not really thought at all. Delusional ideas are NOT thought, but you CAN think that you believe in them.

G. The Two Decisions

12   But you are wrong. The function of thought comes FROM God and is IN God. As part of HIS thought, you cannot think APART from Him. Irrational thought is a thought DISORDER.

God Himself orders your thought, because your thought was created BY Him.

Guilt feelings are always a sign that you do not know this.

They also show that you believe you CAN think apart from God, and WANT to.

13   Every thought disorder is attended by guilt at its inception, and MAINTAINED by guilt in its continuance.

Guilt is inescapable for those who believe that they order their OWN thought, and must therefore obey its orders.

This makes them feel RESPONSIBLE for their mind ERRORS, without recognizing that by ACCEPTING this responsibility they are really reacting Irresponsibly.

If the sole responsibility of the miracle-worker is to accept the ATONEMENT, [209] and I assure you that it is, then the responsibility for what is atoned FOR CANNOT be yours.

14   This contradiction cannot BE resolved except by accepting *the solution of undoing*. You WOULD be responsible for the effects of all your wrong thinking IF IT COULD NOT BE UNDONE. The purpose of the Atonement is to save the past in PURIFIED form only. If you accept the remedy FOR a thought-disorder, and a remedy whose efficacy is beyond doubt, how can its symptoms remain?

You have reason to question the validity of symptom cure. But NO ONE believes that the symptoms can remain if the underlying CAUSE is removed.

H. Time and Eternity

1   The CONTINUING will to remain separated is the only possible reason for continuing guilt feelings. We have said this before, but we did not emphasize the destructive results of this decision at that time. ANY decision of the mind will affect both behavior AND experience. And what you will, you EXPECT. This is NOT delusional.

---

209 Chapter 2 C. Healing as Release from Fear, p17

Chapter 5 – Healing And Wholeness

Your mind DOES create your future,[210] and CAN turn it back to full creation at any minute, IF IT ACCEPTS THE ATONEMENT FIRST. It will also turn back to full creation the instant it has done so. Having given up its thought DISORDER, the proper ordering of thought becomes quite apparent.

2   God in His knowledge is not waiting. But His Kingdom IS bereft while YOU wait. All the Sons of God are waiting for your return, just as YOU are waiting for THEIRS. Delay does not matter in eternity, but it IS tragic in time. You have elected to be in time rather than in eternity, and have therefore changed your belief in your status. But election is both free and alterable. You do NOT belong in time. Your place is ONLY in eternity, where God Himself placed you forever.

3   Guilt feelings are the PRESERVERS of time. They induce fears of FUTURE retaliation or abandonment, and thus ensure that the future will remain like the past. This IS the ego's continuity, and gives it a false sense of security through the belief that you cannot escape from it. But you can and MUST. God offers you the continuity of eternity in exchange. When you will to make this exchange, you will simultaneously exchange guilt for peace, viciousness for love, and pain for joy.

4   *My role is only to unchain your will and make it free. Your egos cannot accept this freedom,* and will oppose your free decision at every possible moment, and in every possible way.

And as its maker, you KNOW what it can do, because you GAVE IT the ability to do it. The mind does indeed know its power, because the mind does indeed know God. Remember the Kingdom always, and remember that you who are part of it cannot BE lost. The mind that was in me IS in you, for God creates with perfect fairness. Let the Holy Spirit remind you always of His fairness, and let me teach you how to share it with your brothers. How else can the chance to claim it for yourself be given you?

5   What you do not understand is that the two voices speak for different interpretations of the same thing simultaneously, or almost simultaneously, for the ego always speaks first.

Alternate interpretations are unnecessary until the first one has been made, and speaking itself was unnecessary before the ego was made.

The ego speaks in judgment, and the Holy Spirit reverses its decisions, much as the Supreme Court has the power to reverse the lower court's decision about the laws of this world.

6   The ego's decisions are ALWAYS wrong, because they are based on a complete fallacy which they are made to uphold. NOTHING it perceives is interpreted correctly.

---

[210] Chapter 1 B. Principles Of Miracles Principle 13; Principle 14
    Chapter 3 C. Atonement Without Sacrifice, p34

H. Time and Eternity

Not only does it cite scripture for its purpose, but it even interprets scripture as a witness for itself. The Bible is a fearful thing to the ego, because of its prejudiced judgment. Perceiving it as fearful, it interprets it fearfully. *Having made YOU afraid, you do not appeal to the higher court, because you believe its judgment would be AGAINST you.*

7 We need cite only a few examples to see how the ego's interpretations have mislead you. A favorite ego quotation is "As ye sow, so shall ye reap." [211] Another is "Vengeance is mine sayeth the Lord." [212] Still another is "I will visit the sins of the fathers unto the third and the fourth generation." [213] And also, "The wicked shall perish." [214] There are many others, but if you will let the Holy Spirit re-interpret these in its own light, they will suffice.

8 "As ye sow, so shall ye reap" merely means that what you believe to be worth cultivating you will cultivate in yourself. Your judgment of what is worthy DOES make it worthy for you.

9 "Vengeance is mine sayeth the Lord" is easily explained if you remember that ideas increase only by being shared. This quotation therefore emphasizes the fact that vengeance CANNOT be shared. Give it therefore to the Holy Spirit, who will undo it in you because it does not BELONG in your mind, which is part of God.

10 "I will visit the sins of the fathers unto the third and fourth generation," as interpreted by the ego, is particularly vicious. It is used, in fact, as an attempt to guarantee its survival beyond itself. Actually, all it really means is that the Holy Spirit in later generations retains the power to interpret CORRECTLY what former generations have thought, and thus release THEIR thoughts from the ability to produce fear ANYWHERE in the Sonship.

11 "The wicked shall perish" is merely a statement of fact, if the word "perish" is properly understood. Every loveless thought MUST be undone, and even the word "undone" is fearful to the ego, which interprets "I am undone" as "I am destroyed."

---

211 Galatians 6:7 Be not deceived; God is not mocked: for whatsoever a man soweth, that shall he also reap. 8 For he that soweth to his flesh shall of the flesh reap corruption; but he that soweth to the Spirit shall of the Spirit reap life everlasting.

212 Romans 12:19 Dearly beloved, avenge not yourselves, but rather give place unto wrath: for it is written, Vengeance is mine; I will repay, saith the Lord.

213 Exodus 34:7 Keeping mercy for thousands, forgiving iniquity and transgression and sin, and that will by no means clear the guilty; visiting the iniquity of the fathers upon the children, and upon the children's children, unto the third and to the fourth generation.

214 Psalm 37:20 But the wicked shall perish, and the enemies of the Lord shall be as the fat of lambs: they shall consume; into smoke shall they consume away.

Chapter 5 – Healing And Wholeness

The ego will NOT be destroyed, because it is part of YOUR thought. But because it is uncreative, and therefore unsharing, it WILL be re-interpreted entirely, to release you from fear.

12 The part of your thought which you have given TO the ego will merely return to the Kingdom, where your whole mind BELONGS. The ego is a form of ARREST, but arrest is merely delay. It does NOT involve the concept of police at all, although the ego welcomes that interpretation. You CAN delay the completion of the Kingdom, but you CANNOT introduce the concept of ASSAULT into it.

13 When I said "I am come as a light into the world," [215] I surely came to share this light with you. Remember the symbolic reference we made before to the ego's dark glass, and remember also that we said "Do not look there." [216] It is still true that "Where you look to find yourself is up to you."

The Higher Court will not condemn you. It will merely dismiss the case against you. There can BE no case against a child of God, and every witness to guilt in God's creations is bearing false witness to God Himself.

14 Appeal everything you believe gladly to God's own Higher Court, because it speaks for Him, and therefore speaks truly. It WILL dismiss the case against you, however carefully YOU have built it. The case may be fool-proof, but it is NOT God-proof. The voice for God will not hear it at all, because it can only witness truly. Its verdict will always be "Thine is the Kingdom," because it was given you to remind you of what you ARE.

15 Your patience with each other is your patience with your selves. Is not a child of God worth patience? I have shown you infinite patience, because my will IS that of our Father, from whom I learned of infinite patience. His voice was in me, as it is in you, speaking for patience towards the Sonship, in the name of its Creator.

What you need to learn now is that only infinite patience CAN produce immediate effects. This is the way in which time is exchanged for eternity. Infinite patience calls upon infinite Love, and by producing results NOW renders time unnecessary.

16 To say that time is temporary is merely redundant. We have repeatedly said that time is a learning device which will be abolished when it is no longer useful. The Holy Spirit, who speaks for God in time, also knows that time is meaningless. He reminds you of this in every passing moment of time, because it is His special function to return YOU to eternity and remain to bless YOUR creations there. He is the only blessing you can truly give, because He is so truly blessed. And because He has been given you so freely by God, you must give Him as you received Him.

---

215 John 12:46 I am come a light into the world, that whosoever believeth on me should not abide in darkness.
216 Chapter 4 E. The Escape From Fear a. This Need Not Be, p13

I. The Eternal Fixation

1   The concept of "set" is among the better psychological percepts. Actually, it is used quite frequently in the Bible, and also here, under many different terms. "God will keep him in perfect peace whose mind is stayed (or set) on Thee because he trusteth in Thee."[217]

2   The pronouns here are confusing without explanation, and the attempt to shift "Thee" to "Him" is a misinterpretation. The statement means that God's peace is set in the Holy Spirit, because it is fixed on God. It is also fixed in you. You, then, ARE fixed in the peace of God.

3   The concept of "fixation" is a very helpful one, which Freud understood perfectly. Unfortunately, he lost his understanding because he was afraid, and as you know all too well, fear is incompatible with good judgment. Fear DISTORTS thinking, and therefore DISorders thought. Freud's system of thought was extremely ingenious, because Freud was extremely ingenious. A mind MUST endow its thoughts with its own attributes. This is its inherent STRENGTH, even though it may misuse its power.

4   Freud lost much of the potential value of his own thought system because, much like Cayce, he did NOT include himself in it. This IS a dissociated state, because the thinker cuts himself off from his thoughts. Freud's thought was so conflicted that he could not have retained his sanity as HE saw it WITHOUT dissociating. This is why the many contradictions which are quite apparent in his thinking became increasingly less apparent to HIM.

5   A man who knows what fixation REALLY means and does NOT yield to it is terribly afraid. Fixation is the pull of God, on whom your mind IS fixed because of the Holy Spirit's irrevocable set. "Irrevocable" means "cannot be called back or redirected."

    The irrevocable nature of the Holy Spirit's set is the basis for its unequivocal voice. The Holy Spirit NEVER changes its mind. Clarity of thought CANNOT occur under conditions of vacillation. Unless a mind is fixed in its purpose, it is NOT clear. But clarity literally means the state of light, and enlightenment IS understanding. It stands UNDER perception because you have denied it as the REAL foundation of thought. This is the basis for ALL delusional systems.

6   The concept of fixation, as Freud saw it, has a number of real learning advantages. First, it recognizes that man CAN be fixated at a point in development which does NOT accord with a point in time. This clearly could have been a means toward real release from the time belief, had Freud pursued it with an open mind. But Freud suffered all his

---

[217] Isaiah 26:3 Thou wilt keep him in perfect peace, whose mind is stayed on thee: because he trusteth in thee.

Chapter 5 – Healing And Wholeness

life from refusal to allow eternity to dawn upon his mind, and enlighten it truly. As a result, he overlooked NOW entirely, and merely saw the continuity of past and future.

7   Second, although he misinterpreted what the Holy Spirit told him, or better, reminded him of, he was too honest to deny more than he had to, to keep his fear in tolerable bounds, as he perceived the situation. Therefore, he EMPHASIZED that the point in development at which the mind is fixated is more real to ITSELF than the external reality with which it DISagrees. This again could have been a powerful RELEASE mechanism, had Freud not decided to involve it in a strong defense system because he perceived it as an attack.

8   Third, although Freud interpreted fixation as irrevocable danger points to which the mind can always regress, the concept can also be interpreted as an irrevocable call to sanity which the mind cannot LOSE. Freud saw return as a threat to maturity because he did not understand prodigality. He merely interpreted it as squandering. Actually, "prodigal" also means careful. This confusion between careful and careless led him to confuse the escape from care with something desirable. In fact, he even went so far as to equate it quite literally WITH desire.

9   But throughout his thought-system, the "threat" of fixation remained, and could never be completely eliminated by any living human being anywhere. Essentially, this was the basis of his pessimism. This was personally as well as theoretically the case. Freud tried every means his very inventive mind could devise to set up a form of therapy which could enable the mind to escape from fixation forever, even though he KNEW this was impossible. The knowledge plagued his belief in his own thought-system at every turn, because he was both an honest man and a healer. He was therefore only PARTIALLY insane at the perceptual level, and was unable to relinquish the hope of release.

10   The reason for this amount of detail is because YOU are in the same position. You were eternally fixated on God in your creation, and the pull of this fixation is so strong that you will never overcome it. The reason is perfectly clear. The fixation is on a level that is so high that it cannot BE surmounted. You are ALWAYS being pulled back to your Creator because you belong in Him.

11   Do you REALLY believe you can make a voice that can drown out His? Do you REALLY believe that you can devise a thought-system which can separate you from His? Do you REALLY believe that you can plan for your safety and joy better than He can? You need be neither careful nor careless. You need merely cast all your cares upon Him because He careth for YOU. [218] You ARE His care because He loves you. His voice reminds you always that all hope is yours BECAUSE of His care.

---

218 1 Peter 5:7 Casting all your care upon him; for he careth for you.

I. The Eternal Fixation

12 You CANNOT choose to escape His care, because that is not His will. But you CAN choose to accept His care, and use the infinite power OF His care for all those He created BY it. There have been many healers who did not heal themselves. They have not moved mountains by their faith because their faith was not WHOLE. Some of them have healed the sick at times, but they have not raised the dead. Unless the healer heals HIMSELF, he does NOT believe that there is no order in miracles. He has not learned that EVERY mind that God created is equally worthy of being healed because GOD CREATED IT WHOLE.

13 You are asked merely to return to God the mind as HE created it. He asks you only for what He gave, knowing that this giving will heal YOU. Sanity IS wholeness. And the sanity of your brothers IS yours. Why should you listen to the endless insane calls which you think are made upon you, when you KNOW the voice of God Himself is in you? God commended His Spirit to you, and asks that you commend yours to Him. He wills to keep it in perfect peace because you are of one mind and Spirit with Him.

14 Excluding yourself from the Atonement is the ego's last-ditch defense of its own existence. It reflects both the ego's need to separate, and your willingness to side with its separateness. This willingness means that YOU DO NOT WANT TO BE HEALED.

When I told Bill that there is "just one more thing," he heard me very well. I hope he will hear me as well now. His intelligent mis-hearing of "river" as "rivet" showed that, even though he wanted release, he was not able to cope with it at the time.

15 But the time IS now. You have not been asked to work out the Plan of Salvation yourselves, because, as I told you before, the Remedy is NOT of your making. God Himself gave you the perfect correction for everything you have made which is not in accord with His Holy Will. I have made His Plan perfectly clear and perfectly explicit to you, and have also told you of your part in His Plan and how urgent it is that you fulfill it.

16 There is time for delay, but there need not be. God weeps at the sacrifice of His children who believe they are lost to Him.

The "one more thing" that Bill must learn is merely that he is NOT the one more. He is both ONE and AT ONE. If he will learn this NOW, he will be willing in accord with the last judgment, which is really only the Biblical reminder of the inevitability of self-INCLUSION. This is what "Physician, heal thyself" really means. Bill has frequently observed for HIMSELF that this is hard to do. He has, however, been perfectly aware of JUST what YOU should do about it.

17 You might ask him for me whether he does not think he might be dissociating HIMSELF from his own awareness, since he is so clear about the remedy for YOU. You might also remind him that to whatever extent he separates himself from you, he is

Chapter 5 – Healing And Wholeness

separating himself from ME. This IS a collaborative venture. Let me therefore return his own ideas to him, so that you can share them and thus help each other to help me.

18   But let me first remind you of something I told you myself.

Whenever you are not wholly joyous, it is because you have reacted with a lack of love to some Soul which God created. [219] Perceiving this as sin, you become defensive because you EXPECT ATTACK. The decision to react in that way, however, was YOURS, and can therefore be undone. It CANNOT be undone by repentance in the usual sense, because this implies guilt. If you allow yourself to feel guilty, you will reinforce the error, rather than allowing it to be undone FOR you.

19   Decisions CANNOT be difficult. This is obvious if you realize that you must ALREADY have made a decision NOT to be wholly joyous if that is what you feel. Therefore, the first step in the undoing is to recognize that YOU ACTIVELY DECIDED WRONGLY, BUT CAN AS ACTIVELY DECIDE OTHERWISE.

20   Be very firm with yourselves in this, and keep yourselves fully aware of the fact that the UNDOING process, which does NOT come from you, is nevertheless WITHIN you because God placed it there. YOUR part is merely to return your thinking to the point at which the error was made, and give it over to the Atonement in peace. Say to yourselves the following, as sincerely as you can, remembering that the Holy Spirit will respond fully to your slightest invitation:

>   I must have decided wrongly because I am NOT at peace.
>   I made the decision myself, but I can also decide otherwise.
>
>   I WILL to decide otherwise, because I WANT to be at peace.
>
>   I do NOT feel guilty, because the Holy Spirit will undo ALL the consequences of my wrong decision IF I WILL LET HIM.
>
>   I WILL to let Him by allowing Him to decide for God for me.

---

[219] This Chapter A. Introduction, p2
   Also, this Chapter B. Healing As Joining, p1

Chapter 6 – Attack And Fear

A. Introduction

1   The relationship of anger to attack is obvious, but the inevitable association of anger and FEAR is not always so clear. Anger ALWAYS involves PROJECTION OF SEPARATION, which must ultimately be accepted as entirely one's own responsibility.

Anger cannot occur unless you believe that:

> You have BEEN attacked;
> the attack was JUSTIFIED;
> and you are in no way responsible for it.

Given these three wholly irrational premises, the equally irrational conclusion that a brother is worthy of attack rather than of love follows. What can be expected from insane premises EXCEPT an insane conclusion?

2   The way to undo an insane conclusion is always to consider the sanity of the premises on which it rests:

> You cannot BE attacked,
> attack HAS no justification,
> and you ARE responsible for what you believe.

You have been asked to take me as your model for learning. And we have often said that an extreme example is a particularly helpful learning device. [220] EVERYONE teaches, and teaches all the time. This is a responsibility which he assumes inevitably, the moment he has accepted any premises at all. And NO ONE can organize his life without ANY thought system. Once he has developed a thought system of any kind, he lives by it and TEACHES it.

3   You have been chosen to teach the Atonement precisely BECAUSE you have been EXTREME examples of allegiance to your thought systems, and therefore have developed the capacity FOR allegiance. It has indeed been misplaced.

Bill had become an outstanding example of allegiance to apathy, and you have become a startling example of fidelity to variability. But this IS a form of faith, which

---

[220] Chapter 4 C. The Ego and False Autonomy, p4

Chapter 6 – Attack And Fear

you yourselves had grown willing to redirect. You cannot doubt the STRENGTH of your devotion when you consider how faithfully you observed it. It was quite evident that you had ALREADY developed the ability to follow a better model, if you could ACCEPT it.

B. The Message of the Crucifixion

1   We have not dwelt upon the crucifixion, because of its fearful connotations. The only emphasis we laid upon it was that it was NOT a form of punishment. [221] But we know that nothing can be really explained only in negative terms.

There is a positive interpretation of the crucifixion which is wholly devoid of fear, and therefore wholly benign in what it teaches, if it is properly understood. It is nothing more than an extreme example. Its value, like the value of any teaching device, lies solely in the kind of learning it facilitates.

It can be, and has been, misunderstood. But this is only because the fearful are apt to perceive fearfully.

2   I told you before that you can always call on me to share my decision and thus MAKE IT STRONGER. [222] I also told you that the crucifixion was the last foolish journey that the Sonship need take, [223] and that it should mean RELEASE from fear to anyone who understands it. While we emphasized the Resurrection only before, [224] the purpose of the crucifixion and how it actually LED to the Resurrection was not clarified at that time. Nevertheless, it has a definite contribution to make to your own lives, and if you will consider it WITHOUT fear, it will help you understand your own role as teachers.

3   You have reacted for years AS IF you were being crucified. This is a marked tendency of the separated, who ALWAYS refuse to consider what they have done to THEMSELVES. Projection means anger, anger fosters assault, and assault promotes fear.

The real meaning of the crucifixion lies in the APPARENT intensity of the assault of some of the Sons of God upon a brother. This, of course, is impossible, and must be fully understood AS an impossibility. In fact, unless it IS fully understood as ONLY that, I cannot serve as a real model for learning.

4   Assault can ultimately be made ONLY on the body. There is little doubt that one BODY can assault another, and can even destroy it. But if destruction ITSELF is impossible, then ANYTHING that is destructible cannot be real. Therefore, its

---

221 Chapter 3 C. Atonement without Sacrifice, p1-2
222 Chapter 5 D. The Voice for God, p9, p12
223 Chapter 4 A. Introduction, p9
224 Chapter 3 C. Atonement without Sacrifice, p1, p11
    Chapter 3 G. The Loss of Certainty, p1, p31

B. The Message of the Crucifixion

destruction does NOT justify anger. To the extent to which you believe it DOES, you MUST be accepting false premises and TEACHING THEM TO OTHERS.

The message which the crucifixion was intended to teach was that it is not necessary to perceive ANY form of assault in persecution because you cannot BE persecuted. If you respond with anger, you MUST be equating yourself with the destructible, and are therefore regarding yourself insanely. I have made it perfectly clear that I am like you, and you are like me. But our fundamental equality can be demonstrated only through joint decision.

5   You are free to perceive yourselves as persecuted if you chose. But you might remember when you DO choose to react that way that I WAS persecuted as the world judges, and did NOT share this evaluation for myself. And because I did not share it, I did NOT strengthen it. I therefore offered a DIFFERENT interpretation of attack, and one which I DO want to share with you. If you will BELIEVE it, you will help me TEACH it.

6   We have said before, "As you teach so shall you learn." [225]

If you react as if you are persecuted, you ARE teaching persecution.

This is not a lesson which the Sons of God should WANT to teach if they are to realize their own salvation. Rather teach your own perfect immunity, which IS the Truth in you, and KNOW that it cannot be assailed. Do not protect it yourselves, or you have believed that it IS assailable.

You are not asked to BE crucified, because that was part of my own teaching contribution. You are merely asked to follow my example in the face of much less extreme temptations to misperceive, and NOT to accept them falsely as justifications for anger.

7   There can BE no justification for the unjustifiable. Do not believe there is, and do not TEACH that there is. Remember always that what you believe you WILL teach.

Believe with me, and we will become equal as teachers. YOUR resurrection is your re-awakening. I am the model for rebirth, but rebirth itself is merely the dawning on your minds of what is already in them.

God placed it there Himself, and so it is true forever. I believed in it, and therefore made it forever true for me. Help me to teach it to our brothers in the name of the Kingdom of God.

But first believe that it is true for you, or you will teach amiss.

---

[225] Chapter 5 F. Therapy and Teaching, p14

Chapter 6 – Attack And Fear

8   My brothers slept during the so-called "agony in the garden," [226] but I could not be angry with them, because I had learned I could not BE abandoned. Peter swore he would never deny me, but he did so three times. [227] It should be noted that he did offer to defend me with the sword, [228] which I naturally refused, not being at all in need of bodily protection. I AM sorry when my brothers do not share my decision to hear (and be) only one voice, because it weakens them as teachers AND learners. But yet I know that they cannot really betray themselves or me, and that it is still on them that I MUST build my church. [229]

9   There is no choice in this, because only you can BE the foundation of God's church. A church is where an altar is, and the presence of the altar is what makes it a church. Any church which does not inspire love has a hidden altar which is not serving the purpose for which God intended it. I must found His church on you because you, who accept me as a model are literally my disciples. Disciples are followers, but if the model they follow has chosen to SAVE THEM PAIN IN ALL RESPECTS, they are probably unwise NOT to follow him.

10   *I elected, both for your sake AND mine, to demonstrate that the most outrageous assault, as judged by the ego, did not matter.* As the world judges these things, but NOT as God knows them, I was betrayed, abandoned, beaten, torn, and finally killed. It was

---

226 Luke 22:39 And he came out, and went, as he was wont, to the mount of Olives; and his disciples also followed him. 40 And when he was at the place, he said unto them, Pray that ye enter not into temptation.
41 And he was withdrawn from them about a stone's cast, and kneeled down, and prayed,
42 Saying, Father, if thou be willing, remove this cup from me: nevertheless not my will, but thine, be done.
43 And there appeared an angel unto him from heaven, strengthening him.
44 And being in an agony he prayed more earnestly: and his sweat was as it were great drops of blood falling down to the ground.
45 And when he rose up from prayer, and was come to his disciples, he found them sleeping for sorrow,
46 And said unto them, Why sleep ye? rise and pray, lest ye enter into temptation.
47 And while he yet spake, behold a multitude, and he that was called Judas, one of the twelve, went before them, and drew near unto Jesus to kiss him.
Also, Matthew 26:36

227 Luke 22:33 And he said unto him, Lord, I am ready to go with thee, both into prison, and to death.
34 And he said, I tell thee, Peter, the cock shall not crow this day, before that thou shalt thrice deny that thou knowest me.

228 Luke 22:49 When they which were about him saw what would follow, they said unto him, Lord, shall we smite with the sword?
John 18:10 Then Simon Peter having a sword drew it, and smote the high priest's servant, and cut off his right ear. The servant's name was Malchus.
11 Then said Jesus unto Peter, Put up thy sword into the sheath: the cup which my Father hath given me, shall I not drink it?

229 Matthew 16:18 And I say also unto thee, That thou art Peter, and upon this rock I will build my church; and the gates of hell shall not prevail against it.

B. The Message of the Crucifixion

perfectly clear that this was only because of the projection of others onto me, because I had not harmed anyone and had healed many. We are still equal as learners, even though we need not have equal experiences. The Holy Spirit is glad when you can learn enough from MINE to be re-awakened by them. That was their only purpose, and that is the only way in which I can be perceived as the Way, the Truth, and the Light. [230]

11   When you hear only one voice, you are never called on to sacrifice. On the contrary, by enabling YOURSELVES to hear the Holy Spirit in others, you can learn from their experiences and gain from them WITHOUT experiencing them. That is because the Holy Spirit IS one, and anyone who listens is inevitably led to demonstrate His way for ALL. You are not persecuted, nor was I. You are not asked to repeat my experience, because the Holy Spirit which we SHARE, makes this unnecessary. But to use my experiences constructively for yourselves, you must still follow my example in how to perceive them.

12   My brothers and yours are constantly engaged in justifying the unjustifiable. My one lesson, which I must teach as I learned, is that no perception which is out of accord with the judgment of the Holy Spirit CAN be justified. I undertook to show this was true in a very extreme case, merely because this would serve as a good teaching aid to those whose temptations to give in to anger and assault would NOT be as extreme.

13   I will, with God Himself, that none of His Sons should suffer. Remember that the Holy Spirit is the communication link between God the Father and His separated Sons. If you will listen to His voice, you will know that you cannot either hurt or BE hurt, but that many need your blessing to help them hear this for themselves. When you perceive only this need in them, and do not respond to any others, you will have learned of me, and be as eager to share your learning as I am. The crucifixion CANNOT be shared, because it is the symbol of projection. But the Resurrection IS the symbol of sharing, because the re-awakening of every Son of God is necessary to enable the Sonship to know its wholeness. Only this IS knowledge.

14   The message of the crucifixion is very simple and perfectly clear:

"Teach ONLY love, for that is what you ARE."

If you interpret it in any other way, you are using it as a weapon for assault rather than as the call to peace for which it was intended. The Apostles often misunderstood it, and always for the same reason that makes anyone misunderstand anything. Their own

---

[230] John 14:6 Jesus saith unto him, I am the way, the truth, and the life: no man cometh unto the Father, but by me.

Chapter 6 – Attack And Fear

imperfect love made them vulnerable to projection, and out of their own fear they spoke of the wrath of God as His RETALIATORY weapon. They also could not speak of the crucifixion entirely without anger, because their own sense of guilt had made them angry.

15   There are two glaring examples of upside down thinking in the New Testament, whose whole Gospel is only the message of love. These are not at all like the several slips into impatience which I made, because I had learned the Atonement prayer, which I also came to teach, too well to engage in upside down thinking myself. If the Apostles had not felt guilty, they never could have quoted ME as saying, "I come not to bring peace but a sword." [231] This is clearly the exact opposite of everything I taught.

16   Nor could they have described my reactions to Judas Iscariot as they did, if they had really understood ME. They could not have believed that I could have said, "Betrayest thou the Son of Man with a kiss?" [232] unless I BELIEVED IN BETRAYAL. The whole message of the crucifixion was simply that I did NOT. The "punishment" which I am said to have called forth upon Judas was a similar reversal. Judas was my brother and a Son of God, as much a part of the Sonship as myself. Was it likely that I would condemn him when I was ready to demonstrate that condemnation is impossible?

17   I am very grateful to the Apostles for their teaching, and fully aware of the extent of their devotion to me. But as you read their teachings, remember that I told them myself that there was much they would understand later, because they were NOT wholly ready to follow me at the time. I emphasize this only because I do not want you to allow ANY fear to enter into the thought system toward which I am guiding you. I do NOT call for martyrs but for TEACHERS.

18   Bill is an outstanding example of this confusion, and has literally believed for years that teaching IS martyrdom. This is because he thought, and still thinks at times, that teaching leads to crucifixion rather than to re-awakening. The upside down nature of this association is so obvious that he could only have made it BECAUSE he felt guilty.

> No-one is "punished" for sins, and the Sons of God are not sinners. ANY concept of "punishment" [233] involves the projection of blame, and REINFORCES the idea that blame is justified. The behavior that results is a LESSON IN BLAME, just as all behavior teaches the beliefs that motivate it.

19   The crucifixion was a complex of behaviors arising out of clearly opposed thought systems. As such, it is the perfect symbol of conflict between the ego and the Son of

---

231 Matthew 10:34 Think not that I am come to send peace on earth: I came not to send peace, but a sword.
232 Luke 22:48 But Jesus said unto him, Judas, betrayest thou the Son of man with a kiss?
233 Chapter 2 F. The Meaning of the Last Judgment, p2

B. The Message of the Crucifixion

God. It was as much intrapersonal as interpersonal then, just as it is now, and it is still just as real. But BECAUSE it is just as real now, its lesson, too, has equal reality WHEN IT IS LEARNED.

I do not need gratitude any more than I needed protection. But YOU need to develop your weakened ability to BE grateful, or you cannot appreciate God. [234] HE does not need your appreciation, but you DO.

20   You cannot love what you do not appreciate, and FEAR MAKES APPRECIATION IMPOSSIBLE. Whenever you are afraid of what you are, you do not appreciate it, and will therefore reject it. As a result, you will TEACH REJECTION.

The power of the Sons of God is operating all the time, because they were created as creators. Their influence on EACH OTHER is without limit, and MUST be used for their joint salvation. Each one MUST learn to teach that all forms of rejection are utterly meaningless.

21   The separation IS the notion of rejection. As long as you teach this, YOU still believe it. This is NOT as God thinks, and you must think as He thinks if you are to know Him again.

C. The Uses of Projection

1   Any split in will MUST involve a rejection of part of it, and this IS the belief in separation. The wholeness of God, which IS His peace, cannot be appreciated EXCEPT by a whole mind, which recognizes the wholeness of God's creation and BY this recognition knows its Creator.

2   Exclusion and separation are synonymous. So are separation and dissociation. We have said before that the separation was and IS dissociation, and also that once it had occurred, projection became its main defense, or the device which KEEPS IT GOING.

The reason, however, may not be as clear to you as you think. What you project you disown, and therefore DO NOT BELIEVE IS YOURS. You are therefore EXCLUDING yourself from it, by the very statement you are making that you are DIFFERENT from someone else. Since you have also judged AGAINST what you project, you attack it because you have already attacked it BY rejecting it. By doing this UNCONSCIOUSLY, you try to keep the fact that you must have attacked yourself FIRST out of awareness, and thus imagine that you have made yourself safe.

---

[234] Chapter 4 G. The Constant State, p16

Chapter 6 – Attack And Fear

3   Projection will ALWAYS hurt you.

It reinforces your belief in your own split mind, and its ONLY purpose is to KEEP THE SEPARATION GOING.

It is solely a device of the ego to make you feel DIFFERENT from your brothers and separated FROM them.

The ego justifies this on the wholly spurious grounds that it makes you seem better than they are, thus obscuring equality WITH them still further.

4   Projection and attack are inevitably related, because projection is ALWAYS a means of JUSTIFYING attack. Anger without projection is impossible. The ego uses projection ONLY to distort your perception of both yourself AND your brothers. It begins by excluding something you think exists in you which you do not want, and leads directly to your excluding yourself from your brothers.

5   But we know that there is another use of projection. Every ability of the ego has a better counterpart, because its abilities are directed by the mind, which has a better voice. [235] The Holy Spirit, as well as the ego, utilizes projection but since their goals are opposed, so is the result.

The Holy Spirit begins by perceiving YOU as perfect. KNOWING this perfection is shared, it RECOGNIZES it in others, thus strengthening it in both. Instead of anger, this arouses love FOR both because IT ESTABLISHES INCLUSION.

Perceiving equality, it perceives equal needs. This invites Atonement automatically, because Atonement IS the one need which is universal.

6   To perceive YOURSELF in this way is the ONLY way in which you can find happiness in this world. This is because it is the acknowledgement that you are NOT in this world, and the world IS unhappy. How else can you find joy in a joyless place EXCEPT by realizing that YOU ARE NOT THERE? You cannot be ANYWHERE that God did not put you, and God created you as part of HIM. That is both WHERE you are and WHAT you are. This is COMPLETELY unalterable. It is total inclusion. You cannot change this now or ever. It is forever true. It is NOT a belief, but a fact.

7   Anything that God creates is as true as He is. Its truth lies only in its perfect inclusion in Him Who alone IS perfect. To deny this in any way is to deny yourself AND Him, because it is impossible to accept one without the other.

The perfect equality of the Holy Spirit's perception is the counterpart of the perfect equality of God's knowing. The ego's perception has no counterpart in God, but the Holy

---

[235] Chapter 3 G. The Loss of Certainty, p1
    Chapter 2 B. The Re-interpretation of Defenses b. The Atonement As Defense, p21 - 24

C. The Uses of Projection

Spirit remains the bridge between perception and knowledge. [236] By enabling you to use perception in a way that PARALLELS knowledge, you will ultimately meet it and KNOW it.

8   The ego prefers to believe that parallel lines do not meet, and conceives of their meeting as impossible. But you might remember that even the human eye perceives them as if they DO meet in the distance, which is the same as IN THE FUTURE, if time and space are one dimension. The later mathematics support the interpretation of ultimate convergence of the parallel theoretically. EVERYTHING meets in God, because everything was created BY Him and IN Him. God created His Sons by extending His Thought and retaining the extensions of His Thought in His Mind. ALL His Thoughts are thus perfectly united within themselves and with each other because they, were created neither partially nor in part.

9   The Holy Spirit enables you to PERCEIVE THIS WHOLENESS NOW. You can no more pray for yourselves alone than you can find joy for yourself alone. Prayer is a re-statement of INCLUSION, directed by the Holy Spirit under the laws of God. God created you to create. You cannot EXTEND His Kingdom until you KNOW of its wholeness. But thoughts begin in the mind OF THE THINKER, from which they extend outward. This is as true of God's thinking as it is of yours. Because your minds are split, you can also perceive as well as think, but perception cannot escape from the basic laws of mind. You perceive FROM your mind, and extend your perceptions outward.

10   Although perception of any kind is unnecessary, YOU made it and the Holy Spirit can therefore use it well. He can INSPIRE perception and lead it toward God by making it PARALLEL to God's way of thinking, and thus guaranteeing their ultimate meeting.

This convergence SEEMS to be far in the future ONLY because your mind is NOT in perfect alignment with the idea, and therefore DOES NOT WANT IT NOW. The Holy Spirit USES time, but does NOT believe in it. Coming from God, He uses EVERYTHING for good, but does not BELIEVE in what is not true.

11   Since the Holy Spirit IS in your minds, then your minds MUST be able to believe ONLY what is true. The Holy Spirit can speak only for this, because he speaks for God. He tells you to return your whole mind to God, BECAUSE IT HAS NEVER LEFT HIM. If it has never left Him, you need only perceive it AS IT IS to BE returned. *The full awareness of the Atonement, then, is the recognition that the separation NEVER OCCURRED.* The ego CANNOT prevail against this, because it is an explicit statement that the EGO never occurred.

---

236 Chapter 4 G. The Constant State, p15
      Chapter 5 E. The Guide to Salvation, p1

Chapter 6 – Attack And Fear

12   The ego can accept the idea that RETURN is necessary, because it can so easily make the idea seem so difficult.

But the Holy Spirit tells you that even RETURN is unnecessary, because what never happened CANNOT involve ANY problem. But it does NOT follow that YOU cannot make the idea of return both necessary AND difficult. God made nothing either necessary OR difficult. But YOU have perceived both AS IF they were part of His perfect creations. Yet it is surely clear that the perfect NEED nothing, and CANNOT experience perfection as a difficult accomplishment because that is what they ARE.

13   This is the way in which you MUST perceive God's Creations, bringing all of your perceptions into the one parallel line which the Holy Spirit sees. This line is the direct line of communication with God, and lets YOUR mind converge with HIS. There is NO CONFLICT ANYWHERE in this perception, because it means that ALL perception is guided by the Holy Spirit, whose mind is fixed on God. ONLY the Holy Spirit can resolve conflict, because ONLY the Holy Spirit is conflict-free. He perceives ONLY what is true in YOUR mind, and extends outward to ONLY what is true in other minds.

14   The difference between the ego's use of projection and projection as the Holy Spirit uses it is very simple.

The ego projects to EXCLUDE and therefore to deceive.

The Holy Spirit projects by RECOGNIZING HIMSELF in EVERY mind, and thus perceives them as ONE.

Nothing conflicts in the Holy Spirit's perception, because what the Holy Spirit perceives IS the same. Wherever He looks He sees Himself, and because He is UNITED, He offers the whole Kingdom always. This is the one message which God gave TO Him, and for which He must speak because that is what He IS. The peace of God lies in that message, and so the peace of God lies in YOU.

15   The great peace of the Kingdom shines in your mind forever, but it must shine OUTWARD to make YOU aware of it.

The Holy Spirit was given you with perfect impartiality, and only by perceiving Him impartially can you perceive Him at all. The ego is legion, but the Holy Spirit is one. No darkness abides ANYWHERE in the Kingdom, so your part is only to allow no darkness to abide in your OWN mind.

> This alignment with Light is unlimited, because it is in alignment with the Light of the world. Each of us IS the Light of the world, and by joining our minds IN this Light, we proclaim the Kingdom of God together and AS ONE.

D. The Relinquishment of Attack

1   We have used many words as synonymous which are not ordinarily regarded as the same. We began with having and being, and recently have used others. Hearing and being is an example, to which we can also add teaching and being, learning and being, and, above all, PROJECTING and being.

    This is because, as we have said before, every idea begins in the mind of the thinker and extends outward. [237] Therefore, what extends FROM the mind IS STILL IN IT, and FROM what it extends IT KNOWS ITSELF. This is its natural talent.

2   The word "knows" is correct here, even though the ego does NOT know, and is not concerned with BEING at all. The Holy Spirit still holds knowledge safe through its impartial perception. By attacking nothing, it presents no barrier at all to the communication of God. Therefore, being is never threatened. Your Godlike mind can never be defiled. The ego never was and never will be part of it.

3   But through the ego you CAN hear and learn and teach and project WHAT IS NOT TRUE. From this, which YOU have made, you have taught yourselves to believe you ARE NOT WHAT YOU ARE. You CANNOT teach what you have not learned. And what you teach you strengthen in yourselves BECAUSE you are sharing it. Every lesson which you teach YOU are learning.

4   That is why you must teach only ONE lesson. If you are to be conflict free yourselves, you must learn ONLY from the Holy Spirit, and teach ONLY by Him. You ARE only love, but when you denied this you made what you ARE something you must LEARN. We said before that the message of the Crucifixion was teach ONLY love, for that is what you ARE. [238] This is the ONE lesson which is perfectly unified, because it is the only lesson which IS one. And only BY teaching it can YOU learn it.

5   "As you teach so will you learn." If that is true, and it is true indeed, you must never forget that what you teach is teaching YOU.

    What you project you BELIEVE.

    The only REAL safety lies in projecting ONLY the Holy Spirit, because as you see His gentleness in others your own mind perceives ITSELF as totally harmless. Once it can accept this fully, it does NOT see the need to PROTECT ITSELF. The protection of God then dawns upon it, assuring it that it is perfectly safe forever.

---

237 Chapter 5 F. Therapy and Teaching, p15
238 This chapter: B. The Message of the Crucifixion, p14

Chapter 6 – Attack And Fear

6 The perfectly safe ARE wholly benign. They bless because they know they ARE blessed. Without anxiety, the mind is wholly kind, and because it PROJECTS beneficence, it IS beneficent.

Safety is the COMPLETE RELINQUISHMENT OF ATTACK.

No compromise is possible in this. Teach attack in any form, and YOU HAVE LEARNED IT AND IT WILL HURT YOU. But your learning is not immortal, and you can unlearn it BY NOT TEACHING IT. Since you cannot NOT teach, your salvation lies in teaching exactly the opposite of EVERYTHING THE EGO BELIEVES. This is how YOU will learn the truth that will make you free, and keep you so as others learn it of YOU.

7 The only way to HAVE peace is to TEACH peace.

By learning it through projection, it becomes a part of you that you KNOW, because you cannot teach what you have dissociated. Only thus can you win back the knowledge you threw away.

An idea which you SHARE you MUST HAVE.

It awakens in you through the CONVICTION of teaching. Remember that if teaching is being and learning is being, then teaching is learning. EVERYTHING you teach YOU are learning.

Teach only love, and learn that love is yours and YOU are love.

E. The Only Answer

1 Remember that the Holy Spirit is the ANSWER, not the question. The ego always speaks first, because it is capricious and does NOT mean its maker well. This is because it believes, and correctly, that its maker may withdraw his support from it at any moment. If it meant you well, it would be glad, as the Holy Spirit will be glad when He has brought you home and you no longer need His guidance. The ego does NOT regard itself as part of you. Herein lies its primary perceptual error, the foundation of its whole thought system.

2 When God created you, He made you part of Him. That is why attack WITHIN the Kingdom is impossible. But YOU made the ego without love, and so it does not love YOU. You could not remain WITHIN the Kingdom without love, and since the Kingdom IS love, you believe you are WITHOUT it.

E. The Only Answer

This enables the ego to regard itself as SEPARATE AND OUTSIDE ITS MAKER, thus speaking for the part of your mind that believes YOU are separate and outside the Mind of God.

3   The ego, then, raised the first question that was ever asked, but it can never answer it. That question, which was "What are you?" was the beginning of doubt. The ego has never answered ANY questions since, though it has raised a great many. The most inventive activities of the ego have never done more than OBSCURE THE QUESTION, because you HAVE the answer, and THE EGO IS AFRAID OF YOU.

You cannot really understand conflict until YOU fully understand one basic fact that the ego does not know. The Holy Spirit does not speak first, but He ALWAYS answers. EVERYONE has called upon Him for help at one time or another, and in one way or another, AND HAS BEEN ANSWERED. Since the Holy Spirit answers truly, He answers FOR ALL TIME, and that means that EVERYONE HAS THE ANSWER NOW.

4   The ego cannot hear the Holy Spirit, but it DOES feel that part of the same mind that made it is AGAINST it. It interprets this wholly as a justification for ATTACKING its maker. The ego believes that the best defense is attack, and WANTS YOU TO BELIEVE THIS. Unless you DO believe it, you will not side with it. And the ego feels badly in need of allies, though not of brothers.

5   Perceiving something alien to itself in your MIND, the ego turns to the body, NOT the mind as its ally BECAUSE the body is not part of you. This makes the body the ego's friend. But it is an alliance frankly based on separation. If you side with this alliance, you WILL be afraid, because you are siding with an alliance OF fear. The ego and the body conspire AGAINST your minds, and because they realize that their "enemy" CAN end them both merely by knowing they are not part of him, they join in the attack together.

This is perhaps the strangest perception of all, if you consider what it really involves. The ego, which is not real, attempts to persuade the mind, which IS real, that it IS its own learning device, and that the learning device is more real than IT is. No-one in his right mind could POSSIBLY believe this, and no-one in his right mind DOES believe it.

6   Hear, then, the one answer of the Holy Spirit to ALL the questions which the ego raises:

> You are a Child of God, a priceless part of His Kingdom,
> which He created as part of Him.
> Nothing else exists, and ONLY this is real.

Chapter 6 – Attack And Fear

> You have chosen a sleep in which you have had bad dreams,
> but the sleep is not real, and God calls you to awake.
> There will be nothing left of your dream when you hear Him,
> because you WILL be awake.

Your dreams have contained many of the ego's symbols, and they have confused you. But that was only because you were asleep and DID NOT KNOW.

7 When you awake, you will see the Truth around you and in you, and you will no longer believe in dreams, because they will have no reality for you. But the Kingdom and all that you have created there will have great reality for you, because they are beautiful and true. In the Kingdom, where you are and what you are is perfectly certain. There is no doubt there, because the first question was never asked. Having finally been wholly answered, IT HAS NEVER BEEN. BEING alone lives in the Kingdom, where everything lives in God without question. The time that was spent on questioning in the dream has given way to the Creation and to its Eternity.

8 YOU are as certain as God, because you are as true as He is. But what was once quite certain in your minds has become only the ABILITY for certainty. The introduction of abilities into being was the beginning of UNcertainty, because abilities are POTENTIALS, not accomplishments. Your abilities are totally useless in the presence of God's accomplishments and also of yours. Accomplishments are RESULTS which HAVE BEEN achieved. When they are perfect, abilities are meaningless.

9 It is curious that the perfect must now be perfected. In fact, it is impossible. But you must remember that when you put yourselves in an impossible situation, you believed that the impossible WAS possible. [239]

10 Abilities must be DEVELOPED, or you cannot use them. [240] This is not true of anything that God created, but it is the kindest solution possible to what YOU have made.

In an impossible situation, you can develop your abilities to the point where they CAN GET YOU OUT OF IT.

---

[239] Chapter 3 G. The Loss of Certainty, p11 - 14
[240] Chapter 3 F. Conflict and the Ego, p1
  This chapter: C. The Uses of Projection, p5

E. The Only Answer

You have a guide to how to develop them, but you have no commander EXCEPT YOURSELF.

This leaves YOU in charge of the Kingdom, with both a guide to FIND it and a MEANS to keep it.

You have a model to follow who will strengthen YOUR command, and never detract from it in any way.

You therefore retain the central place in your perceived enslavement, a fact which ITSELF demonstrates that you are NOT enslaved.

11   You are in an impossible situation only because you thought it was possible to be in one. You WOULD be in an impossible situation if God showed you your perfection, and PROVED to you that you were wrong. This would demonstrate that the perfect were inadequate to bring THEMSELVES to the awareness of their perfection, and thus side with the belief that those who have everything need help, and are therefore helpless.

12   This is the kind of reasoning that the ego engages in, but God, who KNOWS that His creations are perfect does NOT insult them. This would be as impossible as the ego's notion that it has insulted Him.

That is why the Holy Spirit NEVER commands. To command is to assume INequality, which the Holy Spirit demonstrates does not exist. Fidelity to premises is a law of the mind, and everything God created is faithful to His laws. But fidelity to other laws is also possible, not because the laws are true, but because YOU MADE THEM.

13   What would be gained if God proved to you that you have thought insanely? Can God lose His own certainty? We have frequently stated that what you teach you ARE. Would you have God teach you that you have sinned? If He confronted the self you have made with the Truth He created FOR you, what could you be but afraid? You would doubt your sanity, which is the one thing in which you can FIND the sanity He gave you. God does not teach. To teach is to imply a lack which God KNOWS is not there. God is not conflicted. Teaching aims at change, but God created ONLY the changeless.

14   The separation was not a loss of perfection, but a failure in COMMUNICATION. A harsh and strident form of communication arose as the ego's voice. It could not shatter the peace of God, but it COULD shatter YOURS. God did not blot it out, because to eradicate it would be to attack it. Being questioned, He did not question. He merely gave the Answer.

15   God's answer IS your teacher.

F. "To Have, Give All to All"

1   Like any good teacher, He DOES know more than you know NOW, but He teaches only to make you equals. This is because you had ALREADY taught wrong, having believed what was not true. YOU DID NOT BELIEVE IN YOUR OWN PERFECTION. Could God teach you that you had made a split mind when He knows your mind only as whole?

2   What God DOES know is that His communication channels are not open to Him, so that He cannot impart His joy and know that His Children are wholly joyous. This is an ongoing process, not in time, but in eternity. God's extending outward, though not His completeness, was blocked when the Sonship does not communicate with Him as one. [241] So He thought, "My Children sleep, and must be awakened."

3   How can you wake children better and more kindly than with a gentle Voice that will not frighten them, but will merely remind them that the night is over and the Light has come?

>   You do not inform them that the nightmares which frightened them so badly were not real, because children BELIEVE in magic.

>   You merely reassure them that they are safe NOW.

>   Then you train them to RECOGNIZE THE DIFFERENCE between sleeping and waking, so that THEY will understand they need not be afraid of dreams.

      Then when bad dreams come, they will call on the Light THEMSELVES to dispel them.

4   A wise teacher teaches through approach, NOT avoidance. He does not emphasize what you must avoid to escape from harm as much as what you need to learn to have joy. This is true even of the world's teachers. Consider the confusion that a child would experience if he were told,

---

[241] Chapter 1 B. Principles of Miracles Principle 48; Principle 50, p4
  Chapter 4 H. Creation and Communication, p2 – p7
  Chapter 5 D. The Voice for God, p4

F. "To Have, Give All to All"

"Do not do THIS because it might hurt you and make you unsafe, but if you do THAT you will escape from harm and be safe, and then you will not be afraid."

All of this could be included in only three words:

"Do only that."

That simple statement is perfectly clear, easily understood, and very easily remembered.

5 The Holy Spirit NEVER itemizes errors, because He does not frighten children, and those who lack wisdom ARE children. But He ALWAYS answers their call, and His dependability makes THEM more certain. Children DO confuse fantasy and reality, and they ARE frightened because they do not know the difference.

6 The Holy Spirit makes NO distinction among dreams. He merely shines them away. His light is ALWAYS the call to awake, WHATEVER you may have been dreaming. Nothing lasting lies in dreams, and the Holy Spirit, shining with the light from God Himself, speaks only for what lasts forever.

7 When your body and your ego and your dreams are gone, you will know that YOU will last forever. Many think that this is accomplished through death, but NOTHING is accomplished through death because death is nothing. EVERYTHING is accomplished through life, and life is of the mind and in the Mind.

The body neither lives nor dies, because it cannot contain you who ARE life. If we share the same mind, YOU CAN OVERCOME DEATH BECAUSE I DID. Death is an attempt to resolve conflict by not willing at all. Like any other impossible solution which the ego attempts, IT WILL NOT WORK.

8 God did not make the body, because it is destructible, and therefore not of the Kingdom. The body is the symbol of the WHAT YOU THINK YOU ARE. It is clearly a separation device, and therefore does not exist. The Holy Spirit, as always, takes what you have made and translates it into a learning device FOR you. Again, as always, it re-interprets what the ego uses as an argument FOR separation into an argument AGAINST it.

9 If the mind can heal the body, but the body cannot heal the mind, then the mind MUST BE STRONGER. Every miracle demonstrates this. We have said that the Holy Spirit is the MOTIVATION for miracles. This is because He ALWAYS tells you that

Chapter 6 – Attack And Fear

ONLY the mind is real, because only the mind CAN BE SHARED. The body IS separate, and therefore CANNOT be part of you. To be of one mind is meaningful, but to be of one body is meaningless. By the laws of mind, then, the body IS meaningless.

10   To the Holy Spirit THERE IS NO ORDER OF DIFFICULTY IN MIRACLES. [242] This is FAMILIAR enough to you by now, but it has not yet become believable. Therefore, you do not understand it and cannot USE it.

We have too much to accomplish on behalf of the Kingdom to let this crucial concept slip away. It is a real foundation stone of the thought system I teach and want YOU to teach. You cannot perform miracles without believing it, because it is a belief in perfect equality.

11   Only one equal gift CAN be offered to the equal Sons of God, and that is FULL APPRECIATION. Nothing more and nothing less. Without a range, order of difficulty IS meaningless, and there must BE no range in what you offer to each other. The Holy Spirit, which leads to God, translates communication into being, just as He ultimately translates perception into knowledge.

12   You DO NOT LOSE WHAT YOU COMMUNICATE. The ego uses the body for attack, for pleasure, and for pride. The insanity of this perception makes it a fearful one. The Holy Spirit sees it only as a means of COMMUNICATION. And because communicating IS sharing, it becomes communion. You might argue that fear as well as love can be communicated, and therefore can be shared. But this is not so real as it sounds. Those who communicate fear are promoting attack, and attack always BREAKS communication, and therefore makes communion impossible.

13   Egos DO join together in temporary allegiance, but always for WHAT EACH ONE CAN GET SEPARATELY.

The Holy Spirit communicates only WHAT EACH ONE CAN GIVE TO ALL.

He never takes ANYTHING back, because He wants YOU to keep it.

Therefore, His teaching begins with the lesson:

To HAVE, GIVE all TO all.

14   This is a very preliminary step, and THE ONLY ONE YOU MUST TAKE YOURSELF.

It is not even necessary that you COMPLETE the step yourself, but it IS necessary that you turn in that direction.

---

242 Chapter 1 B. Principles Of Miracles Principle 1

F. "To Have, Give All to All"

Having willed to go that way:
> You place YOURSELF in charge of the journey, where you and ONLY you must remain.

15 This step APPEARS to exacerbate conflict rather than resolve it, because it is the BEGINNING step in reversing your perception and turning it right side up. This conflicts with the upside down perception which you have not yet abandoned, or the change in direction would not have been necessary. Some people remain at this step for a very long time, experiencing VERY acute conflict. Many try to accept the CONFLICT, rather than to take the next step toward its resolution. But having taken the first step, they WILL be helped. Having willed what they CANNOT complete alone, THEY ARE NO LONGER ALONE.

16 You, Helen, had taken this step, and because you believed in it, you taught it to Bill, who still believed in the solution of sleep. You were not consistent in teaching it, but you did so often enough to enable him to learn it. Once HE learned it, he could teach YOU how to become more consistently awake, and thus begin to waken HIMSELF. This placed him, too, in command of the journey. His recognition of the direction it must take was perfectly stated when he INSISTED ON COLLABORATION.

17 You, H., had taken a giant step INTO conflict, but B. turned you both forwards TOWARD THE WAY OUT. The more he teaches this, the more he will learn it.

G. "To Have Peace, Teach Peace to Learn It"

1 All the separated ones have a basic fear of retaliation and abandonment. This is because they BELIEVE in attack and rejection, so this is what they perceive and teach and LEARN.

These insane concepts are clearly the result of their own dissociation and projection. What you teach you are, but it is quite apparent that you can teach wrongly, and therefore TEACH YOURSELVES WRONG. Many thought that I was attacking them, even though it is quite apparent that I was NOT. An insane learner learns strange lessons.

2 What you must understand is that, when you do not SHARE a thought system, you ARE weakening it.
> Those who BELIEVE in it therefore perceive this as an ATTACK ON THEM. [243]

This is because everyone identifies himself WITH his thought system, and EVERY thought system centers on WHAT YOU BELIEVE YOU ARE. If the center of the

---

[243] i.e. mob mentality 'truism:' "If you are not for us, you are against us."

Chapter 6 – Attack And Fear

thought system is TRUE, only truth extends outward from it. But if a lie is at its center, only DECEPTION proceeds from it.

3   All good teachers realize that only fundamental change will last. But they do NOT begin at that level.

Strengthening MOTIVATION for change is their first and foremost goal. It is also their last and final one.

Increasing motivation for change IN THE LEARNER is all that a teacher NEED do to GUARANTEE change.

This is because a change in motivation IS a change of mind, and this will INEVITABLY produce fundamental change BECAUSE the mind IS fundamental.

4   The first step in the reversal or undoing process, then, is the UNDOING of the getting concept. Accordingly, the Holy Spirit's first lesson was: To HAVE, GIVE all TO all. We said that this is apt to INCREASE conflict temporarily, and we can clarify this still further now. At this point, the equality of having and being is not yet perceived. Until it IS, having still appears to be the OPPOSITE of being. Therefore, the first lesson SEEMS to contain a contradiction because it is BEING LEARNED BY A CONFLICTED MIND. This MEANS conflicting motivation, and so the lesson CANNOT be learned consistently as yet.

5   Further, the mind of the learner projects its own split, and therefore does NOT perceive consistent minds in others, making him suspicious of THEIR motivations. This is the real reason why in many respects the first lesson is the hardest to learn. Still strongly aware of the ego in himself, and responding primarily TO the ego in others, he is being taught to react to BOTH as if what he DOES believe IS NOT TRUE.

6   Upside down as always, the ego perceives the first lesson as insane. In fact, this is its only alternative here, because the other one, which would be much LESS acceptable, would obviously be that IT is insane. The ego's judgment, then, is predetermined by what it IS, though not more so than is any other product of thought. The fundamental change will still occur with the change of mind IN THE THINKER.

7   Meanwhile, the increasing clarity of the Holy Spirit's voice makes it impossible for the learner NOT TO LISTEN. For a time, then, he IS receiving conflicting messages AND ACCEPTING BOTH.

This is the classic "double bind" in communication, which you wrote about yourselves quite recently, and with good examples too. It is interesting that Helen claimed at the time that she had never heard of it and did not understand it. You might remember our brother's insistence on its inclusion. Helen thought he had become (quite)

G. "To Have Peace, Teach Peace to Learn It"

irrational on this point, but it was quite strongly reinforced in HIS mind, and so he wanted to teach it in his text. This, of course, was a very good way for YOU to learn it.

8   The way out of conflict between two opposing thought systems is clearly TO CHOOSE ONE AND RELINQUISH THE OTHER.

If you identify WITH your thought system, and you cannot escape this, and if you accept two thought systems which are in COMPLETE DISagreement, peace of mind IS impossible. If you TEACH both, which you will surely do as long as you ACCEPT both, you are teaching conflict and LEARNING it. But you DO want peace, or you would not have called upon the voice for PEACE to help you. His LESSON is not insane, but the CONFLICT IS.

9   There can BE no conflict between sanity and insanity, because only one is true, and therefore only ONE is REAL. The ego tries to persuade you that it is up to YOU to decide which voice is true. But the Holy Spirit teaches you that truth was created by God, and YOUR decision CANNOT change it. As you begin to realize the quiet power of His Voice AND ITS PERFECT CONSISTENCY, it MUST dawn on your minds that you are trying to undo a decision which was made irrevocably FOR you. That is why we suggested before that there was help in reminding yourselves to allow the Holy Spirit to decide for God for YOU. [244]

10   You are NOT asked to make insane decisions, although you are free to THINK you are. But it MUST be insane to believe IT IS UP TO YOU to decide what God's Creations ARE. The Holy Spirit perceives the conflict EXACTLY AS IT IS.

Therefore, His second lesson is:

To HAVE peace, TEACH peace to LEARN it.

11   This is still a preliminary step, because having and being are still not equated but it is more advanced than the first step, which is really only a thought REVERSAL. The second step is a positive affirmation of WHAT YOU WANT. This, then IS a step in the direction OUT of conflict, because it means that alternatives have been considered, and ONE has been chosen as MORE DESIRABLE.

12   But the evaluation "more desirable" still implies that the desirable has degrees. Therefore, although this step is essential for the ultimate decision, it is clearly NOT the final one.

---

[244] Chapter 5 I. The Eternal Fixation, p20

Chapter 6 – Attack And Fear

13   It should be clear that the recognition of the lack of order in miracles has not yet been accepted, because NOTHING is difficult that is WHOLLY DESIRED.

To desire wholly is to CREATE, and creating CANNOT be difficult if God Himself created you AS a creator. The second step, then, is still perceptual but it is nevertheless a giant step toward the unified perception that parallels God's knowing.

14   As you take this step and HOLD THIS DIRECTION, you will be pushing toward the center of your thought system, where the FUNDAMENTAL change will occur. You are only beginning this step now, but you have started on this way by realizing that ONLY ONE WAY IS POSSIBLE. You do not yet realize this consistently, and so your progress is intermittent, but the second step is easier than the first, because it FOLLOWS. The very fact that you have accepted THAT is a demonstration of your growing awareness that the Holy Spirit WILL lead you on.

H. "Be Vigilant Only for God and His Kingdom"

1   For your own salvation you MUST be critical, because YOUR salvation IS critical to the whole Sonship. We said before that the Holy Spirit IS evaluative, and MUST be. Yet His evaluation does not extend BEYOND you, or you WOULD share it.

In YOUR mind, and your mind ONLY, He sorts out the true from the false, and teaches you to judge every thought that you allow to ENTER in the light of what God PUT there.

Whatever is IN ACCORD with this light He retains, to strengthen the Kingdom in YOU.

When it is PARTLY in accord with truth He accepts it and purifies it.

But what is OUT OF ACCORD ENTIRELY He rejects by judging against. This is how He keeps the Kingdom perfectly consistent and perfectly unified.

2   But what you must remember is that what the Holy Spirit REJECTS the ego ACCEPTS. This is because they are in fundamental disagreement about everything, because they are in fundamental disagreement about WHAT YOU ARE.

The ego's beliefs on this crucial issue vary, and that is why it promotes different moods.

The Holy Spirit NEVER varies on this point, and so the ONE mood that He engenders is joy.

He PROTECTS this by rejecting everything that does NOT foster joy, and so He alone can keep you wholly joyous.

H. "Be Vigilant Only for God and His Kingdom"

3   *The Holy Spirit does not teach your mind to be critical of other minds*, because He does not want you to teach your errors and LEARN THEM YOURSELVES. He would hardly be consistent if He allowed you to STRENGTHEN what you must learn to avoid.

In the mind of the THINKER, then, He IS judgmental, but only in order to unify it so IT CAN perceive WITHOUT judgment.

This enables the mind to TEACH without judgment and therefore learn to BE without judgment. *The UNdoing is necessary only in YOUR mind, so that you cannot PROJECT it.* God Himself has established what you can project with perfect safety.

Therefore, the Holy Spirit's third lesson is:

Be vigilant ONLY for God and HIS Kingdom.

4   This is a major step toward FUNDAMENTAL change. Yet it is still a lesson in thought REVERSAL, because it implies that there is something you must be vigilant AGAINST. It has advanced far from the first lesson which was PRIMARILY a reversal, and also from the second, which was essentially the identification of what is MORE desirable.

This step, which follows from the second as the second does from the first, emphasizes the DICHOTOMY between the desirable and the UNdesirable. It therefore makes the ULTIMATE choice inevitable. But while the first step seems to INCREASE conflict, and the second still ENTAILS it to some extent, this one calls for CONSISTENT EFFORT AGAINST IT.

5   We said already that you can be as vigilant AGAINST the ego as FOR it. [245]

This lesson teaches not that you CAN be, but that you MUST be.

It does not concern itself with order of difficulty, but with CLEAR-CUT PRIORITY FOR VIGILANCE. This step is unequivocal in that it teaches THERE MUST BE NO EXCEPTIONS, but it does NOT deny that the temptations to MAKE exceptions will occur. Here, then, your consistency is called on DESPITE chaos. But chaos and consistency CANNOT coexist for long, because they are MUTUALLY EXCLUSIVE. As long as you must be vigilant against ANYTHING, however, you are not recognizing this, and are holding the belief that you can CHOOSE EITHER ONE.

6   By teaching you WHAT to choose, the Holy Spirit will ultimately be able to teach you that YOU NEED NOT CHOOSE AT ALL. This will finally liberate your will FROM

---

245 Chapter 4 E. The Escape from Fear, p1
  Chapter 4 E. The Escape from Fear a. This Need Not Be, p5, p9

Chapter 6 – Attack And Fear

choice, and direct it towards creation WITHIN the Kingdom. Choosing through the Holy Spirit will only lead you TO it. You create by what you ARE, but this IS what you must learn. The way to learn it is INHERENT in the third step, which brings together the lessons inherent in the others, and goes beyond them towards real integration.

7   If you allow yourselves to HAVE in your minds only what God put there, you are acknowledging your mind as God created it. Therefore, you are accepting it AS IT IS. And since it IS whole, you are teaching peace BECAUSE you have believed in it. *The final step will still be taken FOR you by God.*

But by the third step, the Holy Spirit has PREPARED you FOR God. He is GETTING YOU READY to translate having into being by the very nature of the steps you must take WITH Him.

You learn first that having rests on GIVING and NOT getting.

Next you learn that you learn what you TEACH, and that you WANT TO LEARN PEACE.

This is the CONDITION for identifying WITH the Kingdom, because it is the condition OF the Kingdom.

8   But you have believed that you are WITHOUT the Kingdom, and have therefore excluded yourself FROM it in your belief. It is therefore essential to teach you that YOU must be INCLUDED, and the BELIEF THAT YOU ARE NOT is the ONLY thing that you must exclude.

9   The third step is thus one of PROTECTION for your minds by allowing you to identify ONLY with the center, where God placed the altar to HIMSELF. We have already said that altars are BELIEFS, but God and His creations are BEYOND belief because they are beyond question. The Voice FOR God speaks only for BELIEF beyond question, but this IS the preparation for BEING without question.

10   As long as belief in God and His Kingdom is assailed by ANY doubts in your minds, His perfect Accomplishment is NOT apparent to you. This is why you MUST be vigilant ON GOD'S BEHALF. The ego speaks AGAINST His Creation, and therefore DOES engender doubt.

You cannot go BEYOND belief UNTIL you believe wholly. No one can EXTEND a lesson he has NOT LEARNED FULLY. Transfer, which IS extension, is the measure of learning because it is the MEASURABLE RESULT. This, however, does NOT mean that what it transfers TO is measurable. On the contrary, unless it transfers to the whole Sonship, which is immeasurable because it was created BY the Immeasurable, the learning itself MUST be incomplete.

H. "Be Vigilant Only for God and His Kingdom"

11   To teach the WHOLE Sonship WITHOUT EXCEPTION demonstrates that you PERCEIVE ITS WHOLENESS and have learned that it IS One. Now you must be vigilant to HOLD its Oneness in your minds because if you allow doubt to enter, YOU will lose awareness of its wholeness, and WILL BE UNABLE TO TEACH IT.

12   The wholeness of the Kingdom does NOT depend on your perception, but your AWARENESS of its wholeness DOES. It is only your awareness that NEEDS protection, because your BEING cannot be assailed. Yet a real sense of being CANNOT be yours while you are doubtful of what you ARE. THIS IS WHY VIGILANCE IS ESSENTIAL. Doubts ABOUT being MUST not enter your mind, or you CANNOT know what you are with certainty.

13   Certainty is OF God for YOU. Vigilance is not necessary for truth, but it IS necessary AGAINST ILLUSION. Truth is WITHOUT illusions, and therefore WITHIN the Kingdom. Everything OUTSIDE the Kingdom IS ILLUSION. But you must learn to ACCEPT truth because YOU THREW IT AWAY. You therefore saw yourself AS IF you were WITHOUT it.

By making another Kingdom WHICH YOU VALUED, you did NOT keep the Kingdom of God alone in your minds, and thus placed part of your mind OUTSIDE of it. What you have made has thus DIVIDED YOUR WILL and given you a sick mind that MUST be healed. Your vigilance AGAINST this sickness IS the way to heal it.

14   Once YOUR mind is healed, it radiates health and thereby TEACHES healing. This establishes you as a teacher who teaches LIKE me. Vigilance was required of me as much as of you. But remember that those who will to teach the same thing MUST be in agreement about what they believe.

15   The third step, then, is a statement of what you WANT to believe, and entails a willingness to RELINQUISH EVERYTHING ELSE. I told you that you were just beginning the second step, but I also told you that the third one FOLLOWS it. The Holy Spirit WILL enable you to go on IF YOU FOLLOW HIM. Your vigilance is the sign that you WANT Him to guide you.

Vigilance DOES require effort, but only to teach you that effort ITSELF is unnecessary.

You have exerted GREAT effort to preserve what you made BECAUSE it is NOT true. Therefore, you must now turn your effort AGAINST it. Only this can cancel out the NEED for effort, and call upon the BEING which you both HAVE and ARE.

THIS recognition is wholly WITHOUT effort, because it is ALREADY true and needs no protection. It is in the perfect safety of God. Therefore, inclusion is total and Creation is WITHOUT LIMIT.

Chapter 7 - The Consistency Of The Kingdom

A. Introduction

1   The creative power of both God AND His Creations is limitless, but it is NOT in reciprocal relationship. You DO communicate fully WITH God, as He does with YOU. This is an ongoing process in which you SHARE, and BECAUSE you share it, you are inspired to create LIKE God.

    But in Creation you are NOT in a reciprocal relation TO God, because He created YOU, but you did NOT create Him. We have already stated that only in this respect your creative power differs from His. Even in this world there is a parallel. Parents give birth to children, but children do NOT give birth to parents. They DO, however, give birth to their children, and thus give birth AS their parents do.

2   If you created GOD and He created you, the KINGDOM could not increase through its OWN creative thought. Creation would therefore be limited, and you would NOT be co-creators WITH God. As God's creative Thought proceeds FROM Him TO you, so must YOUR creative thoughts proceed FROM you to YOUR creations. In this way only can ALL creative power EXTEND OUTWARD.

    God's accomplishments are NOT yours. But yours are LIKE His. HE created the Sonship, and YOU increase it. You HAVE the power to ADD to the Kingdom, but NOT to add to the Creator OF the Kingdom.

3   You claim this power when you have become wholly vigilant for God AND the Kingdom. BY ACCEPTING this power as YOURS, you have learned to be what you ARE. YOUR creations belong in YOU, as YOU belong in God. You are part of God, as your sons are part of His Sons. To create is to love. Love extends outward simply because it cannot be contained. Being limitless, it DOES NOT STOP. It creates forever, but NOT in time. God's creations have ALWAYS BEEN, because HE has always been. YOUR creations have always been, because you can create only as HE creates.

4   Eternity is yours because He created you eternal.

B. Bargaining versus Healing

1   The ego demands RECIPROCAL rights, because it is competitive rather than loving. It is always willing to make a deal, but it cannot understand that to be LIKE another means that NO DEALS ARE POSSIBLE.

B. Bargaining versus Healing

To gain you must GIVE, not bargain. To bargain is to LIMIT giving, and this is NOT God's Will. To will WITH God is to create like HIM. God does not limit HIS gifts in ANY way. You ARE His gifts, and so your gifts must be like HIS.

2 Your gifts TO the Kingdom are like His to YOU. I gave ONLY love to the Kingdom, because I believed that was what I WAS. What you believe you are DETERMINES your gifts, and if God created you by extending HIMSELF AS you, you can only extend YOURSELF as He did. Only joy increases forever. Joy and Eternity are INSEPARABLE. God extends outward beyond limits and beyond time, and you, who are co-creators with Him, extend His Kingdom forever and beyond limit.

Eternity is the indelible stamp of Creation. The eternal are in peace and joy forever.

3 To think like God is to share His certainty of WHAT YOU ARE. And to CREATE like Him is to share the perfect love He shares with YOU. To this the Holy Spirit leads you, that your joy may be complete because the Kingdom of God is whole. We have said that the last step in the re-awakening of knowledge is taken by God. [246]

This is true, but it is hard to explain in words, because words are symbols, and nothing that is true NEEDS to be explained. However, the Holy Spirit always has the task of translating the useLESS into the useFUL, the meaningLESS into the meaningFUL, and the temporary into the timeLESS. He CAN, therefore, tell you something about this last step, but this one you must know yourself, because BY it you know what you are. This IS your being.

4 God does not take steps because His Accomplishments are NOT gradual. He does not teach, because His Creations are changeless. He does nothing LAST because He Created FIRST and FOR ALWAYS. It must be understood that the word "first" as applied to Him is NOT a time concept. He is first here only in the sense that He is first in the Holy Trinity Itself. He is the Prime Creator because HE created His co-creators. Because He DID, time applies neither to Him NOR to what He created.

5 The "last step" that God was said to take was therefore true in the beginning, is true now, and will be true forever. What is timeless IS ALWAYS THERE because its BEING is eternally changeless. It does NOT change by increase, because it was forever created TO increase. If you perceive it as NOT increasing, you do not know what it IS. You also do not know what created it, or who HE is. God does not REVEAL this to you, because it was never hidden. His light was never obscured, because it is His Will to SHARE it. How can what is fully shared be withheld and then revealed?

---

[246] Chapter 5 C. The Mind of the Atonement, p2

Chapter 7 - The Consistency Of The Kingdom

6   To heal is the ONLY kind of thinking in this world that resembles the Thought of God, and because of the elements which they SHARE, can transfer TO it. [247]

When a brother perceives himself as sick, he IS perceiving himself as NOT WHOLE, and therefore IN NEED. If you, too, see him this way, you are seeing him as if he were ABSENT from the Kingdom or separated FROM it, thus making the Kingdom ITSELF obscure to BOTH OF YOU. Sickness and separation are not of God, but the Kingdom IS. If *you* obscure the Kingdom, *you* are perceiving WHAT IS NOT OF GOD.

C. The Laws of Mind

1

    To heal, then, is to correct perception in your brother AND yourself by SHARING THE HOLY SPIRIT WITH HIM.

    This places you both WITHIN the Kingdom and restores ITS wholeness in your minds. This PARALLELS creation because it UNIFIES BY INCREASING, and INTEGRATES BY EXTENDING.

2   WHAT YOU PROJECT YOU BELIEVE. [248] This is an immutable law of mind in this world as well as in the Kingdom.

However, its CONTENT is somewhat different in this world from what it REALLY is, because the thoughts it governs are VERY different from the thoughts in the Kingdom. Laws must be adapted to circumstances, if they are to maintain order.

3   The outstanding characteristic of the laws of mind, as they operate in this world, is that by obeying them, and I assure you that you MUST obey them, you can arrive at diametrically opposed results. This is because the laws have adapted to the circumstances of this world, in which diametrically opposed outcomes are BELIEVED in. The laws of mind govern thoughts, and you DO respond to two conflicting voices.

You have heard many arguments on behalf of "the freedoms," which would indeed have BEEN freedom if man had not chosen to FIGHT for them. That is why they perceive "the freedoms" as many instead of ONE.

4   But the argument that underlies the DEFENSE of freedom is perfectly valid. Because it is true, it should not be FOUGHT for, but it SHOULD be sided WITH. Those who are AGAINST freedom believe that its outcome will hurt them, which CANNOT be true. But those who are FOR freedom, even if they are misguided in HOW they defend it, are siding with the one thing in this world which IS true. Whenever anyone can listen

---

247 Chapter 5 C. The Mind of the Atonement, p7 - 8
    Chapter 5 F. Therapy and Teaching, p16
248 Chapter 6 D. The Relinquishment of Attack, p5

C. The Laws of Mind

fairly to both sides of ANY issue, he WILL make the right decision. This is because he HAS the answer. Conflict can indeed be projected, but it MUST be intrapersonal [249] first.

5   The term "intraPERSONAL" is an ego term, because "personal" implies of ONE person, and NOT of others. "Interpersonal" has a similar error, because it implies something that exists between DIFFERENT individuals. When we spoke before of the extremely PERSONAL nature of revelation, [250] we followed this statement immediately with a description of the inevitable outcomes of the revelation in terms of SHARING. A PERSON conceives of himself as separate, largely because he perceives OF himself as bounded by a body. ONLY if he perceives as a MIND can he overcome this. THEN he is free to use terms like "intraMENTAL" and "interMENTAL" WITHOUT seeing them as different and conflicting, because minds CAN be in perfect accord.

6   OUTSIDE the Kingdom, the law which prevails INSIDE it is ADAPTED to:

"what you project you believe."

7   This is its TEACHING form, because outside the Kingdom teaching is mandatory because learning is essential. This form of the law clearly implies that you will learn what YOU are from what you have projected onto others and therefore believe THEY are.

IN the Kingdom, there is no teaching OR learning, because there is no BELIEF. There is only CERTAINTY. God and His Sons, in the surety of Being, KNOW that what you project you ARE.

8   That form of the law is NOT adapted at all, being the Law of Creation. God Himself created the law by creating BY it. And His Sons, who create LIKE Him, follow it gladly, knowing that the INCREASE of the Kingdom depends on it, just as THEIR creation did.

Laws must be communicated, if they are to be helpful. In effect, they must be TRANSLATED for those who speak a different language. But a good translator, though he MUST alter the FORM of what he translates, NEVER changes the meaning. In fact, his whole PURPOSE is to change the form SO THAT the original meaning IS retained.

9   The Holy Spirit IS the translator of the Laws of God to those who do NOT understand them. YOU could not do this yourselves because conflicted minds CANNOT be faithful to one meaning, and will therefore CHANGE THE MEANING TO PRESERVE THE FORM. The Holy Spirit's purpose in translating is naturally EXACTLY the opposite. He translates ONLY to preserve the original meaning in ALL respects and in ALL languages. Therefore, He OPPOSES differences in form as

---

[249] Intra-personal: occurring within the same mind i.e my mind; my own conflicting thoughts.
   Inter-personal: occurring in relationship; between two 'separate' minds i.e. differing thoughts between you and I.
[250] Chapter 1 B. Principles Of Miracles Principle 35, p8

Chapter 7 - The Consistency Of The Kingdom

meaningful, and emphasizes always that THESE DIFFERENCES DO NOT MATTER. The meaning of His message is ALWAYS the same, and ONLY the meaning matters.

10   God's Law of Creation, in perfect form, does NOT involve the USE of truth to convince His sons OF truth. [251] The EXTENSION of truth, which IS the Law of the Kingdom, rests only on the knowledge of WHAT TRUTH IS. This is your INHERITANCE, and requires no learning at all. But when you DISinherited YOURSELVES, you BECAME learners. No-one questions the intimate connection of learning and memory. Learning is impossible WITHOUT memory, because it CANNOT be consistent UNLESS it is remembered.

11   That is why the Holy Spirit IS a lesson in remembering. We said before that He teaches remembering and FORGETTING, [252] but the forgetting aspect is only TO MAKE THE REMEMBERING CONSISTENT. You forget to REMEMBER BETTER. You will NOT understand His translations while you listen to two ways of perceiving them. Therefore, you must forget or relinquish one to UNDERSTAND the other. This is the only way you can LEARN consistency, so that you can finally BE consistent. What can the perfect consistency of the Kingdom MEAN to the confused? It MUST be apparent that confusion INTERFERES with meaning, and therefore PREVENTS THE LEARNER FROM APPRECIATING IT.

12   There is NO confusion in the Kingdom, because there IS only one meaning. This Meaning comes from God and IS God. Because it is also YOU, you share it and EXTEND it AS YOUR CREATOR DID. This needs no translation, because it is perfectly understood, but it DOES need extension because it MEANS extension. Communication here is perfectly direct and perfectly united. It is totally without strain, because nothing discordant EVER enters. That is why it IS the Kingdom of God. It belongs to Him and is therefore LIKE Him. That IS its reality, and nothing CAN assail it.

D. The Unified Curriculum

1   To heal is to liberate totally. We once said there is no order in miracles because they are all MAXIMAL EXPRESSIONS OF LOVE. [253] This has no range at all. The non-maximal only APPEARS to have a range. This is because it SEEMS to be meaningful to measure it FROM the maximum and identify its position by HOW MUCH IT IS NOT THERE. Actually, this does not mean ANYTHING.

It is like negative numbers in that the concept can be used theoretically, but it has NO application practically. It is true that if you put three apples on the table and then

---

251 Chapter 1 B. Principles Of Miracles Principle 11
252 Chapter 5 D. The Voice for God, p4
253 Chapter 1 B. Principles Of Miracles Principle 1, Principle 3

D. The Unified Curriculum

took them AWAY, the three apples are NOT THERE. But it is NOT true that the table is now MINUS three apples. If there is NOTHING on the table, it does NOT matter what WAS there in terms of amount. The "nothing" is neither greater nor less because of what is ABSENT.

2 That is why "all" and "nothing" are dichotomous, WITHOUT A RANGE. This is perfectly clear in maximal test performance and for EXACTLY the reason you emphasize. You cannot interpret AT ALL, unless you assume either MAXIMAL motivation or its COMPLETE ABSENCE. Only in these two conditions can you validly COMPARE responses, and you MUST assume the former, because if the LATTER is true, the subject WILL NOT DO ANYTHING. Given VARIABLE motivation he WILL do something, but you CANNOT UNDERSTAND WHAT IT IS.

3 The RESULTS of tests are evaluated relatively, ASSUMING maximal motivation. But this is because we are dealing with ABILITIES, where degree of development IS meaningful. This does NOT mean that what ability is used FOR is necessarily either limited OR divided. But one thing is certain. Abilities are POTENTIALS for learning, and you will apply them to WHAT YOU WANT TO LEARN. Learning is EFFORT, and effort MEANS will.

4 You will notice that we have used the term "abilities" as a plural, which is correct. This is because abilities began with the ego, which perceived them as a POTENTIAL FOR EXCELLING. This is how the ego STILL perceives them and uses them. It does NOT want to teach everyone all it has learned, because that would DEFEAT its purpose in learning. Therefore, it does not REALLY learn at all. The Holy Spirit teaches YOU to use what the ego has made to TEACH the opposite of what the ego has LEARNED. The KIND of learning is as irrelevant as is the particular ability which was applied TO the learning.

5 You could not have a better example of the Holy Spirit's unified purpose than this course. The Holy Spirit has taken very diversified areas of YOUR past learning, and has applied them to a UNIFIED curriculum. The fact that this was NOT the ego's reason for learning is totally irrelevant. YOU made the effort to learn, and the Holy Spirit has a unified goal for ALL effort. He ADAPTS the ego's potentials for excelling to potentials for EQUALIZING. This makes them USELESS for the ego's purpose, but VERY useful for His.

6 If different abilities are applied long enough to one GOAL, the abilities THEMSELVES become unified. This is because they are channelized in one direction, or in one WAY. Ultimately, then, they all contribute to ONE RESULT, and by so doing, their SIMILARITY rather than their differences is emphasized. You can EXCEL in many

Chapter 7 - The Consistency Of The Kingdom

DIFFERENT ways, but you can EQUALIZE in ONE WAY ONLY. Equality is NOT a variable state, by definition.

7   That is why we once said that papers will be easy to write when you have learned THIS course. [254]

To the ego there appears to be no connection, because the EGO is discontinuous.

But the Holy Spirit teaches one lesson and *applies it to ALL individuals in ALL situations.*

Being conflict free, He maximizes ALL efforts and ALL results.

By teaching the power of the Kingdom of God Himself, He teaches you that ALL POWER IS YOURS. *Its application does not matter.* It is ALWAYS maximal. Your vigilance does NOT establish it as yours, but it DOES enable you to use it ALWAYS and in ALL WAYS.

8
>   When I said, "Behold I am with you always," [255] I meant it literally. *I am not absent to ANYONE nor in ANY situation.* BECAUSE I am always with you, YOU are the Way, and the Truth, and the Light.

YOU did not make this power any more than I did. It was created to BE shared, and therefore cannot be meaningfully perceived as BELONGING to anyone AT THE EXPENSE of another. This perception makes it meaningLESS by eliminating or overlooking its real and ONLY meaning.

E. The Recognition of Truth

1   God's MEANING waits in the Kingdom because that is where He placed it. It does NOT wait in time. It merely RESTS there (in the Kingdom) because it BELONGS there, as YOU do. How can you, who ARE God's meaning, perceive yourselves as absent FROM it? You can see yourselves as separated FROM your meaning only by EXPERIENCING YOURSELF AS UNREAL.

This is WHY the ego is insane; it teaches that you are NOT what you ARE. This is so contradictory that it is clearly impossible. It is therefore a lesson which you CANNOT REALLY LEARN, and therefore CANNOT REALLY TEACH. But you ARE always teaching. You MUST, then, be teaching SOMETHING ELSE AS WELL, even though the ego DOES NOT KNOW WHAT IT IS.

---

254 Chapter 2 B. The Re-interpretation of Defenses a. Reinterpretation Of Some "Dynamic" Concepts, p18
255 Matthew 28:20 Teaching them to observe all things whatsoever I have commanded you: and, lo, I am with you always, even unto the end of the world. Amen.

E. The Recognition of Truth

2   The ego, then, IS always being undone, and DOES suspect your motives. Your mind CANNOT be unified in allegiance to the ego, because the mind does NOT BELONG to it. But what is "treacherous" to the ego IS faithful to peace. The ego's "enemy" is therefore YOUR friend. We said before that the ego's friend is not part of you but that is because the ego perceives itself as at war and therefore in need of allies. [256] YOU, who are NOT at war, must look for brothers and RECOGNIZE all you see AS brothers, because ONLY EQUALS ARE AT PEACE.

3   Because God's equal Sons have everything, they CANNOT compete. But if they perceive ANY of their brothers as anything OTHER than their perfect equals, the IDEA of competition HAS entered their minds.

> Do not underestimate your need to be vigilant AGAINST this idea, because ALL your conflicts come FROM it.

It IS the belief that conflicting interests are possible, and therefore means that you have accepted the IMpossible as true. How is that different from saying that you are perceiving YOURSELF as unreal?

4   To be IN the Kingdom is merely to focus your full attention ON it. As long as you believe that you can ATTEND to what is NOT true, you are accepting conflict as your CHOICE. IS IT REALLY A CHOICE? It SEEMS to be, but seeming and reality are hardly the same. You who ARE the Kingdom are not concerned with seeming. Reality is yours because you ARE reality. This is how having and being are ultimately reconciled, NOT in the Kingdom, but IN YOUR MINDS. The altar there is the ONLY reality. It is PERFECTLY clear in its thought, because it is a reflection of PERFECT Thought. It SEES only brothers because it sees ONLY in its own Light.

5   God has lit your minds Himself, and keeps your mind lit BY His light because His light is WHAT YOUR MINDS ARE. This is TOTALLY beyond question. And when YOU questioned it, you WERE answered. The answer merely UNDOES the question by establishing the fact that to QUESTION reality is to question MEANINGLESSLY. That is why the Holy Spirit NEVER questions. Its sole function is to UNdo the questionable, and thus LEAD TO CERTAINTY. The certain are perfectly calm, because they are not in doubt. They do NOT raise questions because NOTHING QUESTIONABLE ENTERS THEIR MINDS. This holds them in perfect serenity because this is what they SHARE, KNOWING what they are.

6   Healing is both an art and a science, as has so often been said. It is an art because it depends on inspiration in the sense that we have already used the term. Inspiration is the opposite of dis-spiriting, and therefore means to make joyful. The dis-spirited are

---

256 Chapter 6 E. The Only Answer, p4

Chapter 7 - The Consistency Of The Kingdom

depressed because they believe that they are literally "without the Spirit," which is an illusion.

You do not PUT the Spirit in them by inspiring them, because that would be "magic," and therefore would not be real healing.

But you DO recognize the Spirit that is ALREADY THERE, and thereby REAWAKEN IT.

This is why the healer is part of the Resurrection and the LIFE. *The SPIRIT is not asleep in the minds of the sick, but the part of the mind that can perceive it and be glad IS.*

7   Healing is also a science because it obeys the laws of God, whose laws are true. BECAUSE they are true, they are perfectly dependable, and therefore universal in application. The real aim of science is neither prediction nor control, but ONLY UNDERSTANDING. This is because it does NOT establish the laws it seeks; CANNOT discover them through prediction, and has NO control over them at all.

Science is nothing more than an approach to WHAT ALREADY IS. Like inspiration, it can be misunderstood as magic, and WILL be whenever it is undertaken as SEPARATE from what already is, and perceived as a means for ESTABLISHING it. To believe this is possible is to believe YOU CAN DO IT. This can ONLY be the voice of the ego.

8   Truth can only be RECOGNIZED, and NEED only be recognized. Inspiration is of the Spirit, and certainty is of God according to His laws. Both therefore come from the same Source, because inspiration comes from the voice FOR God and certainty comes from the laws OF God. Healing does not come DIRECTLY from God, who knows His Creations as perfectly whole. But healing is nevertheless OF God, because it proceeds from His Voice and from His laws. It is their RESULT in a state of mind which does not know Him. The STATE is unknown to Him, and therefore does not exist. But those who sleep are stupefied, or better, UNAWARE. And BECAUSE they are unaware THEY DO NOT KNOW.

9   *The Holy Spirit must work THROUGH you to teach you He is IN you.* This is an intermediary step toward the knowledge that YOU are in God BECAUSE YOU ARE PART OF HIM. The miracles which the Holy Spirit inspires CAN have no order, because every part of Creation IS of one order. This is God's will AND yours.

The laws of God ESTABLISH this, and the Holy Spirit reminds you OF it. When you heal, you are REMEMBERING THE LAWS OF GOD and FORGETTING the laws of the ego. We said before that forgetting is merely a way of REMEMBERING

E. The Recognition of Truth

BETTER. [257] It is therefore NOT the opposite of remembering, when it is properly conceived. Perceived IMproperly, it induces a perception of CONFLICT WITH SOMETHING ELSE, as all incorrect perception does. PROPERLY perceived, it can be used as a way OUT of conflict, as all proper perception can.

10   ALL abilities, then should be given over to the Holy Spirit, WHO KNOWS HOW TO USE THEM PROPERLY.

He can use them ONLY for healing, because He knows you ONLY as whole. BY healing you learn of wholeness, and by learning of wholeness you learn to remember God. You HAVE forgotten Him, but the Holy Spirit still knows that YOUR forgetting MUST be translated into a way of remembering, and NOT perceived as a SEPARATE ability which OPPOSES AN OPPOSITE. This is the way in which the ego tries to use ALL abilities, because its goal is ALWAYS to make YOU believe that YOU are in opposition.

11   The ego's goal is as unified as the Holy Spirit's, and it is BECAUSE of this that their goals can NEVER be reconciled in ANY way or to ANY extent. The ego ALWAYS seeks to divide and separate. The Holy Spirit ALWAYS seeks to unify and HEAL. As you heal, you ARE healed because the Holy Spirit sees NO ORDER OF HEALING. Healing IS the way to undo the belief in differences, because it is the ONLY way of perceiving the Sonship WITHOUT this belief. This perception is therefore IN accord with the laws of God even in a state of mind which is OUT of accord with His.

But the strength of right perception is so great that it brings the mind INTO accord with His, because it yields to His pull which IS in all of you.

12   To oppose the pull or the will of God is not an ability but a real delusion. The ego believes that it HAS this ability, and can offer this ability to YOU as a gift. YOU DO NOT WANT IT. It is NOT a gift. It is NOTHING AT ALL. God HAS given you a gift, which you both HAVE and ARE. When you do not USE it, you do not know you HAVE it. By not knowing this, you do NOT know what you ARE.

Healing, then, is a way of APPROACHING knowledge by THINKING in accordance with the laws of God and RECOGNIZING THEIR UNIVERSALITY. WITHOUT this recognition, you have made the laws themselves meaningless TO you. But the LAWS are not meaningless, because all meaning is contained BY them, and IN them.

---

257 Chapter 5 D. The Voice for God, p4
   This chapter: C. The Laws of Mind, p11

Chapter 7 - The Consistency Of The Kingdom

13   Seek ye FIRST the Kingdom of Heaven, [258] because that is where the laws of God operate truly, and they can operate ONLY truly, because they are the laws of Truth. But SEEK THIS ONLY, because you can FIND nothing else. There IS nothing else. God is all in all in a very literal sense. All being is in Him because He IS all Being. YOU are therefore in Him because YOUR being IS His.

    Healing is a way of FORGETTING the sense of danger that the ego has induced in YOU by not recognizing its (sense of danger's) existence in your brothers. This strengthens the Holy Spirit in BOTH of you, because it is a REFUSAL TO ACKNOWLEDGE FEAR. Love needs only this invitation. It comes freely to ALL the Sonship, because it is what the Sonship IS.

    By their awakening TO it, they merely forget what they are NOT. This enables them to remember what they ARE.

F. Healing and the Changelessness of Mind

1   The body is nothing more than a framework for developing abilities. It is therefore a means for developing potentials, which is quite apart from what the potential is used FOR. This IS a decision. The effects of the ego's decision in this matter are so apparent that they need no elaboration here. But the Holy Spirit's decision to use the body ONLY for communication has such direct connection with healing that it DOES need clarification. The unhealed healer OBVIOUSLY does not understand his own vocation.

2   ONLY minds communicate. Since the ego CANNOT obliterate the impulse to communicate because it is also the impulse to CREATE it can only try to teach you that the BODY can both communicate AND create, and therefore DOES NOT NEED THE MIND. The ego, then, tries to teach you that the body can ACT like the mind, and therefore IS self-sufficient. But we have learned that behavior is NOT the level for either teaching OR learning. [259] This MUST be so, because you CAN act in accordance with what you do NOT believe. But this will weaken you as teachers AND learners because, as has been repeatedly emphasized, you teach what you DO believe. An inconsistent lesson WILL be poorly taught and POORLY LEARNED. If you teach both sickness AND healing, you ARE both a poor teacher and a poor learner.

3   Healing is the one ability that everyone CAN develop, and MUST develop, if he is to BE healed. Healing IS the Holy Spirit's form of communication, and THE ONLY ONE

---

258 Matthew 6:33 But seek ye first the kingdom of God, and his righteousness; and all these things shall be added unto you.
259 Chapter 2 C. Healing as Release from Fear, p20
    Chapter 2 D. Fear as Lack of Love, p7 (p1 – 13)
    Chapter 4 E. The Escape from Fear, p2

F. Healing and the Changelessness of Mind

HE KNOWS. He recognizes no other, because he does NOT accept the ego's confusion of mind and body. Minds CAN communicate, but they CANNOT hurt. The body in the service of the ego can hurt other BODIES, but this CANNOT occur UNLESS the body has ALREADY been confused WITH the mind. This fact, too, can be used either for healing or for magic, but you must realize that magic is ALWAYS the belief that healing is HARMFUL. This is its totally insane premise, and so it proceeds accordingly.

4   Healing ONLY STRENGTHENS. Magic always tries to weaken. Healing perceives NOTHING in the healer that everyone else does not share WITH him. Magic ALWAYS sees something special in the healer, which he believes he can offer as a gift to someone who does NOT have it. He may believe that this gift comes from God TO him, but it is quite evident that he does NOT understand God if he thinks HE has something that others DO NOT. You might well ask why SOME healing CAN result from this kind of thinking, and there is a real reason for this.

5   However misguided the "magical healer" may be, and however much he may be trying to strengthen his ego, HE IS ALSO TRYING TO HELP. He IS conflicted and unstable, but AT TIMES he is offering SOMETHING to the Sonship, and the ONLY thing the Sonship can ACCEPT IS healing. When the so-called healing "works," then, the impulse both to help and BE helped have coincided. This is co-incidental, because the healer may NOT be experiencing HIMSELF as truly helpful at the time, and the belief that he IS, in the mind of ANOTHER, HELPS HIM. [260]

6   The Holy Spirit does NOT work by chance, and the healing that is of HIM ALWAYS works. And unless the healer ALWAYS heals BY Him, the results WILL vary. But healing itself IS consistence, because ONLY consistence is conflict-free, and only the conflict-free ARE whole. By accepting exceptions, and acknowledging that he can SOMETIMES heal and SOMETIMES not, the healer is OBVIOUSLY accepting INconsistency. He is therefore IN conflict and TEACHING conflict.

7   Can ANYTHING of God NOT be for all and always? Love is incapable of ANY exceptions. Only if there is fear does the whole IDEA of exceptions of any kind seem to be meaningful. Exceptions ARE fearful because they were made BY fear. The "fearful healer" is a contradiction in terms, and is therefore a concept that ONLY a conflicted

---

260 [Tim Note: This applies to all healing: doctors, medicine, herbs, 'energy work.' There is an intention in the 'patient' to want to be healed, to be whole; there is an intention in the healer to help, to see healing happen. Those intentions are channels of the higher mind to perform miraculous healing, as all true healing is. But when used unconsciously like this, (1) the minds can limit the healing change of mind, and, (2) they can attribute the solution to the physical when healing has been seen, which severely counters true healing – change of mind – that could also have occurred. Use whatever is helpful, but keep the perspective of what is really going on in mind at all times. The inner healing awareness grows in predominance as any healing occurs - if we let it.]

Chapter 7 - The Consistency Of The Kingdom

mind could POSSIBLY perceive as meaningful. Fear does NOT gladden. Healing DOES. Fear ALWAYS makes exceptions. Healing NEVER does. Fear produces dissociation because it induces SEPARATION. Healing ALWAYS induces harmony because it proceeds from integration.

8   Healing is predictable BECAUSE it can be counted on. EVERYTHING that is of God can be counted on, because everything of God is WHOLLY REAL. HEALING can be counted on BECAUSE it is inspired by His voice, and is in accord with His laws. But if healing IS consistence, it CANNOT be inconsistently understood. Understanding MEANS consistence, because GOD means consistence. And because that IS His Meaning, it is also YOURS. YOUR meaning CANNOT be out of accord with His, because your whole meaning, and your ONLY meaning, comes FROM His and is LIKE His. God CANNOT be out of accord with HIMSELF, and YOU cannot be out of accord with Him. You cannot separate your SELF from YOUR Creator, who created YOU by sharing HIS Being WITH you.

9   The unhealed healer wants gratitude FROM his brothers, but he is NOT grateful to them. This is because he thinks he is giving something TO them, and is NOT receiving something equally desirable in return. His TEACHING is limited because he is LEARNING so little. His HEALING lesson is limited by his own ingratitude, which is a lesson in sickness.

> Learning is constant and so vital in its power for change that a Son of God can recognize his power in an instant, and change the world in the next. That is because by changing HIS mind he has changed the most powerful device that was ever created FOR change.

10   This in no way contradicts the changelessness of mind as GOD created it. But YOU think that you HAVE changed it, as long as you learn through the ego. This DOES place you in a position of needing to learn a lesson which SEEMS contradictory: you must learn to change your mind ABOUT your mind. Only by this can you learn that it IS changeless.

11   When you heal, that is exactly what you ARE learning (doing). You are recognizing the changeless mind in your brother by perceiving (knowing) that he could NOT have changed his mind. That is how you perceive the Holy Spirit in him. It is ONLY the Holy Spirit in him that never changes His mind. He himself must think he CAN, or he would not perceive himself as sick. He therefore does not know what his self IS.

If YOU see only the changeless in him, you have not really changed him at all.

> But by changing your mind about HIS FOR him, you help him undo the change his ego thinks it has made in him.

F. Healing and the Changelessness of Mind

As you can hear two voices, so you can see in two ways. One way shows you an image, or better, an idol which you may worship out of fear, but which you will never love. The other shows you only truth, which you will love because you will UNDERSTAND it. Understanding is APPRECIATION, because what you understand you can identify WITH, and by making it part of YOU you have accepted it with love.

This is how God Himself created YOU; in understanding, in appreciation, and in love.

12   The ego is totally unable to understand this, because it does NOT understand what it makes. It does NOT appreciate it, and it does NOT love it. It incorporates to TAKE AWAY. It literally believes that every time it deprives someone of something IT has increased. We have spoken often of the INCREASE of the Kingdom by YOUR creations,[261] which can only BE created as YOU were.

13   The whole glory and perfect joy that IS the Kingdom lies in you to give. Do you not WANT to give it? You CANNOT forget the Father because I am with you and I CANNOT forget Him. To forget ME is to forget yourself and Him who created you. Our brothers ARE forgetful. That is why they need your remembrance of Me and Him who created Me. Through this remembrance you can change THEIR minds about themselves, as I can change YOURS.

> *Your minds are so powerful a light that you can look into theirs and enlighten them, as I can enlighten yours.*

14   I do not want to share my BODY in communion because this is to share nothing. Would I try to share an illusion with the most holy children of a most Holy Father? *But I do want to share my MIND with you* because we ARE of one Mind, and that Mind IS ours.

See ONLY this Mind everywhere, because only this IS everywhere and in everything. It IS everything, because it encompasses all things within ITSELF. Blessed are you who perceive only this, because you perceive only what is true. Come therefore unto me and learn of the truth in YOU.

---

[261] Chapter 5 B. Healing as Joining, p4
  Chapter 5 D. The Voice for God, p12
  Chapter 5 E. The Guide to Salvation, p16
  This chapter: A. Introduction, p2
  This chapter: C. The Laws of Mind, p8

Chapter 7 - The Consistency Of The Kingdom

15

The mind WE share IS shared by all our brothers, and as we see them truly, they WILL be healed. Let YOUR minds shine with mine upon their minds, and by our gratitude to them make THEM aware of the light in THEM.

This light will shine back upon YOU and on the whole Sonship because this IS your proper gift to God. He will accept it and give it to the Sonship, because it is acceptable to Him, and therefore to His Sons. This is the true communion of the Spirit Who sees the altar of God in everyone, and by bringing it to YOUR appreciation calls upon you to love God and His Creation.

G. From Vigilance to Peace

1   You can think of the Sonship ONLY as one. This is part of the law of Creation, and therefore governs ALL thought. You can PERCEIVE the Sonship as fragmented, but it is IMPOSSIBLE for you to see something in part of it that you will not attribute to ALL of it. That is why attack is NEVER discrete. And why attack MUST be relinquished entirely. If it is NOT relinquished entirely, it is not relinquished at all.

Fear and love are equally reciprocal.
They make or create [262] depending on whether the ego or the Holy Spirit begets or inspires them, but they WILL return to the mind of the thinker, and they WILL affect his total perception.

That includes his perception of God, of His Creations, and of his own. He will not appreciate ANY of these if he regards them fearfully. He will appreciate ALL of them if he regards them with love.

2   The mind that accepts attack CANNOT love. This is because it believes that it can DESTROY love, and therefore does not understand what love IS. If it does not understand what love IS, it CANNOT perceive itself as loving. This loses the awareness of being; induces feelings of unreality; and results in utter confusion.

---

[262] **Chapter 3 G. The Loss of Certainty, p2**
   Chapter 3 I. Creating versus the Self-Image, p2
   Chapter 4 A. Introduction, p4
   Chapter 4 D. Love without Conflict, p18
   Chapter 5 G. The Two Decisions, p11
   Chapter 6 E. The Only Answer, p10, 12, 13

G. From Vigilance to Peace

Your own thinking has done this, because of its power. But your own thinking can also save you FROM this, because its power is not of your making.

Your ability to DIRECT your thinking as you will IS part of its power. If you do not believe you can do this, you have DENIED the power of your thought, and thus rendered it powerLESS in your belief.

3   The ingeniousness of the ego to preserve itself is enormous, but it stems from the power of the mind WHICH THE EGO DENIES.

This means that the ego attacks WHAT IS PRESERVING IT, and this MUST be a source of extreme anxiety. This is why it NEVER knows what it is doing. This is perfectly logical, though clearly insane.

The ego draws upon the one source which is totally inimical to its existence FOR its existence. Fearful of perceiving the POWER of this source, it is forced to DEPRECIATE it. This threatens its OWN existence, a state which it finds intolerable.

4   Remaining logical but still insane, the ego resolves this completely insane dilemma in a completely insane way. It does not perceive ITS existence as threatened, by projecting the threat onto YOU, and perceiving your BEING as NONexistent. This ensures ITS continuance, if you side WITH it, by guaranteeing that you will NOT know your OWN safety. The ego CANNOT AFFORD TO KNOW ANYTHING. Knowledge is total, and the ego DOES NOT BELIEVE IN TOTALITY. This unbelief is its own origin, and while the ego does not love YOU, it IS faithful to its own antecedent, begetting as it was begotten.

5   Mind ALWAYS REproduces as it was produced. Produced by fear, the ego REproduces fear. This IS its allegiance, and this allegiance makes it treacherous to love BECAUSE you are love. Love IS your power, which the ego MUST deny. It must also deny everything which this power gives TO you, BECAUSE it gives you everything. No-one who has everything WANTS the ego. Its own maker, then, DOES NOT WANT IT. Rejection is therefore the only decision which the ego could POSSIBLY encounter if the mind which made it knew ITSELF. And if it recognized ANY part of the Sonship, it WOULD know itself.

6   The ego therefore opposes ALL appreciation, ALL recognition, ALL sane perception, and ALL knowledge. It perceives their threat as total because it senses the fact that all commitments which the mind makes ARE total. Forced therefore to detach itself from you who ARE mind, it is willing to attach itself to anything ELSE. But there IS nothing else.

Chapter 7 - The Consistency Of The Kingdom

It does NOT follow, however, that the mind cannot make illusions. But it DOES follow that if it makes illusions it will BELIEVE in them, because THAT IS HOW IT MADE THEM.

7   The Holy Spirit undoes illusions without attacking them merely because He cannot perceive them at all. They therefore do not exist for Him. He resolves the APPARENT conflict which they engender by perceiving CONFLICT as meaningless. We said before that the Holy Spirit perceives the conflict EXACTLY AS IT IS, and it IS meaningless.

The Holy Spirit does not want you to UNDERSTAND conflict. He wants you to realize that BECAUSE conflict is meaningLESS it cannot BE understood. WE have already said that understanding brings appreciation, and appreciation brings love. Nothing else CAN be understood because nothing else is real and therefore nothing else HAS meaning.

8   If you will keep in mind what the Holy Spirit offers you, you cannot be vigilant for anything BUT God and His Kingdom. The ONLY reason why you find this difficult is because you think there IS something else. Belief does not require vigilance UNLESS it is conflicted. If it IS, there ARE conflicting components within it which have engendered a state of war, and vigilance has therefore BECOME essential. Vigilance has no place at all in peace. It is necessary ONLY AGAINST beliefs which are NOT true, and would never have been called upon by the Holy Spirit if you had not believed the untrue yourselves.

9   But you CANNOT deny that when you BELIEVE something you HAVE made it true FOR YOU. When YOU believe what God DOES NOT KNOW, your thought seems to CONTRADICT His, and this makes it appear AS IF YOU ARE ATTACKING HIM. We have repeatedly emphasized that the ego DOES believe it can attack God, and tries to persuade you that YOU have done this. If the mind CANNOT attack, the ego proceeds perfectly logically to the position that YOU cannot be mind. By not seeing you as YOU are, it can see ITSELF as it WANTS to be.

Aware of its weakness, the ego wants your allegiance, but NOT as you really are. The ego therefore wants to engage your mind in its OWN delusional system, because otherwise the light of YOUR understanding WILL dispel it.

10   The ego wants no part of truth, because the truth is that IT is not true. If truth is total, the UNtrue CANNOT exist. Commitment to either MUST be total, because they cannot co-exist in your minds WITHOUT splitting them. If they cannot coexist in peace, and if you WANT peace, you MUST give up the IDEA of conflict ENTIRELY, and for ALL TIME. This requires vigilance ONLY as long as YOU DO NOT RECOGNIZE WHAT IS TRUE. While you believe that two totally contradictory thought systems SHARE truth,

G. From Vigilance to Peace

your need for vigilance is apparent. Your minds ARE dividing their allegiance between two kingdoms, and YOU are totally committed to neither.

11 Your identification with the Kingdom is totally beyond question except by you WHEN YOU ARE THINKING INSANELY. What you are is NOT established by your perception, and is NOT influenced BY it at all. ALL perceived problems in identification at ANY level ARE NOT PROBLEMS OF FACT. But they ARE problems in UNDERSTANDING, because they MEAN that you perceive WHAT you can understand as UP TO YOU TO DECIDE. The ego believes THIS totally, being fully committed TO it. But it is NOT TRUE. The ego is therefore totally committed to UNtruth, perceiving in total contradiction to the Holy Spirit and to the knowledge of God.

12 You can be perceived with meaning ONLY by the Holy Spirit, because your being IS the knowledge of God. ANY belief that you accept which is APART from this WILL obscure God's voice in you, and will therefore obscure God TO you. Unless you perceive His Creation truly, you CANNOT know the Creator, because God and His Creation ARE NOT SEPARATE.

> The Oneness of the Creator and the Creation IS your wholeness, your sanity, and your limitless power.

> This limitless power is God's gift to you, because it is WHAT YOU ARE.

> *If you dissociate your mind FROM it, you are perceiving the most powerful force in the universe of thought AS IF it were weak, because you do NOT believe YOU are part of it.*

13 *Perceived WITHOUT your part IN it, God's Creation IS perceived as weak,* and those who SEE themselves as weakened DO attack. The attack MUST be blind, because there is nothing TO attack. Therefore, they make up images, perceive them as unworthy, and attack them for their unworthiness.

> That is all the world of the ego is.
> NOTHING.
> It has no meaning. It does not exist.

> Do not TRY to understand it, because if you do you are believing that it CAN be understood, and therefore is capable of being appreciated and loved. This WOULD justify it, but it CANNOT BE justified.

Chapter 7 - The Consistency Of The Kingdom

YOU cannot make the meaningLESS meaningFUL. This can ONLY be an insane attempt.

14   Allowing INsanity to enter your minds means that you have not judged sanity AS WHOLLY DESIRABLE. If you WANT something else, you WILL MAKE something else. But because it IS something else it WILL attack your thought system and divide your allegiance. You CANNOT create in this divided state, and you MUST be vigilant AGAINST this divided state because ONLY peace CAN BE extended.

Your divided minds ARE blocking the extension of the Kingdom, and its extension IS your joy. If you do not extend the Kingdom, you are NOT thinking with your Creator and creating as He created.

15

In this depressing state, the Holy Spirit reminds you gently that you are sad because you are not fulfilling your function as co-creators WITH God, and are therefore depriving YOURSELVES of joy.

This is not God's will, but YOURS. If your will is out of accord with God's, YOU ARE WILLING WITHOUT MEANING. But because ONLY God's will is unchangeable, no REAL conflict of will is possible. This is the Holy Spirit's perfectly consistent teaching. Creation, not separation, IS your will BECAUSE it is God's. And nothing that opposes this means anything at all.

Being a perfect Accomplishment, the Sonship can only accomplish perfectly, EXTENDING the joy in which it was created, and identifying itself with both its Creator and its creations, KNOWING they are One.

H. The Total Commitment

1   Whenever you deny a blessing to a brother, YOU will feel deprived.

This is because denial is as total as love. It is as impossible to deny part of the Sonship as it is to love it in part. Nor is it possible to love it totally AT TIMES. You CANNOT be totally committed SOMETIMES. Remember a very early lesson, - - "never underestimate the power of denial." [263] It has no power in ITSELF, but YOU can give it the power of YOUR mind, whose power is without limit of ANY kind. If you use it to

---

263 Chapter 2 B. The Re-interpretation of Defenses, p13
    Chapter 3 I. Creating versus the Self-Image, p12

H. The Total Commitment

deny reality, reality is gone FOR YOU. REALITY CANNOT BE PARTLY APPRECIATED. That is why denying any part of it means you have lost awareness of ALL of it.

2   That is the negative side of the law as it operates in this world. But denial is a defense, and so it is as capable of being used positively as it is of being used destructively. Used negatively, it WILL be destructive, because it will be used for attack.

But in the service of the Holy Spirit, the law becomes as beneficent as all of the laws of God. Stated positively, the law requires you only to recognize PART of reality to appreciate ALL of it. Mind is too powerful to be subject to exclusion. You will NEVER be able to exclude yourself from what you project.

3   When a brother acts insanely, he is offering you an opportunity to bless him. His need is YOURS.

> *YOU need the blessing you can offer him. There is no way for you to have it EXCEPT by giving it.*

This IS the law of God, and it HAS NO EXCEPTIONS.

What you deny you LACK, not because it IS lacking, but because you have denied it in another, and therefore are not aware of it in YOU. Every response you make is determined by what you think you ARE. *And what you WANT to be IS what you think you are.* Therefore, what you WANT to be determines every response you make.

4   You do NOT need God's blessing, because that you have forever. But you DO need YOURS. The picture you see of yourselves is deprived, unloving, and very vulnerable. You CANNOT love this. But you can very easily escape FROM it, or better, leave it behind. You are NOT there, and that is not YOU. Do not see this picture in anyone, or you HAVE accepted it as you.

ALL illusions about the Sonship are DISPELLED together, as they were MADE together.

> *Teach no-one that HE is what YOU do not want to be.*
> Your brother is the mirror in which you will see the image of yourself as long as perception lasts. And perception WILL last until the Sonship knows itself as whole.

5   You MADE perception, and it MUST last as long as you WANT it. Illusions are investments. They will last as long as you value them. Values are relative, but they are powerful because they are MENTAL JUDGMENTS.

Chapter 7 - The Consistency Of The Kingdom

The only way to dispel illusions is to withdraw ALL investment from them, and they will HAVE no life for you because you have put them OUT OF YOUR MIND. While you include them IN it, you are GIVING them life. Except there is nothing there to receive your gift.

6   The gift of life IS yours to give, because it was given YOU. You are unaware of YOUR gift BECAUSE you do not give it. You CANNOT make nothing live, because it cannot BE enlivened. Therefore, you have NOT extended the gift you both have and are, and so you do NOT know your being. All confusion comes from not extending life, because this is NOT the will of your Creator. You CAN do nothing apart from Him, and you DO do nothing apart from him. Keep His Way to remember yourselves, and teach His Ways lest you forget yourself.

Give only honor to the sons of the living God, and count yourself among them gladly.

7   ONLY honor is a fitting gift for those whom God Himself created worthy of honor and whom He honors. Give them the appreciation which God accords them always, because they are His Beloved Sons in whom He is well pleased. [264] You CANNOT be apart from them, because you are not apart from Him. Rest in His love, and protect your rest by loving. But love EVERYTHING He created, of which YOU are part, or you cannot learn of His peace and accept His gift FOR yourself and AS yourself.

You CANNOT know your own perfection until you have honored all those who were created LIKE you.

8   One Child of God is the only teacher sufficiently worthy to teach another. One Teacher is in all your minds, and He teaches the same lesson to all. He always teaches you the inestimable worth of EVERY Son of God, teaching it with infinite patience born of the Love of Him for whom He speaks.

Every attack is a call for His patience, because ONLY His patience can translate attack into blessing. Those who attack DO NOT KNOW THEY ARE BLESSED. They attack BECAUSE THEY BELIEVE THEY ARE DEPRIVED. *Give therefore of YOUR abundance, and teach them THEIRS.* Do not share their delusions of scarcity, or you will perceive YOURSELF as lacking.

---

264 Matthew 3:17 And lo a voice from heaven, saying, This is my beloved Son, in whom I am well pleased.
    Matthew 17:5 While he yet spake, behold, a bright cloud overshadowed them: and behold a voice out of the cloud, which said, This is my beloved Son, in whom I am well pleased; hear ye him.
    Also, Mark 1:11, Mark 9:7, Luke 3:22, Luke 9:35
    1 John 3:2 Beloved, now are we the sons of God, and it doth not yet appear what we shall be: but we know that, when he shall appear, we shall be like him; for we shall see him as he is.

H. The Total Commitment

9 Attack could never PROMOTE attack unless you perceived it as a means of depriving you of SOMETHING YOU WANT. But you cannot lose ANYTHING unless YOU do not value it and therefore DO NOT WANT IT. This makes you feel DEPRIVED of it, and by projecting YOUR rejection, you believe that others are TAKING IT FROM YOU. One MUST be fearful if he believes that his brother is attacking him to tear the Kingdom of Heaven from him.

10 This is the ultimate basis for ALL of the ego's projection. Being the part of your mind which does NOT believe it is responsible for ITSELF, and being without allegiance to God, it is incapable of trust. Projecting its insane belief that YOU have been treacherous to YOUR Creator, it believes that your brothers, who are as incapable of this as you are, are out to TAKE GOD FROM YOU.

Whenever a brother attacks another, THIS IS WHAT HE BELIEVES. *Projection ALWAYS sees YOUR will in others.* If you will to separate YOURSELF from God, that is what you will think others are doing TO you.

11 You ARE the will of God. Do not accept anything else AS YOUR will, or you ARE denying what you are. Deny THIS and you WILL attack, because you believe you have BEEN attacked.

But see the love of God in you, and you will see it everywhere because it IS everywhere. See His abundance in everyone, and you will know that you are in Him WITH them.

They are part of you as you are part of God. *YOU are as lonely without understanding this as God Himself is lonely when His Sons do not know Him.* The peace of God IS understanding this.

12 There is only one way out of the world's thinking, just as there was only one way INTO it. Understand totally by understanding TOTALITY. Perceive ANY part of the ego's thought system as wholly insane, wholly delusional, and wholly undesirable, and you have CORRECTLY EVALUATED ALL OF IT. This correction enables you to perceive ANY part of Creation as wholly real, wholly perfect, and WHOLLY DESIRABLE. Wanting this ONLY, you will HAVE this only, and giving this only, you will BE only this. The gifts you offer to the ego are ALWAYS experienced as sacrifices.

But the gifts you offer to the Kingdom are gifts to YOU. They will always be treasured by God, because they belong to His Beloved Sons who belong to Him. All power [265] and glory [266] are yours because the Kingdom is His.

---

265 Matthew 28:18 And Jesus came and spake unto them, saying, All power is given unto me in heaven and in earth.

266 Colossians 1:27 To whom God would make known what is the riches of the glory of this mystery among the Gentiles; which is Christ in you, the hope of glory:

Chapter 7 - The Consistency Of The Kingdom

I. The Defense of Conflict

1   We once said that without projection there can be no anger, but it is also true that without projection there can be no love.

Projection is a fundamental law of the mind, and therefore one which ALWAYS operates.
It is the law by which you create and were created. It is the law which unifies the Kingdom and keeps it in the mind of God.

To the ego, the law is perceived as a way of getting RID of something it does NOT want.
To the Holy Spirit, it is the fundamental law of sharing, by which you give what you value in order to keep it in your OWN minds.

2   Projection to the Holy Spirit is the law of extension.
To the ego, it is the law of deprivation.
It therefore produces abundance or scarcity, depending on how you choose to apply it.

This choice IS up to you, *but it is NOT up to you to decide whether or not you will UTILIZE projection.* [267] Every mind MUST project, because that is how it lives, and every mind IS life.

The ego's use of projection must be fully understood before the INEVITABLE association between projection and anger can be finally Unmade.

3   The ego ALWAYS tries to preserve conflict. It is very ingenious in devising ways which SEEM to diminish conflict only because it does NOT want you to find it so intolerable that you will INSIST on giving it up. Therefore, it tries to persuade you that IT can free you OF conflict, lest you give IT up and free YOURSELF. The ego, using its own warped version of the laws of God, uses the power of the mind ONLY to defeat the mind's real purpose. It projects conflict FROM your mind to OTHER minds, in an attempt to persuade you that you have gotten RID of it. This has a number of fallacies which may not be so apparent.

4   Strictly speaking, conflict cannot BE projected, precisely BECAUSE it cannot be fully shared. Any attempt to keep PART of it and get rid of ANOTHER part does not

---

267 Chapter 2 E. The Correction for Lack of Love, p7 – 8, p15 - 16

I. The Defense of Conflict

really mean ANYTHING. Remember that a conflicted teacher is a poor teacher AND A POOR LEARNER. His lessons are confused, and their transfer value severely limited BY his confusion.

5   A second fallacy is the idea that you can GET RID of something you do not want BY giving it away. GIVING it is how you KEEP it. The belief that by giving it OUT you have excluded from WITHIN is a complete distortion of the power of EXTENSION.

6   That is why those who project from the ego are vigilant for their OWN safety. THEY ARE AFRAID THAT THEIR PROJECTIONS WILL RETURN AND HURT THEM. They DO believe they have blotted them out of their OWN minds, but they also believe they are trying to creep back INTO them. This is because their projections have NOT left their minds, and this, in turn, forces them to engage in compulsive activity in order NOT to recognize this.

7   You cannot perpetuate an illusion about another WITHOUT perpetuating it about yourself. There is no way out of this, because it is IMPOSSIBLE to fragment the mind. To fragment is to break into pieces, and mind CANNOT attack. The belief that it CAN, a fallacy which the ego ALWAYS makes, underlies its whole use of projection. This is because it does not understand what the mind IS, and therefore does not understand what YOU are.

Yet ITS existence IS dependent on your mind, because it is a BELIEF. The ego IS therefore a confusion in identification, which never had a consistent model, and never developed consistently. *It is the distorted product of the misapplication of the laws of God by distorted minds which are misusing their own power.*

8   DO NOT BE AFRAID OF THE EGO. It DOES depend on your mind, and as you made it by believing in it, so you can dispel it by withdrawing belief FROM it.

> Do NOT project the responsibility for your belief in it onto ANYONE else, or you will PRESERVE the belief.

> When you are willing to accept sole responsibility for the ego's existence YOURSELF, you will have laid aside all anger and all attack, because they COME from an attempt to PROJECT RESPONSIBILITY FOR YOUR OWN ERRORS.

But having ACCEPTED the errors as yours, DO NOT KEEP THEM. Give them over quickly to the Holy Spirit to be undone completely, so that ALL their effects will vanish from your minds and from the Sonship AS A WHOLE. He will teach you to perceive BEYOND belief, because truth IS beyond belief and His perception IS true.

Chapter 7 - The Consistency Of The Kingdom

9   The ego can be completely forgotten at ANY time, because it was always a belief that is totally incredible. No-one can KEEP a belief he has judged to be unbelievable. The more you learn ABOUT the ego, the more you realize that it cannot BE believed. The incredible cannot BE understood because it IS unbelievable. The utter meaninglessness of ALL perception which comes from the unbelievable MUST be apparent, but it is NOT beyond belief because it was made BY belief.

10   The whole purpose of this course is to teach you that the ego is unbelievable and will forever BE unbelievable. You who made the ego by BELIEVING the unbelievable CANNOT make this judgment alone. By accepting the Atonement for YOURSELF, you are deciding AGAINST the belief that you can BE alone, thus dispelling the idea of separation and affirming your true identification with the whole Kingdom as literally PART OF YOU. This identification is as beyond doubt as it is beyond belief. Your wholeness HAS no limits, because its being is in Infinity.

J. The Extension of the Kingdom

1   Only you can limit your creative power, but God wills to release it. He no more wills you to deprive yourselves of YOUR creations than He wills to deprive Himself of His.

2   Do not withhold your gifts to the Sonship, or you withhold yourself from God. Selfishness is of the ego but self-fullness is of the Soul because that is how He created it. *The Holy Spirit is the part of the mind that lies between the ego and the Soul*, mediating between them ALWAYS IN FAVOR OF THE SOUL. To the ego this is partiality, and it therefore responds as if it were the part that is being sided AGAINST.

    To the Soul this is truth, because it knows its own fullness and cannot conceive of ANY part from which it is excluded. *The soul KNOWS that the consciousness of all its brothers is included in its own, as IT is included in God.* The power of the whole Sonship AND OF ITS CREATOR is therefore its OWN fullness, rendering its Creation and its creating equally whole and equal in perfection.

3   The ego cannot prevail against a totality which includes God, and any totality MUST include God. Everything He created is given ALL His power because it is part of Him and shares His Being WITH Him. Creating is the OPPOSITE of loss, as blessing is the opposite of sacrifice. Being MUST be extended. That is how it retains the knowledge of itSELF. The soul yearns to share ITS Being as ITS Creator did. Created BY sharing, its will is to create. It does NOT wish to CONTAIN God, but to EXTEND HIS BEING.

4   The extension of God's Being is the Soul's only function. ITS fullness cannot be contained any more than can the fullness of its Creator. Fullness IS extension. The ego's whole thought system BLOCKS extension, and therefore blocks YOUR ONLY

J. The Extension of the Kingdom

FUNCTION. It therefore blocks your joy and THIS is why you perceive yourselves as unfulfilled. Unless you create, you ARE unfulfilled. But God does NOT know unfulfillment, and therefore you MUST create.

YOU may not know your own creations, but this can no more interfere with their reality than your unawareness of your Soul can interfere with its being.

5   The Kingdom is forever extending, because it is in the Mind of God. YOU do not know your joy because you do not know your own self-fullness. Exclude ANY part of the Kingdom FROM yourself, and you are NOT whole. A split mind CANNOT perceive its fullness, and needs the miracle OF its wholeness to dawn upon it and heal it. This reawakens its wholeness IN it and restores it to the Kingdom because of its ACCEPTANCE of wholeness. The full appreciation of its self-fullness makes selfishness impossible, and extension inevitable.

That is why there is perfect peace in the Kingdom. Every Soul IS fulfilling its function, and ONLY complete fulfillment IS peace.

6   Insanity APPEARS to add to reality, but no-one would claim that what it adds is true. Insanity is therefore the NONextension of truth, which blocks joy because it blocks Creation and therefore blocks self-FULFILLMENT. The unfulfilled MUST be depressed, because their self-fullness is UNKNOWN to them.

Your creations are protected FOR you because the Holy Spirit, Who is in your minds, knows of them, and can bring them INTO your awareness whenever you will let Him. They ARE there as part of your own being, because YOUR fulfillment INCLUDES them. The creations of every Son of God are yours, because every creation belongs to everyone, being created for the Sonship as a whole.

7   You have not failed to add to the inheritance of the Sons of God, and thus have not failed to secure it for yourselves. If it was the will of God to give it to you, He gave it forever. If it was His will that you have it forever, He gave you the means for keeping it, and YOU HAVE DONE SO. Disobeying God's will is meaningful only to the insane. In truth, it is impossible.

8   Your self-fullness is as boundless as God's. Like His, it extends forever and in perfect peace. Its radiance is so intense that it creates in perfect joy, and only the whole can be born of its wholeness. Be confident that you have never lost your identity and the extension which maintains it in wholeness and peace.

Miracles are AN EXPRESSION OF THIS CONFIDENCE. They are reflections both of your own proper identification WITH your brothers, and of your own awareness that YOUR identification IS maintained by extension. The miracle is A LESSON IN TOTAL PERCEPTION. By including ANY part of totality in the lesson, you HAVE included the whole.

Chapter 7 - The Consistency Of The Kingdom

9   You have said that, when you think (write) of the Kingdom and your own creations which belong to it, you are describing WHAT YOU DO NOT KNOW. This is true in a sense, but no more true than your failure to acknowledge the whole result of the ego's premises. The Kingdom is the result of premises, as much as this world is. You HAVE carried the ego's reasoning to its logical conclusion, which is TOTAL CONFUSION ABOUT EVERYTHING. But you do not really BELIEVE this, or you could not possibly maintain it. If you REALLY saw this result, you COULD not want it. The ONLY reason why you could possibly want ANY part of it is because YOU DO NOT SEE THE WHOLE OF IT.

10   You therefore ARE willing to look at the ego's premises but NOT at their logical outcome. Is it not possible that you have done the same thing with the premises of God? Your creations ARE the logical outcome of His premises. HIS thinking has established them FOR you. They are therefore THERE, EXACTLY where they belong. They belong to your mind, as part of your identification with HIS. But your state of mind and your recognition of WHAT IS IN YOUR MIND depends, at any given moment, on what you believe ABOUT your mind. Whatever these beliefs may be, they are the premises which will determine WHAT YOU ACCEPT INTO YOUR MINDS.

11   It is surely clear that you can both accept into your minds what is NOT really there, and DENY WHAT IS. [268] Neither of these possibilities requires further elaboration, although both are clearly indefensible even if YOU elect to defend them. But the function which God Himself GAVE your minds through His you may DENY but you CANNOT prevent. They are the logical outcome of what you ARE. The ability to SEE a logical outcome depends on the WILLINGNESS TO SEE IT, but its TRUTH has nothing to do with your willingness at all. Truth is GOD'S will. SHARE His Will, and you will share what He KNOWS. Deny His Will AS YOURS, and you are denying His Kingdom AND yours.

12   The Holy Spirit will direct you ONLY so as to avoid all pain. The UNDOING of pain must OBVIOUSLY avoid this. No-one would surely OBJECT to this goal IF HE RECOGNIZED IT. The problem is NOT whether what He says is true, but whether or not you want to LISTEN to what He says.

K. The Confusion of Strength and Weakness

1   You no more recognize what is painful than you know what is joyful, and are, in fact, very apt to confuse them. The Holy Spirit's main function is to teach you to TELL THEM APART.

---

268 Chapter 3   D. Miracles as Accurate Perception, p2
    Chapter 5   G. The Two Decisions, p6

K. The Confusion of Strength and Weakness

2   However strange it may seem that this is necessary, it obviously IS. The reason is equally obvious. What is joyful to you IS painful to the ego, and as long as you are in doubt about what YOU are, you WILL be confused about joy and pain. This confusion is the cause of the whole idea of sacrifice. Obey the Holy Spirit, and you WILL be giving up the ego, but you will be SACRIFICING nothing. On the contrary, you will be gaining EVERYTHING. But if you BELIEVED this there would BE no conflict. That is why you need to DEMONSTRATE THE OBVIOUS TO YOURSELF. It is NOT obvious to you.

3   You REALLY believe that doing the opposite of God's will CAN be better for you. You also believe that it is POSSIBLE to do the opposite of God's will. Therefore, you believe that an impossible choice IS open to you, which is both very fearful and very desirable. But God WILLS. He does NOT wish. YOUR will is as powerful as His because it IS His. The ego's wishes do not mean anything, because the ego wishes for the impossible. You CAN wish for the impossible, but you can only WILL with God. This is the ego's weakness and YOUR strength.

4   The Holy Spirit ALWAYS sides with YOU and with your STRENGTH. As long as you avoid His guidance in any way, you WANT TO BE WEAK. But weakness IS frightening. What else, then, can this decision mean except that you WANT to be fearful? The Holy Spirit NEVER asks for sacrifice, but the ego ALWAYS does. When you are confused about this VERY clear distinction in motivation, it CAN only be due to projection. Projection of this kind IS a confusion in motivation, and given THIS confusion, TRUST becomes impossible.

5   No-one obeys gladly a guide he does not trust. But this does not mean that the GUIDE is untrustworthy. In this case, it ALWAYS means that the FOLLOWER IS. However, this, too, is merely a matter of his own belief. Believing that HE can betray, he believes that everything can betray HIM. But this is ONLY because he has ELECTED TO FOLLOW FALSE GUIDANCE.

Unable to follow THIS guidance WITHOUT fear, he associates fear WITH guidance, and refuses to follow ANY guidance at all. If the result of this decision is confusion, this is hardly surprising.

6   The Holy Spirit is perfectly trustworthy, as YOU are. God Himself trusts you and therefore your trustworthiness IS beyond question. It will always remain beyond question, however much you may question it. I trust MY choices ONLY because they ARE God's Will. We said before that YOU are the will of God. His will is not an idle wish, and your identification WITH His Will is not optional because it IS what you are. Sharing His will WITH me is not really open to choice at all, though it may SEEM to be. The whole separation lies in this fallacy. And the ONLY way out of the fallacy is to decide that YOU DO NOT HAVE TO DECIDE ANYTHING.

Chapter 7 - The Consistency Of The Kingdom

7   Everything has been given you by GOD'S decision. This IS His Will, and you can NOT undo it. Even the relinquishment of your false decision-making prerogative, which the ego guards so jealously, is not accomplished by your wish. It was accomplished FOR you by the Will of God, who has not left you comfortless. His Voice WILL teach you how to distinguish between pain and joy, and lead you out of the confusion YOU have made. There IS no confusion in the mind of a Son of God, whose will MUST be the will of the Father, because the Father's Will IS His Son.

8   Miracles are IN ACCORD with the Will of God, whose will you do NOT know because you are confused about what YOU will. This MEANS that you are confused about what you are. If you ARE God's will and do NOT ACCEPT His will, you can ONLY be not accepting what you are. But if your joy IS what you are, you ARE denying joy. The miracle therefore is a lesson in WHAT JOY IS. Being a lesson in SHARING, it is a lesson in love, which IS joy. Every miracle is thus a lesson in Truth, and by OFFERING truth YOU are learning the difference between pain and joy.

L. The State of Grace

1   The Holy Spirit will ALWAYS guide you truly, because YOUR joy IS His. This is His will for everyone, because He speaks for the Kingdom of God which IS joy. Following Him is therefore the easiest thing in the world, and the only thing which IS easy, because it is NOT of the world and is therefore NATURAL. The world goes AGAINST your nature, because it is out of accord with God's laws. The world perceives orders of difficulty in EVERYTHING. This is because the ego perceives nothing as wholly desirable. By DEMONSTRATING to yourselves that THERE IS NO ORDER OF DIFFICULTY IN MIRACLES, you will convince yourselves that in your NATURAL state there IS no difficulty, because it is a state of Grace.

2   Grace is the natural state of every Son of God. When he is NOT in a state of grace he IS out of his natural environment, and does NOT function well. Everything he does becomes a strain, because he was not created for the environment which he has made. He therefore CANNOT adapt to it, nor can he adapt IT to HIM. There is no point in trying. A Son of God is happy ONLY when he knows he is WITH God. That is the only environment in which he will not experience strain, because that is where he belongs. It is also the only environment that is worthy of him, because his own worth is beyond ANYTHING that he can make.

3   Consider the Kingdom which YOU have made, and judge its worth fairly. Is it worthy to be a home for a Child of God? Does it protect his peace, and shine love upon him? Does it keep his heart untouched by fear, and allow him to give always without any

L. The State of Grace

sense of loss? Does it teach him that this giving IS his joy, and that God Himself thanks him for his giving?

4   That is the only environment in which you can be happy. You cannot make it, any more than you can make yourselves. But it has been created for you, as you were created for it. God watches over His children and denies them nothing. But when they deny Him they do NOT know this, because THEY deny themselves everything. *You who could give the love of God to everything you see and touch and remember are literally denying Heaven to yourselves.* I call upon you again to remember that I have chosen you to teach the Kingdom TO the Kingdom. There are no exceptions to this lesson because the lack of exceptions IS the lesson.

5   Every Son who returns to the Kingdom with this lesson in his heart has healed the Sonship and given thanks to God. Everyone who learns this lesson has become the perfect teacher, because he has learned it of the Holy Spirit, who wants to teach him everything He knows.

When a mind has only light, it KNOWS only light. [269] Its own radiance shines all around it, and extends out into the darkness of other minds, transforming them into majesty. The majesty of God is there, for YOU to recognize and appreciate and KNOW.

6   Perceiving the majesty of God AS your brother is to accept your OWN inheritance. God gives only equally. If you recognize His gift to anyone ELSE, you have acknowledged what He has given YOU. Nothing is as easy to perceive as truth. This is the perception which is immediate, clear, and natural. You have trained yourselves NOT to see it, and this HAS been very difficult for you. OUT of your natural environment you may well ask, "what is truth?" because truth IS the environment by which and for which you were created. You do not know yourselves because you do not know YOUR Creator. You do not know YOUR creations, because you do not know your brothers who created them WITH you.

7   We said before that only the whole Sonship is a worthy co-creator with God, because only the whole Sonship can create LIKE Him. Whenever you heal a brother by recognizing his worth, you are acknowledging HIS power to create and YOURS. HE cannot have lost what YOU recognize, and you MUST have the glory you see in HIM. He is a co-creator with God with YOU. Deny his creative power and you are denying yours AND THAT OF GOD WHO CREATED YOU. You cannot deny part of the truth. You do not know your creations because you do not know their creator. You do not know yourselves because you do not know YOURS.

---

[269] Matthew 6:22 The light of the body is the eye: if therefore thine eye be single, thy whole body shall be full of light.

Chapter 7 - The Consistency Of The Kingdom

8   Your creations cannot establish your reality, any more than YOU can establish God's. But you can KNOW both. *Being is known by sharing.* Because God shared His Being with you, you can know Him. But you must also know all He created to know what THEY have shared. Without your Father you will not know your fatherhood. The Kingdom of God includes all His Sons and their children, who are like the Sons as they are like the Father. Know then the Sons of God, and you will know ALL Creation.

Chapter 8 – The Journey Back

A. Introduction

1   You are hampered in your progress by your demands to know what you do not know. This is actually a way of hanging on to deprivation.

You cannot reasonably object to following instructions in a course FOR knowing, on the grounds that you do not know. The need for the course is implicit in your objection.

Knowledge is not the motivation for learning this course. PEACE is. As the PREREQUISITE for knowledge, peace MUST be learned. This is ONLY because those who are in conflict are not peaceful, and peace is the CONDITION of knowledge because it is the condition of the Kingdom.

2   Knowledge will be restored when YOU meet its conditions. This is not a bargain made by God, who made no bargains at all. It is merely the result of your misuse of His Laws on behalf of a will that was not His. Knowledge IS His Will. If you are OPPOSING His Will, how CAN you have knowledge? I have told you what knowledge OFFERS you, but it is clear that you do NOT regard this as wholly desirable. If you did, you would hardly be willing to throw it away so readily, when the ego asks for your allegiance.

3

> The distraction of the ego SEEMS to interfere with your learning, but it HAS no power to distract unless you GIVE it the power. The ego's voice is an hallucination. You cannot expect the EGO to say "I am not real." Hallucinations ARE inaccurate perceptions of reality.

But you are NOT asked to dispel them alone. You are merely asked to evaluate them in terms of their results TO YOU. If you DO NOT WANT THEM on the basis of LOSS OF PEACE, they will be removed from your mind FOR you. Every response to the ego is a call to war, and war DOES deprive you of peace.

4   Yet in this war THERE IS NO OPPONENT. THIS is the re-interpretation of reality which you must make to secure peace, and the ONLY one you need ever make.

B. The Direction of the Curriculum

1   Those whom you PERCEIVE as opponents are PART of your peace, which YOU are giving up by attacking them. How can you have what YOU give up? You SHARE to have, but you do NOT give it up yourselves.

Chapter 8 – The Journey Back

When you GIVE UP peace, you are EXCLUDING yourself FROM it. This is a condition which is so ALIEN to the Kingdom that you CANNOT understand the state which prevails WITHIN it.

2 Your past learning MUST have taught you the wrong things, simply because it has not made you happy. On this basis alone, its value should be questioned. If learning aims at CHANGE, and that is ALWAYS its purpose, are you satisfied with the changes YOURS has brought you? Dissatisfaction with the learning outcome MUST be a sign of learning failure, because it means that you did NOT get what you WANT.

3 The curriculum of the Atonement IS the opposite of the curriculum you have established for yourselves, but SO IS ITS OUTCOME. If the outcome of yours has made you unhappy, and if you WANT a different outcome, a change in the curriculum is obviously necessary.

4 The first change that MUST be introduced is a change in DIRECTION. A meaningful curriculum CANNOT be inconsistent. If it is planned by two teachers, each believing in diametrically opposed ideas, it CANNOT be integrated. If it is carried out by these two teachers simultaneously, EACH ONE MERELY INTERFERES WITH THE OTHER. This leads to fluctuation, but NOT to change. The volatile HAVE no direction. They cannot choose one, because they CANNOT relinquish the others EVEN IF THE OTHERS DO NOT EXIST. Their conflicted curriculum teaches them that ALL directions exist, and gives them no RATIONALE for choice.

5 The total senselessness of such a curriculum must be fully recognized before a real change in direction becomes possible. You CANNOT learn simultaneously from two teachers who are in TOTAL DISAGREEMENT ABOUT EVERYTHING. Their joint curriculum presents an IMPOSSIBLE learning task. They are teaching you ENTIRELY different things in ENTIRELY different ways, which WOULD be possible except for the crucial fact that both are teaching you about YOURSELF. Your REALITY is unaffected by both. But if you LISTEN to both, your mind will split on WHAT YOUR REALITY IS.

C. The Rationale for Choice

1 There IS a rationale for choice. Only ONE teacher KNOWS what your reality is. If learning that is the PURPOSE of the curriculum, you MUST learn it of Him. The ego does NOT KNOW WHAT IT IS TRYING TO TEACH. It is trying to teach you what you are WITHOUT KNOWING IT. The ego is expert ONLY in confusion. It does not understand ANYTHING ELSE. As a teacher, then, it is totally confused and TOTALLY CONFUSING.

C. The Rationale for Choice

2	Even if you could disregard the Holy Spirit entirely, which is quite impossible, you could learn nothing from the ego, because the ego KNOWS nothing. Is there ANY possible reason for choosing a teacher such as this? Does the TOTAL disregard of ANYTHING it teaches make anything BUT sense? Is THIS the teacher to whom a Son of God should turn to find HIMSELF? The ego has never given you a sensible answer to anything.

Simply on the grounds of your own experience with the ego's teaching, should not this alone disqualify it as your future teacher?

3	But the ego has done more harm to your learning than this alone. Learning is joyful if it leads you along your natural path, and facilitates the development of WHAT YOU HAVE. But when you are taught AGAINST your nature, you will lose by your learning, because your learning will IMPRISON you. Your will is IN your nature, and therefore CANNOT go AGAINST it. The ego cannot teach you anything as long as your will is free, because you WILL NOT LISTEN TO IT. It is NOT your will to be imprisoned, BECAUSE your will is free.

4	That is why the ego IS the denial of free will. It is NEVER God Who coerces you, because He SHARES His Will WITH you. His voice teaches ONLY His Will, but that is not the Holy Spirit's lesson, because that is what you ARE. The LESSON is that your will and God's CANNOT be out of accord because they ARE one. This is the UNdoing of EVERYTHING the ego tries to teach. It is not, then, only the DIRECTION of the curriculum which must be unconflicted, but also the CONTENT.

5	The ego wants to teach you that you want to OPPOSE God's Will. This unnatural lesson CANNOT be learned, but the ATTEMPT to learn it is a violation of your own freedom, and makes you AFRAID of your will BECAUSE it is free. The Holy Spirit opposes ANY imprisoning of the will of a Son of God, KNOWING that the will of the Son IS the Father's. He leads you steadily along the path of freedom, teaching you how to disregard, or look beyond EVERYTHING that would hold you back.

6	We said before that the Holy Spirit teaches you the difference between pain and joy. [270] That is the same as saying that He teaches you the difference between imprisonment and freedom. YOU CANNOT MAKE THIS DISTINCTION WITHOUT HIM. That is because you have taught YOURSELF that imprisonment IS freedom. [271] Believing them to be the same, how can you tell them apart? Can you ask the part of your mind that taught you to believe they ARE the same to teach you the DIFFERENCE?

---

270 Chapter 7 K. The Confusion of Strength and Weakness, p7
271 Chapter 2 A. Introduction, p28
    Chapter 2 C. Healing as Release from Fear, p11

Chapter 8 – The Journey Back

7   The Holy Spirit's teaching takes only one direction, and has only one goal. His direction is freedom, and His goal is God. But He cannot conceive of God without YOU, because it was not God's Will to BE without you. When you have learned that your will IS God's, you could no more will to be without Him than He could will to be without YOU. This IS freedom and this IS joy. Deny YOURSELF this, and you ARE denying God His Kingdom, because He created you FOR this.

8   When we said, "all power and glory are yours because the Kingdom is His," [272] this is what we meant:

> The Will of God is without limit, and all power and glory lie within it. It is boundless in strength and in love and in peace. It has no boundaries because its extension is unlimited, and it encompasses all things because it CREATED all things. By CREATING all things, it made them PART OF ITSELF. YOU are the Will of God, because this is how you were created. Because your Creator creates only like Himself, you ARE like Him.

9   You are part of Him who IS all power and glory, and are therefore as unlimited as He is. To what else EXCEPT all power and glory can the Holy Spirit appeal to restore God's Kingdom? His appeal, then, is merely to what the Kingdom is, and for its own acknowledgment of what it is. When you acknowledge THIS, you bring the acknowledgment automatically to everyone, because YOU HAVE ACKNOWLEDGED EVERYONE.

By your recognition you awaken theirs, and through theirs YOURS is extended. Awakening runs easily and gladly through the Kingdom in answer to the call of God. This is the natural response of every Son of God to the Voice of His Creator, because it is the voice for HIS creations and for his own extension.

D. The Holy Encounter

1   Glory be to God in the highest, [273] and to YOU because He has so willed it. Ask and it shall be given you, [274] because it has already BEEN given. Ask for light and learn that you ARE light. If you WANT understanding and enlightenment you WILL learn it,

---

272 Chapter 7   H. The Total Commitment, p12
273 Luke 2:13 And suddenly there was with the angel a multitude of the heavenly host praising God, and saying, 14 "Glory to God in the highest, and on earth peace, good will toward men."
274 Matthew 7:7 Ask, and it shall be given you; seek, and ye shall find; knock, and it shall be opened unto you:
Luke 11:9 And I say unto you, Ask, and it shall be given you; seek, and ye shall find; knock, and it shall be opened unto you

D. The Holy Encounter

because your will to learn it is your decision to listen to the Teacher who KNOWS of light and can therefore TEACH IT TO YOU.

2   There is no limit on your learning, because there is no limit on your MINDS. There is no limit on His will to teach, because He was created by unlimited Will in ORDER to teach. KNOWING His function perfectly, He wills to fulfill it perfectly, because that is His joy AND YOURS. To fulfill the Will of God perfectly is the only joy and peace that can be fully KNOWN, because it is the only function that can be FULLY EXPERIENCED. When this is accomplished, then, there IS no other experience. But the WISH for other experience will block this, because God's Will CANNOT be forced upon you, being an experience of total WILLINGNESS.

3   The Holy Spirit knows how to teach this, but YOU do not. That is why you need Him, and why God gave Him TO you. Only HIS teaching will release your will to God's, uniting it with His power and glory, and establishing them as yours. You will share them as He shares them, because this is the natural outcome of their being. The Will of the Father and of the Son are one together BY THEIR EXTENSION. Their extension is the RESULT of their Oneness, holding THEIR unity by extending their JOINT will.

4   This is perfect creation by the perfectly created in union with the Perfect Creator. The Father MUST give fatherhood to His Sons, because His Own Fatherhood must be extended outward. You who belong in God have the holy function of extending His Fatherhood by placing no limits upon it. Let the Holy Spirit teach you HOW to do this, for you will know what it MEANS of God Himself.

5   *When you meet anyone, remember it is a holy encounter.*

> As you see him, you will see yourself.
> As you treat him, you will treat yourself.
> As you think of him, you will think of yourself.

Never forget this, for in him you will find yourself or lose sight of yourself.

> *Whenever two Sons of God meet they are given another chance at Salvation.*

Do not leave anyone without giving salvation TO him and receiving it yourself. For I am always there WITH you, in remembrance of YOU.

6   The goal of the curriculum, regardless of the teacher you choose, is KNOW THYSELF. There is nothing else to learn. Everyone is looking for himself and the power and glory he thinks he has lost. *Whenever you are with anyone ELSE, you have another opportunity to find them.* Your power and glory are in HIM BECAUSE they are yours. The ego tries to find them in YOURSELF, because it does not know where to look. But

Chapter 8 – The Journey Back

the Holy Spirit teaches you that if you look only at yourself you CANNOT find yourself because that is NOT what you are.

7 Whenever you are with a brother you are learning what you are, because you are TEACHING what you are. He will respond either with pain or with joy, depending on which teacher YOU are following. HE will be imprisoned or released according to your decision, AND SO WILL YOU. Never forget your responsibility to him, because it is your responsibility to YOURSELF. Give him HIS place in the Kingdom, and you will have YOURS. The Kingdom CANNOT be found alone, and you who ARE the Kingdom cannot find YOURSELVES alone.

8

> To achieve the goal of the curriculum, then, you CANNOT listen to the ego. Its purpose is to DEFEAT ITS OWN GOAL. It does not know this, because it does not know anything. But YOU can know this, and you WILL know it if you are willing to look at what the ego has made of YOU.

This IS your responsibility, because once you have really done this you WILL accept the Atonement for yourself. What other choice could you make?

9 *Having made this choice, you will begin to learn and understand why you have believed that when you met someone else, you have thought he WAS someone else.*

> And every holy encounter in which YOU enter fully will teach you THAT THIS IS NOT SO. You can encounter ONLY part of yourself, because you are part of God WHO IS EVERYTHING. His power and glory are everywhere, and you CANNOT be excluded from them. The ego teaches that your strength is in you ALONE. The Holy Spirit teaches that ALL strength is in God and THEREFORE in you.

10 God wills NO-ONE suffer. He does not will ANYONE to suffer for a wrong decision you have made, including YOURSELF. That is why He has given you the means for UNDOING it. Through His power and glory all your wrong decisions are undone COMPLETELY, releasing you AND your brothers from EVERY IMPRISONING THOUGHT ANY part of the Sonship has accepted. Wrong decisions HAVE no power BECAUSE they are not true. The imprisonment which they SEEM to produce is no more true than THEY are.

11 Power and glory belong to God alone. So do YOU. God gives WHATEVER belongs to Him, because He gives OF HIMSELF, and EVERYTHING belongs to Him. Giving of YOUR self is the function He gave you. Fulfilling it perfectly will teach you what YOU

have of HIM. And this will teach you what you are IN Him. You CANNOT be powerLESS to do this, because this IS your power.

Glory is God's gift to you because that is what HE is. See this glory everywhere, to learn what YOU are.

E. The Light of the World

1   If God's Will for you is complete peace and joy, unless you experience ONLY this you MUST be refusing to acknowledge His Will. His Will does not vacillate, being changeless forever. When you are not at peace, it can only be because you do not believe you are IN HIM. Yet He is all in all. His peace IS complete, and you MUST be included in it. His laws govern you because they govern EVERYTHING. You cannot exempt yourself from His laws, although you CAN disobey them. But if you do, and ONLY if you do, you WILL feel lonely and helpless, because you ARE denying yourself everything.

2   I am come as a light into the world [275] which DOES deny itself everything. It does this simply by dissociating itself FROM everything. It is therefore an illusion of isolation, MAINTAINED by fear of the same loneliness which IS its illusion. I have told you that I am with you always even to the end of the world. [276] That is WHY I am the light of the world. If I am with you in the loneliness of the world, THE LONELINESS IS GONE. You CANNOT maintain the illusion of loneliness if you are NOT alone.

3   My purpose, then, IS to overcome the world. [277] I do not attack it, but my light must dispel it because of WHAT IT IS. Light does not ATTACK darkness, but it DOES shine it away. If my light goes with you everywhere, YOU shine it away WITH ME. The light becomes OURS, and you CANNOT abide in darkness, any more than darkness can abide anywhere you go. The remembrance of me [278] IS the remembrance of yourself and of Him Who sent me to you.

---

275 John 8:12 Again therefore Jesus spake unto them, saying, I am the light of the world: he that followeth me shall not walk in the darkness, but shall have the light of life.
John 9:5 As long as I am in the world, I am the light of the world.
John 12:46 I am come a light into the world, that whosoever believeth on me should not abide in darkness.
276 Matthew 28:20 teaching them to observe all things whatsoever I commanded you: and lo, I am with you always, even unto the end of the world.
277 John 16:33 These things have I spoken unto you, that in me ye may have peace. In the world ye have tribulation: but be of good cheer; I have overcome the world.
278 Luke 22:19 And he took bread, and gave thanks, and brake [it], and gave unto them, saying, This is my body which is given for you: this do in remembrance of me.

Chapter 8 – The Journey Back

4   You WERE in darkness [279] until God's Will was done completely by ANY part of the Sonship. When it was, it was perfectly accomplished by ALL. How else could it BE perfectly accomplished?

My mission was simply to UNITE the Will of the Sonship WITH the Will of the Father by being aware of the Father's Will myself.

This is the awareness I came to give YOU, and YOUR problem in accepting it IS the problem of this world. Dispelling it is salvation, and in this sense I AM the salvation of the world. [280]

5   The world MUST despise and reject me [281], because the world IS the belief that love is impossible. YOUR reactions to me ARE the reactions of the world to God. If you will accept the fact that I am with you, you are DENYING the world and ACCEPTING GOD. My will IS His, and YOUR will to hear me IS the decision to hear His Voice and abide in His Will. As He sent me to you, so will I send you to others. But I will go to them WITH you, so we can teach them union and peace.

6   Do you not think the world needs peace as much as you do?

Do you not want to give it to the world as much as you want to receive it?

For unless you do, you will NOT receive it.

If you will to have it of me, you MUST give it.

Rehabilitation does not come from anyone ELSE.

You can have GUIDANCE from without, but you must ACCEPT it from within.

The guidance must become what YOU want, or else it will be meaningless to you.

---

279 John 1:1 In the beginning was the Word, and the Word was with God, and the Word was God.
   2 The same was in the beginning with God.
   3 All things were made by him; and without him was not any thing made that was made.
   4 In him was life; and the life was the light of men.
   5 And the light shineth in darkness; and the darkness comprehended it not.
280 Acts 4:10 Be it known unto you all, and to all the people of Israel, that by the name of Jesus Christ of Nazareth, whom ye crucified, whom God raised from the dead, even by him doth this man stand here before you whole. 11 This is the stone which was set at nought of you builders, which is become the head of the corner. 12 Neither is there salvation in any other: for there is none other name under heaven given among men, whereby we must be saved.
281 Isaiah 53:3 He is despised and rejected of men; a man of sorrows, and acquainted with grief: and we hid as it were our faces from him; he was despised, and we esteemed him not.

E. The Light of the World

That is why rehabilitation is a collaborative venture. I can tell you what to DO, but this will not really help you unless you collaborate by believing that I KNOW what to do. Only then will your MIND will to follow me.

7 Without YOUR will, you cannot be rehabilitated.
MOTIVATION TO BE HEALED is the crucial factor in rehabilitation. Without this, you are deciding AGAINST healing, and your veto of my will FOR you MAKES HEALING IMPOSSIBLE. If healing IS our joint will, unless our wills ARE joined you CANNOT be healed. This is obvious when you consider what healing is FOR.

8 Healing is the way in which the separation is overcome. Separation is overcome by UNION. It CANNOT be overcome by separating. The WILL to unite must be unequivocal, or the will ITSELF is separated or NOT WHOLE.
Your will is the means by which you determine your own condition, because will is the MECHANISM OF DECISION. It is the power by which you separate or join, and experience pain or joy accordingly.

> My will cannot OVERCOME yours, because YOURS IS AS POWERFUL AS MINE. If it were not so, the Sons of God would be unequal.

9 All things BECOME possible through our JOINT will. But my will alone will not help you.
Your will is as free as mine, and God Himself would not go against it.
I cannot will what God does NOT will. I CAN offer you my will to make YOURS invincible by this sharing, but I CANNOT oppose yours without competing with it and thereby violating God's Will for you.
Nothing God created can oppose your will, as nothing God created can oppose His. God GAVE your will its power, which I can only acknowledge in honor of HIS.

10 If you want to be LIKE me, I will help you, knowing that we ARE alike. If you want to be DIFFERENT, I will wait until you change your mind. I can TEACH you, but only you can choose to LISTEN to my teaching. How else can it be, if God's Kingdom IS freedom? Freedom cannot be learned by tyranny of ANY kind, and the perfect equality of ALL God's Sons cannot be recognized through the dominion of one will over another. God's Sons are equal in will, all being the Will of their Father. This is the ONLY lesson I can teach, knowing that it is true.

11 When your will is NOT mine, it is not Our Father's. This means that you have imprisoned YOURS, and have not LET it be free. Of yourselves you can do nothing, because of yourselves you ARE nothing. I am nothing without the Father, and YOU are

Chapter 8 – The Journey Back

nothing without me because by DENYING the Father you deny YOURSELF.[282] I will ALWAYS remember you, and in MY remembrance OF you lies your remembrance of YOURSELF. In our remembrance of EACH OTHER lies our remembrance of God. And in this remembrance lies your freedom, because your freedom is in Him.

12   Join then with me in praise of Him AND you whom He created. This is our gift of gratitude to Him, which He will share with ALL His Creations, to whom He gives equally whatever is acceptable to Him. BECAUSE it is acceptable to Him, it is the gift of freedom, which IS His Will for all His Sons. By OFFERING freedom you will be free, because freedom is the only gift which you can offer to God's Sons, being an acknowledgment of what they are and what HE is.

13   Freedom is creation because it is love. What you seek to imprison you do NOT love. Therefore, when you seek to imprison ANYONE, including YOURSELF, you do not love him and you cannot identify with him. When you imprison yourself, you are losing sight of your true identification with me and with the Father. Your identification IS with the Father and with the Son. It CANNOT be with one and not the other. If you are part of one, you MUST be part of the other because they ARE One.

14   The Holy Trinity is holy BECAUSE It is One. If you exclude YOURSELF from this union, you are perceiving the Holy Trinity as separated. You MUST be included in It, because It IS everything. Unless you take your place in It and fulfill your function AS part of It, It is as bereft as YOU are. No part of It can be imprisoned if Its Truth is to be known.

15   Can you be separated from your identification and be at peace? Dissociation is NOT a solution; it is a DELUSION. The delusional believe that truth will ASSAIL them, and so they DO NOT SEE IT because they prefer the delusion. Judging truth as something they do NOT want, they perceive deception and block knowledge. Help them by offering them YOUR unified will on their behalf, as I am offering you mine on YOURS. Alone we can do nothing, but TOGETHER our wills fuse into something whose power is far beyond the power of its separate parts.

16   By NOT BEING SEPARATE, the Will of God is established IN ours and AS ours. This will is invincible BECAUSE it is undivided. The UNDIVIDED will of the Sonship is the perfect creator, being wholly in the likeness of God, Whose Will it IS. YOU cannot be exempt from it, if you are to understand what it is and what YOU are. By separating

---

[282] John 5:19 Then answered Jesus and said unto them, Verily, verily, I say unto you, The Son can do nothing of himself, but what he seeth the Father do: for what things soever he doeth, these also doeth the Son likewise.
John 5:30 I can of mine own self do nothing: as I hear, I judge: and my judgment is just; because I seek not mine own will, but the will of the Father which hath sent me.

E. The Light of the World

your will from mine, you ARE exempting yourself from the Will of God which IS yourself.

17   But to heal is still to make whole. Therefore to heal is to UNITE with those who are LIKE you, because perceiving this likeness IS to recognize the Father. If YOUR perfection is in Him and ONLY in Him, how can you KNOW it WITHOUT recognizing Him? The recognition of God is the recognition of yourself. There IS no separation of God and His Creation. You will learn this as you learn that there is no separation of YOUR will and mine.

18   Let the love of God shine upon you by your acceptance of me. MY reality is yours and His. By joining YOUR will with mine, you are signifying your awareness that the Will of God is One. His Oneness and ours are not separate, because His Oneness ENCOMPASSES ours. To join WITH me is to restore His power TO you BECAUSE we are sharing it. I offer you only the recognition of His power in you, but in that lies ALL truth. As WE unite, we unite with Him. Glory be to the union of God and His Holy Sons, because all glory lies IN them because they ARE united.

19   The miracles WE do bear witness to the Will of the Father for His Son, and to our joy in uniting WITH His Will FOR us. When you unite with me, you are uniting WITHOUT the ego, because I have renounced the ego in myself, and therefore CANNOT unite with yours. OUR union is therefore the way to renounce the ego in YOURSELVES. The truth in both of us is BEYOND the ego. By willing that, you HAVE gone beyond it toward truth.

20   Our success in transcending the ego is guaranteed by God, and I can share my perfect confidence IN His Promise because I know He gave me this confidence for both of us and ALL of us. I bring His Peace back to all His Children, because I received it of Him for us all. [283] Nothing can prevail against our united wills, because nothing can prevail against God's. Would ye know the Will of God for YOU? Ask it of me, who knows it for you, and you will find it. I will deny YOU nothing, as God denies ME nothing.

21   Ours is simply the journey back to God Who is our home. Whenever fear intrudes anywhere along the road to peace, it is ALWAYS because the ego has attempted to JOIN the journey with us AND CANNOT DO SO. Sensing defeat and angered by it, it regards itself as rejected and becomes retaliative. You are invulnerable to its retaliation BECAUSE I AM WITH YOU. On this journey, you have chosen me as your companion INSTEAD of your ego. Do not try to hold on to both, or you will try to go in different directions and will lose the way.

---

[283] Chapter 5 F. Therapy and Teaching, p10

Chapter 8 – The Journey Back

22 The ego's way is not mine, but it is also NOT YOURS. The Holy Spirit has one direction for ALL minds, and the one He taught me IS yours. Let us not lose sight of His direction through illusions, for ONLY illusions of another direction can obscure the one for which God's Voice speaks in all of us.

 Never accord the ego the power to interfere with the journey, because it HAS none, and the journey is the way to what is TRUE. Leave ALL deception behind, and reach beyond all attempts of the ego to hold you back.

23 I DO go before you, because I AM beyond the ego. Reach therefore for my hand because you WANT to transcend the ego. My will, will NEVER be wanting, and if you want to share it YOU WILL. I give it willingly and gladly, because I need YOU as much as you need ME.

F. The Power of Joint Decision

1 WE are the joint will of the Sonship, whose wholeness is for all. We begin the journey back by setting out TOGETHER, and gather in our brothers as we CONTINUE together.

2 Every gain in our strength is offered to all, so they, too, can lay aside their weakness and add their strength to us. God's welcome waits for us all, and He will welcome us as I am welcoming YOU. Forget not the Kingdom of God for anything the world has to offer. The world can ADD nothing to the power and the glory of God and His Holy Sons, but it CAN blind the Sons to the Father if they behold it. You cannot behold the world and know God. Only one is true.

3 I am come to tell you that the choice of which is true is not yours. If it were, you would have destroyed yourselves. But God did not will the destruction of His Creations, having created them for eternity. His Will has saved you, not from yourselves, but from your illusions of yourselves. He has saved you FOR yourselves. Let us glorify Him Whom the world denies, for over His Kingdom it has no power.

4 No-one created by God can find joy in anything except the eternal. That is not because he is DEPRIVED of anything else, but because nothing else is WORTHY of him. What God AND His Sons create IS eternal, and in this and this only is their joy. Listen to the story of the prodigal son, and learn what God's treasure is and YOURS:

5 This son of a loving father left his home and thought he squandered everything for nothing of any value, though he did not know its worthlessness at the time. He was ashamed to return to his father, because he thought he had hurt

F. The Power of Joint Decision

him. But when he came home the father welcomed him with joy, because only the son himself WAS his father's treasure. HE WANTED NOTHING ELSE.[284]

6   God wants only His Son, because His Son is His only treasure. You want your creations, as He wants His. Your creations are your gift to the Holy Trinity, created in gratitude for YOUR creation. They do not leave you, any more than you have left YOUR Creator. But they EXTEND your creation, as God extended Himself to YOU. Can the Creations of God Himself take joy in what is not real? And what IS real except the Creations of God and those which are created like His? YOUR creations love you as your Soul loves your Father FOR THE GIFT OF CREATION. There IS no other gift that is eternal, and therefore THERE IS NO OTHER GIFT THAT IS TRUE.

7   How, then, can you accept anything else, or GIVE anything else, and expect joy in return? And what else BUT joy would you want? You made neither yourself nor your function. YOU have made only the DECISION to be unworthy of both. But you COULD not make YOURSELF unworthy because YOU ARE THE TREASURE OF GOD. What HE values IS valuable. There CAN be no question of its worth, because its value lies in God's sharing Himself with it and ESTABLISHING ITS VALUE FOREVER. YOUR function is to ADD to God's treasure by creating YOURS. His will TO you is His Will FOR you. He would not withhold creation from you, because HIS joy is in it.

8   You CANNOT find joy EXCEPT as He does. HIS joy lay in creating YOU, and He extends His Fatherhood to you so that you can extend yourself AS HE DID. You do not understand this because you do not understand Him. No one who does not know his function can understand it. And no one CAN know his function unless he knows who he IS. Creation is the Will of God. His Will created you TO CREATE. Your will was not created separate from His, and so it wills as HE wills.

9   An unwilling will does not mean anything, because it is a contradiction in terms which actually leaves nothing. You can make yourself powerless only in a way that has NO MEANING AT ALL. When you THINK you are unwilling to will with God, YOU ARE NOT THINKING. God's will IS thought. It cannot be contradicted BY thought. God does not contradict HIMSELF. And His Sons, who are like Him, cannot contradict themselves OR Him.

But their thought is so powerful that they can even imprison the mind of God's Son IF THEY SO CHOOSE. This choice DOES make the Son's function unknown TO HIM, but never to his Creator. And BECAUSE it is not unknown to his Creator, it is forever knowable to him.

10   There is no question but one you should ever ask of yourself:

"Do I want to know my Father's Will for me?"

---

[284] Luke 15:11-32 The parable of the prodigal son.

Chapter 8 – The Journey Back

HE will not hide it. He has revealed it to me because I asked it of Him, and learned of what He had already given. Our function is to function together, because apart from each other we cannot function at all. The whole power of God's Son lies in all of us, but not in any of us alone.

God would not have us be alone because HE does not will to be alone. That is why He created His Son and gave him the power to create with Him. Our creations are as holy as we are, and we are the Sons of God Himself, and therefore as holy as He is. Through our creations we extend our Love, and thus increase the joy of the Holy Trinity.

You do not understand this for a very simple reason. You who are God's own treasure do not regard yourselves as valuable. Given this belief YOU CANNOT UNDERSTAND ANYTHING.

11 I share with God the knowledge of the value HE puts upon you. My devotion to you is of Him, being born of my knowledge of myself AND Him. We cannot BE separated. Whom God has joined CANNOT be separated, [285] and God has joined all His Sons WITH HIMSELF. Can you be separated from your life and your being? The journey to God is merely the reawakening of the knowledge of where you are always, and what you are forever. *It is a journey without distance, to a goal that has never changed.*

12 Truth can only be EXPERIENCED.

It cannot be described and it cannot be explained.

I can make you aware of the CONDITIONS of truth, but the experience is of God.

> Together we can meet its conditions,
> but truth will dawn upon you of itself.

What God has willed for you IS yours. He has given His Will to His treasure, whose treasure It is. Your heart lies where your treasure is, [286] as His does. You who are beloved of God are wholly blessed. Learn this of me, and free the Holy Will of all those who are as blessed as you are.

---

285 Mark 10:9 What therefore God hath joined together, let not man put asunder.
  Matthew 19:6 So that they are no more twain, but one flesh. What therefore God hath joined together, let not man put asunder.
286 Matthew 6:19 Lay not up for yourselves treasures upon earth, where moth and rust doth corrupt, and where thieves break through and steal:
  20 But lay up for yourselves treasures in heaven, where neither moth nor rust doth corrupt, and where thieves do not break through nor steal:
  21 For where your treasure is, there will your heart be also.
  22 The light of the body is the eye: if therefore thine eye be single, thy whole body shall be full of light.

G. Communication and the Ego-Body Equation

1   Attack is ALWAYS physical. When attack in ANY form enters your mind, you are EQUATING YOURSELF WITH A BODY.

This is the ego's INTERPRETATION of the body. *You do not have to ATTACK physically to accept this interpretation; you ARE accepting it simply by the belief that attack can GET YOU SOMETHING YOU WANT.* If you did NOT believe this, the IDEA of attack would have no appeal to you.

2

When you equate yourself with a body, you will ALWAYS experience depression. When a Child of God thinks of himself in this way, he is belittling himself and seeing his brothers as similarly belittled. Since he can find himself ONLY in them, he has cut himself off from salvation. Remember that the Holy Spirit interprets the body ONLY as a means of communication. Being the communication link between God and His separated Sons, He interprets everything YOU have in the light of what HE is.

3   The ego SEPARATES through the body.
The Holy Spirit reaches THROUGH it to others.

You do not perceive your brothers as the Holy Spirit does because you do not interpret their bodies AND YOURS solely as a means of JOINING THEIR MINDS and uniting them with yours and mine.

This interpretation of the body will change your mind entirely about its value. Of itself it has NONE. If you use it for attack it is harmful to you.

But if you use it ONLY to reach the minds of those who believe they ARE bodies and teach them THROUGH the body that THIS IS NOT SO, you will begin to understand the power of the mind that is in both of you.

If you use the body for this, and ONLY for this, you CANNOT use it for attack. In the service of uniting, it becomes a beautiful lesson in communion, which has value until communion IS.

4   This is God's way of making unlimited what YOU have limited. His Voice does not see the body as YOU do, because He knows the ONLY reality that ANYTHING can have is the service it can render God on behalf of the function HE has given.

Chapter 8 – The Journey Back

Communication ENDS separation.
Attack PROMOTES it.

> The body is ugly or beautiful, savage or holy, helpful or harmful, according to the use to which it is put. And in the body of another you will see the use to which you put YOURS.

5   If the body becomes for you a means which you give to the Holy Spirit to use on behalf of the union of the Sonship, you will not see ANYTHING physical except as WHAT IT IS.

Use it for truth, and you will see it truly.

MISuse it and you WILL misunderstand it, because you have already done so BY misusing it.

Interpret ANYTHING apart from the Holy Spirit, and you will mistrust it. This will lead you to hatred and attack and LOSS OF PEACE.

6   But ALL (sense of) loss comes only from your own misunderstanding. Loss of ANY kind is impossible. When you look upon a brother as a physical entity, HIS power and glory are lost to you and SO ARE YOURS. You HAVE attacked him, and you MUST have attacked yourself first. Do not see him this way for your OWN salvation, which MUST bring him his.

Do not ALLOW him to belittle himself in YOUR mind, but give him freedom from his belief in littleness, and escape from YOURS. As part of YOU, HE is holy. As part of ME, YOU are. To communicate with part of God Himself is to reach beyond the Kingdom to its Creator, through His Voice which He has established as part of YOU.

7   Rejoice, then, that of yourselves you can do nothing. You are not OF yourselves. And He of Whom you ARE has willed your power and glory FOR you, with which you can perfectly accomplish His holy Will for you when you so will it yourself. He has not withdrawn His gifts from YOU, but YOU have withdrawn them from Him. Let no Son of God remain hidden for His Name's sake, because His Name [287] is YOURS.

8   Remember that the Bible says, "The word (or thought) was made flesh." [288] Strictly speaking, this is impossible, since it seems to involve the translation of one order of reality into another. Different orders of reality merely SEEM to exist, just as different

---

287 [Tim Note: The original idea of 'name' meant 'nature of.' It is in this sense that 'in my name' or 'in His Name' is used in the Bible and Course.

288 John 1:14 And the Word became flesh, and dwelt among us (and we beheld his glory, glory as of the only begotten from the Father), full of grace and truth.

G. Communication and the Ego-Body Equation

orders of miracles do. Thought cannot be MADE into flesh except by belief, because thought is NOT physical.

But thought IS communication, for which the body can be used. This is the only NATURAL use to which it can be put. To use the body UNnaturally is to lose sight of the Holy Spirit's purpose, and thus to confuse the goal of His curriculum.

9 There is nothing so frustrating to a learner as to place him in a curriculum which he cannot learn. His sense of adequacy suffers, and he MUST become depressed. Being faced with an impossible learning situation, REGARDLESS of why it is impossible, is the most depressing thing in the world. In fact, it is ultimately WHY the world is depressing. The Holy Spirit's curriculum is NEVER depressing because it is a curriculum in joy.

Whenever the reaction to learning is depression, it is only because the goal of the curriculum has been lost sight of.

10 In the world, not even the body is perceived as whole. Its purpose is seen as fragmented into many functions which bear little or no relationship to each other, so that it appears to be ruled by chaos. Guided by the ego, it IS.

Guided by the Holy Spirit, it is NOT. It becomes ONLY a means by which the part of the mind which you have separated from your Soul can reach beyond its distortions and RETURN to the Soul. The ego's temple thus becomes the temple of the Holy Spirit, where devotion to Him replaces devotion to the ego. In this sense the body DOES become a temple to God, [289] because His Voice abides in it by directing the use TO WHICH YOU PUT IT.

11 *Healing is the result of using the body SOLELY for communication.* Since this IS natural, it heals by making whole, which is also natural. ALL mind is whole, and the belief that part of it is physical or NOT MIND is a fragmented (or sick) interpretation.

Mind CANNOT be made physical, but it CAN be made manifest THROUGH the physical if it uses the body to GO BEYOND itself. By reaching OUT, the mind EXTENDS itself. It does not STOP at the body, for if it does it is blocked in its purpose. A mind which has been blocked has allowed itself to be vulnerable to attack, because it has TURNED AGAINST ITSELF.

12 The removal of blocks, then, is the ONLY way to guarantee help and healing. *Help and healing are the normal expressions of a mind which is working THROUGH the body but not IN it.*

---

[289] 1 Corinthians 3:16 Do you not know that you are the temple of God and that the Spirit of God dwells in you?

Chapter 8 – The Journey Back

If the mind believes the body is its GOAL, it WILL distort its perception OF the body, and by blocking its own extension BEYOND it will INDUCE illness by FOSTERING SEPARATION. Perceiving the body AS A SEPARATE ENTITY cannot BUT foster illness, because it is not true. A medium of communication WILL lose its usefullness if it is used for anything else.

13   To use a medium of communication as a medium of ATTACK is an obvious confusion in purpose. To communicate is to join and to attack is to separate. How can you do both simultaneously WITH THE SAME THING, and NOT suffer? Perception of the body can be unified only by ONE PURPOSE. This releases the mind from the temptation to see it in many lights, and gives it over ENTIRELY to the One Light in which it can be really understood at all.

14   To confuse a learning device with a curriculum GOAL is a fundamental confusion. Learning can hardly be meaningfully arrested at its own aids, and hope to understand them OR its real purpose.

Learning must lead BEYOND the body to the re-establishment of the power of the mind IN it. This can be accomplished ONLY if the mind EXTENDS to other minds, and does not ARREST ITSELF in its extension.

The arrest of the mind's extension is the cause of all illness, because ONLY EXTENSION IS THE MIND'S FUNCTION. Block this, and you have blocked health because you have BLOCKED THE MIND'S JOY.

15   The opposite of joy is depression. When your learning promotes depression INSTEAD of joy, you CANNOT be listening to God's joyous teacher, and you MUST be learning amiss. To see a body as anything EXCEPT a means of pure extension is to limit your mind and HURT YOURSELF. Health is therefore nothing more than united purpose. If the body is brought under the purpose of the mind, it becomes whole because the mind's purpose IS one.

16   Attack can only be an assumed goal of the body, but the body APART from the mind HAS NO PURPOSE AT ALL. You are NOT limited by the body, and thought CANNOT be made flesh. But mind can be manifested through the body if it goes beyond it and DOES NOT INTERPRET IT AS LIMITATION.

Whenever you see another as limited TO or BY the body, you are imposing this limit ON YOURSELF. Are you willing to ACCEPT this, when your whole purpose for learning should be to escape FROM limitations?

17   To conceive of the body as a means of attack of any kind, and to entertain even the possibility that joy could POSSIBLY result, is a clear-cut indication of a poor learner. He has accepted a learning goal in obvious contradiction to the unified purpose of the curriculum, and is interfering with his ability to accept it AS HIS OWN.

G. Communication and the Ego-Body Equation

¹⁸ Joy is unified purpose, and unified purpose is ONLY God's. When yours is unified, it IS His. Interfere with His purpose, and YOU NEED SALVATION. You have condemned yourself, but condemnation is not of God. Therefore, it is not true. No more are any of the RESULTS of your condemnation. When you see a brother as a body, you are condemning him BECAUSE you have condemned yourself. But if ALL condemnation is unreal, and it MUST be unreal because it is a form of attack, then it can HAVE no results.

¹⁹ Do not allow yourselves to suffer from the results of what is not true. Free your minds from the belief that this is possible. In its complete impossibility, and your full awareness OF its complete impossibility, lies your only hope for release. But what other hope would you want?

Freedom from illusions lies only in not BELIEVING them. THERE IS NO ATTACK, but there IS unlimited communication and therefore unlimited power and wholeness. The power of wholeness is EXTENSION. Do not arrest your thought in this world, and you will open your mind to Creation in God.

H. The Body as Means or End

¹ Attitudes toward the body are attitudes toward ATTACK. The ego's definitions of ANYTHING are childish, and are ALWAYS based on what it believes a thing is FOR.

This is because it is incapable of true generalizations, and equates what it sees with the function IT ascribes to it. It does NOT equate it with what it IS.

To the ego, the body IS TO ATTACK WITH. Equating YOU with the body, it teaches that YOU are to attack with, because THIS IS WHAT IT BELIEVES. The body, then, is not the source of its own health. Its condition lies solely in your interpretation of its function.

² The reason why definitions by function are inferior is merely because they may well be inaccurate. Functions are part of being, since they arise FROM it. But the relationship is NOT reciprocal.

The whole does define the part, but the part does NOT define the whole.

This is as true of knowledge as it is of perception. The reason why to KNOW in part is to know entirely is merely because of the fundamental difference between knowledge and perception.

In perception, the whole is built up of parts, which can separate and reassemble in different constellations.

Knowledge never changes, so that its constellation is permanent.

Chapter 8 – The Journey Back

The only areas in which part-whole relationships have any meaning are those in which change is possible. There IS no difference between the whole and the part where change is impossible.

3   The body exists in a world which seems to contain two voices which are fighting for its possession. In this perceived constellation, the body is regarded as capable of shifting its control from one to the other, making the concept of both health and sickness possible. The ego makes a fundamental confusion between means and ends, as it always does. Regarding the body as an end, it has no real use for it at all, because it is NOT an end.

You must have noticed an outstanding characteristic of every end that the ego has accepted as its own. When you have achieved it, IT HAS NOT SATISFIED YOU. This is why the ego is forced to shift from one end to another without ceasing, so that YOU will continue to hope it can offer you something.

4   It has been particularly difficult to overcome the ego's belief in the body as an end because this is synonymous with ATTACK AS AN END. The ego has a REAL INVESTMENT IN SICKNESS. If you are sick, how can you object to the ego's firm belief that you are NOT invulnerable? This is a particularly appealing argument from the ego's point of view, because it obscures the obvious attack which underlies the sickness. If you accepted THIS, and also decided AGAINST attack, you could not give this false witness to the ego's stand. It is hard to perceive this as a false witness, because you do not realize that it IS entirely out of keeping with what YOU want. This witness, then, appears to be innocent and trustworthy only because YOU have not seriously cross-examined him.

5   If you did, you would not consider sickness such a strong witness on behalf of the ego's views. A more honest statement would be as follows:

> Those who WANT the ego are predisposed to defend it.

Therefore, their choice of witnesses should be suspect from the beginning. The ego does not call upon witnesses who might disagree with its case, NOR DOES THE HOLY SPIRIT. We have said before that judgment IS the function of the Holy Spirit, and one which He is perfectly equipped to fulfill. The ego, as a judge, gives anything BUT an impartial trial (judgment.) When the ego calls on a witness, it has ALREADY MADE IT AN ALLY.

It is still true that the body has no function of itself. This is because it is NOT an end. The ego, however, establishes it AS an end because, as such, IT WILL LOSE ITS TRUE FUNCTION.

H. The Body as Means or End

6   This is the purpose of everything the ego does. Its sole aim is to lose sight of the functions of EVERYTHING. A sick body does not make any sense. It COULD not make any sense, since sickness is not what it is FOR.

Sickness is meaningful only if the two basic premises on which the ego's interpretation of the body rests are true. These are specifically:

first, that the body is for attack,

and also that, you ARE a body.

Without this, sickness is completely inconceivable. Sickness is a way of demonstrating that YOU CAN BE HURT. It is a witness to your frailty, your vulnerability, and your extreme need to depend on external guidance. The ego uses this as its best argument for your need for ITS guidance. It dictates endless prescriptions for AVOIDING this catastrophic outcome. The Holy Spirit, perfectly aware of the same data, does not bother to analyze it at all. If the data are meaningless, there is no point in treating them at all.

7   The function of truth is to collect data which are TRUE. There is no point in trying to make sense out of meaningless data. ANY way they are handled results in nothing. The more complicated the results become, the harder it may be to recognize their nothingness, but it is not necessary to examine ALL possible outcomes to which premises give rise to judge the PREMISES truly.

8   A learning DEVICE is NOT a teacher. IT cannot tell you how you feel. YOU do not KNOW how you feel, because YOU HAVE ACCEPTED THE EGO'S CONFUSION, and YOU think A LEARNING DEVICE CAN TELL YOU HOW YOU FEEL. Sickness is merely another example of your insistence on asking for guidance of a teacher who DOES NOT KNOW THE ANSWER. The ego is INCAPABLE of knowing how you feel.

When we said that the ego DOES NOT KNOW ANYTHING, we said the one thing about the ego that is wholly true. But there is a corollary. If knowledge is being, and the ego has no knowledge, then the ego HAS NO BEING.

9   You might ask how the voice of something which does not exist can be so insistent. Have you ever seriously considered the distorting power of something you WANT, even if it is not true? You have had many instances of how what you want can distort what you see and hear. No one can doubt the ego's skill in building up false cases. And no one can doubt your willingness to listen, until YOU will not to tolerate ANYTHING except truth.

10   When YOU lay the ego aside it will be gone. *The Holy Spirit's voice is as loud as your willingness to listen.* It cannot be louder without violating your will, which He seeks to free but never to command.

Chapter 8 – The Journey Back

He will teach you to use your body ONLY to reach your brothers so He can teach His message through you. This will heal them and THEREFORE heal you. Everything used in accordance with its function as HE sees it CANNOT be sick. Everything used otherwise IS.

11
>Do not allow the body to be a mirror of a split mind.
>Do not let it be an image of your own perception of littleness.
>Do not let it reflect your will to attack.

Health is the natural state of anything whose interpretation is left to the Holy Spirit, who perceives no attack on anything.

Health is the result of relinquishing ALL attempts to use the body lovelessly.

It is the beginning of the proper perspective on life, under the guidance of the one teacher who knows what life IS, being the voice for Life Itself.

I. Healing as Corrected Perception

1   We once said that the Holy Spirit is the Answer. [290] He is the answer to EVERYTHING, because He knows what the answer to everything IS. The ego does not know what a REAL question is, although it asks an endless number. But YOU can learn this, as you learn to question the value of the ego and thus establish your ability to EVALUATE its questions.

When the ego tempts you to sickness, do not ask the Holy Spirit to heal the body. For this would merely be to accept the ego's belief that the body is the proper aim for healing. Ask rather that the Holy Spirit teach you the right PERCEPTION of the body, for perception alone can be distorted.

2   ONLY PERCEPTION CAN BE SICK, because perception can be WRONG.
>Wrong perception is DISTORTED WILLING, which WANTS things to be as they are not.

The reality of EVERYTHING is totally harmless, because total harmlessness is the CONDITION of its reality. It is also the condition of your AWARENESS of its reality. You do not have to SEEK reality. It will seek you and FIND you, WHEN YOU MEET ITS CONDITIONS. Its conditions are part of WHAT IT IS.

And this part only is up to you. The rest is of Itself. You need do so little, because It is so powerful that your little part WILL bring the whole to you. Accept, then, your little part, and LET the whole be yours. Wholeness heals BECAUSE it is of the mind.

---

290 Chapter 5 C. The Mind of the Atonement, p10

I. Healing as Corrected Perception

3   All forms of sickness, even unto death, are physical expressions of the FEAR OF AWAKENING.

They are attempts to reinforce UNCONSCIOUSNESS out of fear of CONSCIOUSNESS.

This is a pathetic way of TRYING NOT TO KNOW by rendering the faculties for knowing ineffectual. "Rest in peace" is a blessing for the living, not the dead, because rest comes from waking, not from sleeping. Sleep is withdrawing; waking is JOINING. Dreams are ILLUSIONS of joining, taking on the ego's distortions about what joining means, if you are sleeping under its guidance. But the Holy Spirit, too, has use for sleep, and can use dreams on BEHALF of waking, if you will let Him.

4   How you wake is the sign of how you have used sleep. To whom did you give it? Under which teacher did you place it? Whenever you wake dis-spiritedly, it was NOT of the Spirit. ONLY when you awaken joyously have you utilized sleep ACCORDING TO THE HOLY SPIRIT'S PURPOSE. You can indeed be "drugged by sleep," but this is ALWAYS because you have MISUSED IT ON BEHALF OF SICKNESS. Sleep is no more a form of death than death is a form of unconsciousness. UNCONSCIOUSNESS IS IMPOSSIBLE. You can rest in peace only BECAUSE YOU ARE AWAKE.

5   Healing is release from the fear of waking, and the substitution of the will to wake.

The will to wake is the will to love, since ALL healing involves replacing fear with love. The Holy Spirit cannot distinguish among degrees of error, for if He taught that one form of sickness is more serious than another, He would be teaching that one error can be more REAL than another. But HIS function is to distinguish ONLY between the false and the true, REPLACING the false WITH the true.

6   The ego, which always WEAKENS the will, wants to SEPARATE the body from the mind. This IS an attempt to DESTROY it. But the ego actually believes that it is PROTECTING the body. This is because it believes that MIND IS DANGEROUS, and that to MAKE MINDLESS is to heal. But to make mindless is impossible, since it would mean to make nothing out of what God Created. The ego DESPISES weakness, even though it makes every effort to INDUCE it. IT WANTS ONLY WHAT IT HATES. To the ego this is perfectly sensible. Believing in the power of attack, it WANTS it.

Chapter 8 – The Journey Back

7. You have begun to realize that this is a very practical course, because it means EXACTLY what it says. So does the Bible, if it is properly understood. *There has been a marked tendency on the part of many of the Bible's followers, and also its translators, to be entirely literal about fear and ITS effects, but NOT about love and ITS results.* Thus, "hellfire" means burning, but raising the dead becomes allegorical. Actually, it is PARTICULARLY the references to the outcomes of love that should be taken literally because the Bible is ABOUT love, being about GOD.

8. The Bible enjoins you to be perfect, [291] to heal ALL errors, to take no thought of the body AS SEPARATE, and to accomplish all things IN MY NAME. This is not my name alone, for ours is a shared identification. The name of God's Son is One, and you are enjoined to do the works of love BECAUSE we share this oneness. Our minds are whole BECAUSE they are one. If you are sick, you are withdrawing from me. But you CANNOT WITHDRAW FROM ME ALONE. You can only withdraw from yourself AND me.

9.
> I would not ask you to do things which you CANNOT do, and it is impossible that I could do things YOU cannot do. Given this, and given this QUITE LITERALLY, there CAN be nothing which prevents you from doing EXACTLY what I ask, and EVERYTHING which argues FOR it. I give you NO limits, because God lays none upon you.

   When you limit YOURSELF, we are NOT of one mind, and that IS sickness. But sickness is not of the body, but OF THE MIND. ALL forms of DISfunction are merely signs that the mind has split, and does not accept a UNIFIED PURPOSE.

10. The unification of purpose, then, is the Holy Spirit's ONLY way of healing. This is because it is the only level at which healing MEANS anything. The re-establishing of meaning in a chaotic thought system IS the only way to heal it. We said before that your task is only to meet the conditions [292] FOR meaning, since meaning itself is of God. But your RETURN to meaning is essential TO HIS, because YOUR meaning is PART of His. Your healing, then, is part of HIS health, because it is part of His Wholeness. He cannot lose this, but YOU can not know it. Yet it is still His will for you, and His will MUST stand forever and in all things.

---

291 Matthew 5:48 Ye therefore shall be perfect, as your heavenly Father is perfect.
292 This chapter: A. Introduction p2

J. The Acceptance of Reality

1   Fear of the Will of God is one of the strangest beliefs that the human mind has ever made. This could not possibly have occurred unless the mind was already profoundly split, making it possible for IT to be afraid of what it really is. It is apparent that reality CANNOT "threaten" anything except illusions, because reality can only UPHOLD truth. The very fact that the will of God, which IS what you are, is perceived as fearful TO you demonstrates that you ARE afraid of what you are. It is not, then, the will of God of which you are afraid, but YOURS. Your will is NOT the ego's, and that is why the ego is against you. What seems to be the fear of God is really only the fear of YOUR OWN REALITY.

2   It is impossible to learn anything consistently in a state of panic. If the purpose of this course is to learn what you are, and if you have ALREADY DECIDED that what you are is FEARFUL, then it MUST follow that you will NOT LEARN THIS COURSE. But you might remember that the reason FOR the course is that you do NOT know who you are. If you do not know your reality, how would you know whether it is fearful or not? The association of truth and fear, which would be highly artificial at best, is particularly inappropriate in the minds of those who do not know what truth IS. All that this kind of association means is that you are arbitrarily endowing something quite beyond your awareness with something YOU DO NOT WANT.

3   It is evident, then, that you are judging something of which you are totally unaware. You have set this strange situation up so that it is COMPLETELY IMPOSSIBLE to escape from it WITHOUT a guide who DOES know what your reality is.

The purpose of this Guide is merely to remind you of what YOU want. He is not attempting to force an alien will UPON you. He is merely making every possible effort, within the limits YOU impose upon Him, to RE-ESTABLISH your OWN will in your consciousness. You have IMPRISONED it in your UNconscious, where it remains available, but cannot help you.

When we said that the Holy Spirit's function is to sort out the true from the false in your unconscious, we meant that He has the power to look into what YOU have hidden, and perceive the Will of God there.

4   His perception of this will can make it real to YOU, because HE is in your mind, and therefore He IS your reality. If, then, His perception OF your mind brings its reality TO you, He IS teaching you what you are. The only source of fear in this whole process can ONLY be WHAT YOU THINK YOU LOSE. But it is only what the Holy Spirit sees that you can possibly HAVE. We have emphasized many times that the Holy Spirit will never call upon you to sacrifice anything. But if you ask the sacrifice of reality OF

Chapter 8 – The Journey Back

YOURSELVES, the Holy Spirit MUST remind you that this is not God's will BECAUSE it is not yours.

5   There is NO DIFFERENCE between your will and God's. If you did not have divided wills, you would recognize that willing is salvation because it IS communication. It is impossible to communicate in alien tongues. You and your Creator can communicate through creation, because that, and only that, IS your joint will. Divided wills do not communicate because they speak for different things TO THE SAME MIND. This loses the ability to communicate, simply because confused communication DOES NOT MEAN ANYTHING. A message cannot be said to be communicated UNLESS it makes sense.

6   How sensible can your messages be, when they ask for WHAT YOU DON'T WANT? Yet as long as you are afraid of your will, this is precisely what you WILL ask for.

You may insist that the Holy Spirit does not answer you, but it might be wiser to consider the kind of asker you are. YOU DO NOT ASK ONLY FOR WHAT YOU WANT.

This is SOLELY because you are afraid you might receive it, AND YOU WOULD.

THIS is really why you persist in asking the teacher who could not possibly teach you your will. Of him, you can never learn it, and this gives you the illusion of safety. But you cannot be safe FROM truth, but only IN it. Reality is the ONLY safety.

7   Your will is your salvation BECAUSE IT IS THE SAME AS GOD'S. The separation is nothing more than the belief that it is DIFFERENT. NO mind can believe that its will is STRONGER than God's. If, then, a mind believes that ITS will is different FROM His, it can only decide either that there IS no God, or that GOD'S WILL IS FEARFUL. The former accounts for the atheist, and the latter for the martyr. Martyrdom takes many forms, the category including ALL doctrines which hold that God demands sacrifices of ANY kind.

8   Either basic type of insane decision will induce panic, because the atheist believes he is alone and the martyr believes that God is crucifying him. Both really fear both abandonment AND retaliation, but the former is more reactive against abandonment and the latter against retaliation. The atheist maintains that God has left him, but he does not care. He will, however, become very fearful, and hence very ANGRY, if anyone suggests that God has NOT left him. The martyr, on the other hand, is more aware of guilt, and believing that punishment is inevitable, attempts to teach himself to LIKE it.

J. The Acceptance of Reality

9   The truth is, very simply, that NO-ONE WANTS EITHER ABANDONMENT OR RETALIATION. Many people SEEK both, but it is still true that they do NOT want it. Can you ask the Holy Spirit for "gifts" such as these, and actually expect to RECEIVE them? The Holy Spirit is totally incapable of giving YOU anything that does NOT come from God. *His task is NOT to make anything FOR you.* He CANNOT make you want something you DON'T want. When you ask the Universal Giver for what you do not want, YOU are asking for what CANNOT be given, BECAUSE IT WAS NEVER CREATED. It was never created because it was never your will for YOU.

10   Ultimately everyone must learn the will of God, because ultimately everyone must recognize HIMSELF. This recognition IS the recognition that HIS WILL AND GOD'S ARE ONE. In the presence of Truth, there are no unbelievers and no sacrifices. In the security of Reality fear is totally meaningless. To deny what IS can only SEEM to be fearful. Fear cannot be real without a cause, and GOD is the only Cause. God is Love, and you DO want Him. This IS your will. Ask for THIS and you WILL be answered, because you will be asking only for what BELONGS to you.

11   When you ask the Holy Spirit for what would hurt you, He CANNOT answer, because NOTHING can hurt you and SO YOU ARE ASKING FOR NOTHING. ANY desire which stems from the ego IS a desire for nothing, and to ask for it IS NOT A REQUEST. It is merely a denial in the FORM of a request. The Holy Spirit is not concerned with form at all, being aware only of MEANING. The ego cannot ask the Holy Spirit for ANYTHING, because there is COMPLETE COMMUNICATION FAILURE between them. But YOU can ask for EVERYTHING of the Holy Spirit, because YOUR requests are real, being of your will. Would the Holy Spirit deny the Will of God? And could He fail to recognize it in God's Sons?

12   The energy which you withdraw from Creation you expend on fear.

This is not because your ENERGY is limited, but because YOU HAVE LIMITED IT.

You do not recognize the ENORMOUS waste of energy which you expend in denying truth. What would YOU say of someone who PERSISTED in attempting the impossible, and believed that to ACHIEVE it is SUCCESS? The belief that you MUST HAVE THE IMPOSSIBLE in order to be happy is totally at variance with the principle of Creation. God COULD not will that happiness DEPENDED on what you could never have.

13   *The fact that God is love does not require belief, but it DOES require ACCEPTANCE.* It is indeed possible for you to DENY facts, although it is IMPOSSIBLE for you to CHANGE them.

Chapter 8 – The Journey Back

If you hold your hands over your eyes you will NOT see, because you are interfering with the laws of seeing. If you deny love you will NOT KNOW IT because your cooperation is the LAW OF ITS BEING.

You cannot change laws you did not make, and the laws of happiness were created FOR you, NOT BY you.

14   Attempts of any kind to deny what IS are fearful, and if they are strong they WILL induce panic. WILLING AGAINST reality, though impossible, can be MADE into a very persistent goal, EVEN THOUGH YOU DO NOT WANT IT. But consider the result of this strange decision.

You are DEVOTING your mind to what you DO NOT WANT. How real can this devotion be? If you do not want it, it was never created. If it was never created, it is nothing. Can you REALLY devote yourself to nothing?

15   God, in His devotion to YOU, created you devoted to EVERYTHING, and GAVE you what you are devoted TO. Otherwise, you would not have been created perfect. Reality IS everything, and you therefore have everything BECAUSE you are real. You cannot make the UNreal because the ABSENCE of reality is fearful, and fear cannot BE created. As long as you believe that fear is possible, YOU WILL NOT CREATE. Opposing orders of reality MAKE REALITY MEANINGLESS, and reality is MEANING.

16   Remember, then, that God's Will is ALREADY possible, and nothing else will EVER be. This is the simple acceptance of Reality because only this is real. You cannot DISTORT reality and KNOW WHAT IT IS. And if you DO distort reality you will experience anxiety, depression, and ultimately panic, because you are trying to MAKE YOURSELF UNREAL. When you feel these things do not try to look BEYOND yourself for truth, for truth can only be WITHIN you. Say, therefore,

"Christ is in me, and where He is God MUST be, for Christ is PART of Him."

K. The Answer to Prayer

1   Everyone who has ever tried to use prayer to request something, has experienced what appears to be failure. This is not only true in connection with specific things which might be harmful, but also in connection with requests which are strictly in line with this course. The latter, in particular, might be incorrectly interpreted as "proof" that the course

K. The Answer to Prayer

does not mean what it says. But you must remember that the course does state, and REPEATEDLY, that its purpose is the ESCAPE FROM FEAR.

2 Let us suppose, then, that what you request of the Holy Spirit IS what you really want, but that YOU ARE STILL AFRAID OF IT. Should this be the case, your ATTAINMENT of it would no longer BE what you want, even if IT is. This accounts for why CERTAIN SPECIFIC FORMS of healing are not achieved, even though the STATE of healing IS.

It frequently happens that an individual asks for physical healing, because he is fearful OF BODILY HARM. However, at the same time, if he WERE healed physically, the threat to his thought-system would be considerably MORE fearful to him than its physical EXPRESSION. In this case, he is not really asking for RELEASE from fear, but for the removal of a symptom WHICH HE HAS SELECTED. This request is, therefore, NOT for healing at all.

3 The Bible emphasizes that ALL prayers are answered, and this must be true, if no effort is wasted. The very fact that one has asked the Holy Spirit for ANYTHING, will ensure a response. But it is equally certain that no response, given by the Holy Spirit, will EVER be one which would INCREASE fear. It is even possible that His answer will not be heard at all. It is IMpossible, however, that it will be lost. There are many answers which you have already received, but have NOT YET HEARD. I assure you that they are waiting for you. It is indeed true that no effort is wasted.

4 **If you would know your prayers are answered, never doubt a Son of God.**

Do not question him, and do not confound him, for your faith in him is your faith in YOURSELF.

If you would know God and His Answer, believe in me, whose faith in YOU cannot be shaken. Can you ask of the Holy Spirit truly, and doubt your brother? Believe his words are true, because of the truth which is in him. [293] You will unite with the truth in him, and his words will BE true. As you hear him, you will hear me.

---

[293] [Tim Note: When we look for, and listen to Truth in our brother, we become very present and hear every word and nuance of emotion in him. Yet, we do not process those word for meaning of the human kind. Listening in awareness, we suddenly 'hear' what he is really, either, asking for, or giving to us. This is true even if he is babbling nonsense, accusing or threatening us, or demanding something. It's all about HOW we 'listen.' And our response in words, if called for by TRUTH, may have nothing to do with what he just said in words. This just takes practice.]

Chapter 8 – The Journey Back

5   LISTENING to truth is the only way you can hear it now, and finally KNOW it.

>**The message your brother gives you is UP TO YOU.**
>What does he say to you?
>What would YOU have him say?
>Your decision ABOUT him determines the message YOU receive.

Remember that the Holy Spirit is in him, and His Voice speaks to YOU through him. What can so holy a brother tell you EXCEPT truth?

>But are you LISTENING to it?

6

>Your brother may not know who he is, but there is a Light in his mind which DOES know.
>*This Light can shine into yours, making HIS words true, and you ABLE TO HEAR THEM.*

>His words ARE the Holy Spirit's answer to YOU.
>Is your faith in him strong enough to LET you listen and hear?

>Salvation is of your brother.
>The Holy Spirit extends from your mind to his, and answers YOU.

You cannot hear the Voice for God in yourself alone, because you are NOT alone. And His answer is only for what you ARE.

7   You will not know the trust I have in you, unless you EXTEND it. You will not trust the guidance of the Holy Spirit, or believe that it is for YOU, unless you hear it in others.

It MUST be for your brother, BECAUSE it is for you. Would God have created a Voice for you alone? Could you hear His answer EXCEPT as He answers ALL of God's Sons? Hear of your brother what you would have me hear of YOU, for you would not want ME to be deceived.

8   I love you for the truth in you, as GOD does. Your deceptions may deceive YOU, but they CANNOT deceive ME. Knowing what you ARE, I CANNOT doubt you. I hear only the Holy Spirit in you, Who speaks to me through YOU.

>If you would hear ME, hear my brothers, in whom God's Voice speaks.
>The answer to ALL your prayers lies in them.

K. The Answer to Prayer

You will be answered as you HEAR THE ANSWER IN EVERYONE. Do not listen to anything else, or you will not hear truth.

9   Believe in your brothers BECAUSE I believe in you, and you will learn that my belief in you is justified. Believe in me BY believing in them, for the sake of what God gave them. THEY WILL ANSWER YOU, if you learn to ask truth of them. Do not ask for blessings without blessing THEM, for only in this way can YOU learn how blessed YOU are. By following this way, you ARE looking for the truth in YOU. This is not going BEYOND yourself, but TOWARD yourself. Hear only God's answer in His Sons, and YOU are answered.

10   To disbelieve is to side AGAINST, or to ATTACK. To believe is to accept, and SIDE WITH. To believe is not to be credulous, but to accept and APPRECIATE. What you do NOT believe you do NOT APPRECIATE, and you CANNOT be grateful for what you do not VALUE. There is a price you will pay for judgment, because judgment IS the setting of price. And as you set it, you WILL pay it.

11   If paying is equated with GETTING, you will set the PRICE low, but demand a high RETURN. But you will have forgotten that to price is to VALUE, so that YOUR return is IN PROPORTION TO YOUR JUDGMENT OF WORTH.

If paying is associated with giving, IT CANNOT BE PERCEIVED AS LOSS, and the RECIPROCAL relationship of giving and RECEIVING will be recognized. The price will then be set high, because of the value of the RETURN.

12   To price for GETTING is to LOSE SIGHT OF VALUE, making it inevitable that you will NOT value what you receive. Valuing it little, you will not appreciate it, and you will not WANT it. Never forget, then, that YOU have set the value on what you receive, and have priced it BY what you give. To believe that it is possible to get much FOR little, is to believe that you can bargain with God.

13   God's laws are ALWAYS fair, and PERFECTLY consistent. BY giving, you receive. But to receive is to ACCEPT, NOT to get. It is impossible not to HAVE, but it IS possible NOT TO KNOW YOU HAVE. The recognition of HAVING is the willingness for GIVING, and ONLY by this willingness, can you RECOGNIZE what you have. What you give is therefore the value you put on what you have, being the exact measure of the value you PUT upon it. And this, in turn, is the measure of HOW MUCH YOU WANT IT.

14   You can ASK of the Holy Spirit, then, ONLY by giving TO Him. And you can GIVE to Him only WHERE YOU SEE HIM. If you SEE Him in everyone, consider how much you will be asking OF Him, and HOW MUCH YOU WILL RECEIVE. He will deny you nothing, because you have denied Him nothing, and so you can SHARE EVERYTHING.

Chapter 8 – The Journey Back

This is the way, and the ONLY way, to have His answer, because His answer is all you can ask for and WANT. Say, then, to everyone,

> *"Because I will to know myself,*
> *I see you as God's Son and my brother."*

Made in the USA
Coppell, TX
27 May 2021